Foreword

The Hidden Places is a collection of easy to use travel guides taking you, in this instance, on a relaxed but informative tour of Cornwall - a county of spectacular rugged coastlines, atmospheric fishing ports, secluded villages, narrow winding lanes and strong, romantic seafaring traditions.

This edition of *The Hidden Places of Cornwall* represents a milestone in the publishing of the Hidden Places series as it is the first title to be published *in full colour*. All Hidden Places titles will now be published in colour which will ensure that readers can properly appreciate the attractive scenery and impressive places of interest in Cornwall and, of course, in the rest of the British Isles. We do hope that you like the new format.

Our books contain a wealth of interesting information on the history, the countryside, the towns and villages and the more established places of interest in the county. But they also promote the more secluded and little known visitor attractions and places to stay, eat and drink many of which are easy to miss unless you know exactly where you are going.

We include hotels, inns, restaurants, public houses, teashops, various types of accommodation, historic houses, museums, gardens, garden centres, craft centres and many other attractions throughout Cornwall, all of which are comprehensively indexed. Most places are accompanied by an attractive photograph and are easily located by using the map at the beginning of each chapter. We do not award merit marks or rankings but concentrate on describing the more interesting, unusual or unique features of each place with the aim of making the reader's stay in the local area an enjoyable and stimulating experience.

Whether you are visiting the area for business or pleasure or in fact are living in the county we do hope that you enjoy reading and using this book. We are always interested in what readers think of places covered (or not covered) in our guides so please do not hesitate to use the reader reaction forms provided to give us your considered comments. We also welcome any general comments which will help us improve the guides themselves. Finally if you are planning to visit any other corner of the British Isles we would like to refer you to the list of other **Hidden Places** titles to be found at the rear of the book.

Travel Publishing

D0547921

Regional Map

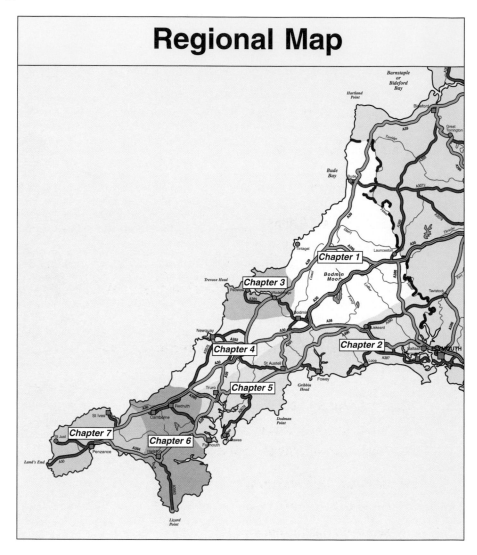

Contents

1 Northeast Cornwall

Separated from the rest of mainland England by the River Tamar, which rises just behind the north coast to the northeast of Bude, and forms the county boundary with Devon, this part of Cornwall, like the rest of the county has been able to preserve its Celtic heritage. The most common reminders are the place names beginning with Tre, Pol and Pen but

Tintagel Castle

there are many ancient monuments to be discovered such as crosses, holy wells and prehistoric sites, particularly on the lonely and bleak expanse of Bodmin Moor.

A mysterious place and the inspiration for Daphne du Maurier's famous novel, Jamaica Inn, the moor not only has a wealth of Iron and Bronze Age monuments but also interesting natural formations that are typified by the curious Cheesewring. Legends abound in such lonely places and the isolated Dozmary Pool is very much linked with the legend of King Arthur, it was here, so many believe, that the great king's sword Excalibur was received by the Lady of the Lake.

Tales of the Arthurian legend continue at Tintagel, a small coastal village where, on a rocky headland known as The Island, stand the romantic remains of Tintagel Castle. Said to be the birthplace of King Arthur, this ancient village has certainly embraced the tales and there is plenty for the King Arthur legend hunter to enjoy. However, the most interesting building here is the Old Post Office which was built long before the Penny Post came into being.

Further up the windswept and dramatic coastline of north Cornwall lies the sheltered beach of Bude. The birthplace of British surfing, this traditional seaside resort has been a favourite holiday destination for many over the years though it was once a bustling port which handled slate from the inland quarries. Also boasting a castle, although Bude's fortification does not have the mysterious quality of Tintagel's castle is renowned for being the first building in the country to have been constructed on sand with its foundations resting on a concrete raft.

Along the shore line from Bude

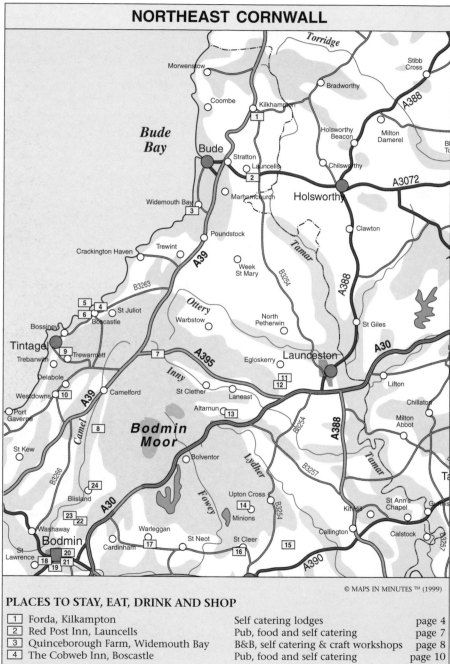

NORTHEAST CORNWALL

© MAPS IN MINUTES ™ (1999)

PLACES TO STAY, EAT, DRINK AND SHOP

BUDE

This traditional seaside resort, with its sweeping expanse of sand, rock pools and Atlantic breakers rolling in from the west, has numerous facilities for beach lovers, surfers and coastal walkers. Said to be the place where British surfing started, Bude has become a very popular surfing centre and this renewed interest in the town has, once again, made it a much favoured holiday destination. During a winter gale this can be a remote and harsh environment but, in summer, with a gentle breeze blowing in off the sea and the possible sighting of dolphins in the sea there can be few more exhilarating places in Cornwall.

Originally a busy north Cornwall port, Bude developed rapidly after the canal to Launceston was opened in the 1820s and, in the 1880s, the completion of the railway started to bring holidaymakers here, who were looking for fresh, bracing air. The **Bude Canal** was an ambitious inland waterway project that was intended to connect the Atlantic with the English Channel via the River Tamar. The only stretch to be completed was that between Bude and Launceston and it was, in many ways, remarkable as the sea lock at the entrance to the canal was the only lock on the whole

length of the canal - although it ran for 35 miles and rose to a height of 350 feet in six miles. To achieve the changes in levels, a

View down on Bude

FORDA,

Kilkhampton, near Bude, Cornwall EX23 9RZ
Tel: 01288 321413 Fax: 01288 321413
e-mail: forda.lodges@virgin.net website: www.cornwall-online.co.uk/forda-lodges

Found in a hidden valley of 17 acres and yet only a few minutes drive from heritage coastline and the fine beaches of North Cornwall, Tamar Lakes and many other attractions, **Forda** is ideally placed for those wishing to explore the county. However, this too is a place for those looking to relax and enjoy peace and quiet as well as indulge in country activities such as fishing, walking, cycling, riding and playing golf.

Whatever the season, the wooded valley in which this holiday village lies has something to offer the visitor - there are three private fishing ponds, walking trails, a wealth of wildfowl and other animals to catch sight of and, of course, the changing colours of the wild flowers and the splendid woods. There is also a games' room, with table tennis, pool, table football and darts, an outdoor play area that includes boules and horseshoes, a laundry room and payphone.

Originally a traditional Cornish farmstead, Forda today is a small and select holiday setting where cleverly designed Scandinavian lodges have been constructed to blend into the surroundings. Providing first class accommodation for up to six people, they have been decorated and furnished with both flair and comfort in mind. The modern kitchens are fully equipped and include a microwave and there is a television and video in the lounge. New arrivals will find a tray of tea, coffee and biscuits ready for them with fresh milk in the fridge, the beds made up and fresh flowers to welcome to their holiday home. Nothing else has been left to chance and, with towels and linen included, as well as fishing in the lakes and electricity, there is nothing else to worry about. Families with children will find that cots, highchairs and stair gates are available and some of the lodges also welcome family pets.

There is also a luxury barn conversion at Forda that sleeps up to nine people and, as well as being equally expertly decorated and furnished, the barn has its own laundry facilities and there is a dishwasher in the kitchen. The English Tourism Council has recently awarded a rating of 5 stars for the barn and 4 stars for the lodges.

Owners, the Chibbett family, live at Forda in the old farmhouse and take great pride in ensuring that all their guests have a relaxing and peaceful holiday in this wonderful and idyllic location. Forda is open all year and special short breaks are available in spring, autumn and winter with special offers also available on long stays in low season. This is a superb holiday location and equally well an excellent place for Christmas and New Year when the lodges can be specially decorated on request.

Canal and Summerleaze Beach, Bude

series of inclined planes, or ramps, were used between the different levels and a wheeled tub boat was pulled up the ramps on metal rails. The longest such canal when it opened in 1823, Bude Canal carried lime rich sea sand that was ideal for fertilising inland farmland whilst, on the journey back towards Bude, cargoes of oats and slate were taken to the ships in Bude harbour. Now open to pleasure craft following the canal's commercial closure in 1912, the **Bude Canal Trail** follows this tranquil backwater into the heart of Cornwall.

Close to the entrance to the canal stands **Bude Castle**, an unusually small fortification that was designed by the local 19th century inventor, Sir Goldsworthy Gurney. However, what makes this now office building particularly interesting is that it is thought to be the first building in Britain to be constructed on sand and, in this case, it rests on a concrete raft. The history of the town and its canal can be explored in the **Stratton Town Museum** which, too, stands on the canalside in a former blacksmith's forge. From shipwrecks, the railways, farming and local geology, the story of Bude and the

surrounding area is told in a vivid series of displays. Room is also set aside to honour two local men, the giant Anthony Payne and the inventor Sir Goldsworthy Gurney.

AROUND BUDE

POUGHILL
1 mile NE of Bude off the A39

The thatched cottages of the old village of Poughill (pronounced Poffil) stand around the originally Norman Church of St Olaf. Noted for its late 15th century carved oak bench ends, keen eyed visitors will also spot that the Royal Arms of Charles II have been incorrectly dated 1655. Opposite the church lies the Church House which was built in 1525.

COOMBE
3 miles N of Bude off the A39

This picturesque village of thatched cottages lies in the Coombe Valley and it is reached via a ford across the valley's stream. Just a mile to the west lies **Duckpool**, where a natural dam of pebbles have contained the stream to create a fresh water pool in Coombe Valley Cove. Whilst care should be taken when swimming from certain parts of the sandy, shingle-backed beach, the woodlands of **Coombe Valley** support a wide variety of birds, plants and small animals.

KILKHAMPTON
4½ miles NE of Bude on the A39

This small hilltop village is thought to have been an important settlement in Saxon times as the surrounding area is littered with ancient burial grounds. Later, in 1088, the manor of Kilkhampton, along with that of Bideford, was awarded to Robert Fitz Hamon (who went on to found Tewkesbury) by William Rufus for his support during Odo's Revolt. The village's tall and elegant church, which was built in the 15th century on the site of the previous Norman church, remains a local landmark.

MORWENSTOW
5½ miles N of Bude off the A39

Found on the harshest stretch of the north

Stone Stile, Morwenstow

Cornwall coast, this tiny village has been used to taking the full brunt of Atlantic storms through the years and, though it can seem at times rather storm-lashed, this is a marvellous place from which to watch the changing moods of the ocean. Not surprisingly shipwrecks have been common along this stretch of coast and, though many floundered as a result of storms, it was not unknown for local criminals to lure unsuspecting ships on to the rocks by lighting lanterns from the cliff tops or the shore.

The village's most renowned inhabitant is the eccentric vicar and poet, Reverend Robert Stephen Hawker, who came here in 1834 and stayed amongst his congregation of "smugglers, wreckers and dissenters" until his death in 1875. A colourful figure dressed in a purple frock coat, a fisherman's jersey and long fisherman's boots, he would spend much of his time walking this area of his beloved county or writing verse and smoking - some accounts say it was opium - in the driftwood hut that he built himself 17 steps down from the top of the precipitous **Vicarage Cliff**.

One of the first people to show concern for the number of merchant vessels that were coming to grief along this perilous stretch of coastline, Hawker would spend much of his time monitoring the sea and would often climb down the cliff to rescue shipwrecked crews. After carrying the bodies of the dead mariners back to the village he would give them a Christian burial.

Hawker's other contribution to Morwenstow was the rectory which he built at his own expense and to his own design. As unique as the man himself, the chimneys of the house represent the towers of various churches he had known, Oxford colleges and, extraordinarily, his mother's gravestone is

remembered by the broad kitchen chimney! His lasting contribution to the church was to reintroduce the annual Harvest Festival and his most famous poem is the rousing Cornish anthem, The Song of Western Men. The National Trust-owned land, between the church and the cliffs, is dedicated to this remarkable man's memory.

Another interesting gentleman of Morwenstow was David Coppinger, a Dane who settled near the village in the 18th century. Based as much on fact as fiction, the story begins when, during a terrible storm, Coppinger dived from a floundering foreign ship and swam through the waves to shore. He then leapt up on to a horse belonging to Dinah, who had come to see the storm, and rode it hard inland to Dinah's house. Here he stayed and, upon her father's death, he married the girl. Coppinger turned the house into the headquarters for his ruthless gang of smugglers and, with neither the local people or the authorities prepared to take action against him, he began to terrorise the area, even taking control of the local roads. At home, he was equally violent and he treated his wife with great cruelty. Eventually the revenue men took control and, realising his days were numbered after many members of his gang had been killed, Coppinger fled from the country on a strange boat that mysteriously appeared at the point where he first arrived in Cornwall.

To the north of the village, and close to the Devon border, lies **Welcombe Mouth**, a graveyard for many ships that floundered on the jagged rocks, and, set back from the shore, Welcombe and Marsland Valleys. This nature reserve, set in the forested valley slopes, is a haven for butterflies.

At **Higher and Lower Sharpnose Points**, to the south of Morwenstow, the erosion caused by the constant bombardment of the sea can be seen clearly as there are boulders strewn along the bottom of these crumbling cliffs and some of the outcrops of harder rocks have begun to form tiny islands.

STRATTON
1½ miles E of Bude on the A3072

Believed to have been founded in Roman times, this old market town was once a port. Situated on a hill, the steeply sloping main street is lined with fine Georgian houses and

RED POST INN AND HOLIDAY PARK,

Red Post, Launcells, near Bude,
Cornwall EX23 9NW
Tel: 01288 381305

Lying close to the Devon border and just a short drive away from the north Cornwall coast, **The Red Post Inn and Holiday Park** has something to offer every member of the family. The famous Red Post Inn dates back to 1531 although it is known that there has been an inn here since the 9th century and, down the ages, the inn has played an important part in the history of the area.

Today, things are a little quieter and, whilst the original thatched inn is now the home of owners, Mike and Pam Hinks and their son Simon, the inn is a wonderful place that is full of atmosphere and character. It is also an inn that is well known and popular for the high standard of its cuisine. The extensive menu does feature many of the usual bar meals and snacks but it is the splendid choice of imaginative home-cooked dishes, prepared from the finest local produce, which make dining here a real culinary treat. To the rear of the inn lies the holiday park, a well equipped site with full amenities that is ideal for those holidaying in caravans, motor homes and tents. As well as providing a superb location in which to enjoy a pleasant holiday, visitors can, of course, enjoy the hospitality of the inn and, for children, there is a wonderful Playquest adventure playground. Meanwhile, the inn also has a two bedroomed luxury cottage nearby that makes an ideal get-away-from-it-all holiday base.

cottages, many of which are still thatched today.

During the Civil War, Stratton was a stronghold of the Royalist and their commander, Sir Bevil Grenville, made The Tree Inn his centre of operations. In May 1643, at the **Battle of Stamford Hill**, Grenville led his troops to victory over the Parliamentarians who had been holding an Iron Age earthworks just northwest of the town. The dead of both sides were buried in unmarked graves in Stratton churchyard.

The Tree Inn was also the birthplace of the legendary Cornish Giant, Anthony Payne. At over seven feet tall, Payne was an excellent choice as Sir Bevil's bodyguard and they fought together at Stamford Hill and, later, at Lansdown Hill near Bath. At this second encounter with the Parliamentarians Grenville was killed and Payne helped the General's son lead the King's Army to victory before carrying his master's body back to Stratton. After the Civil War, Payne continued to live at the Grenville manor house until his death and, when he died, the house had to be altered to allow his coffin in and out. The Tree Inn still remembers Stratton's most

famous son and a life size portrait hangs in the inn's courtyard.

LAUNCELLS
2½ miles E of Bude off the A3072

Set in a delightful wooded combe lies St Swithin's Church, a 15th century building that is remarkable as it has managed to escape the ravages of enthusiastic Victorian restorers. In the churchyard lies the grave of the 19th century physician, scientist and inventor, Sir Goldworthy Gurney, the steam pioneer and builder of the castle at the mouth of the Bude Canal.

MARHAMCHURCH
2 miles SE of Bude off the A39

This hilltop village was founded by St Morwenna (to whom the 14th century parish church is dedicated) as a monastic settlement but today the key feature here is the Bude Canal. This still surviving stretch of waterway lies just below Marhamchurch and this was also the site of one of the canal's ramps which carried the barges on to the continuation of the canal at the top of the hill.

WEEK ST MARY
6 miles SE of Bude off the B3254

This small village was, in medieval times, much larger and, to the west lies Penhallam, the grass covered ruins of a medieval manor house that was surrounded by a protective moat.

TREWINT
6 miles SW of Bude off the A39

This handsome village often played host to John Wesley whilst he was on his preaching tours of Cornwall. His hosts' cottage, **Wesley Cottage**, is a 'one up, one down' building that has been maintained in the 18th century style and visitors can see its specially constructed prophets' room and pilgrims' garden.

POUNDSTOCK
4½ miles S of Bude off the A39

The unusual Guildhouse, found here in a wooded hollow, was constructed in the 14th century, probably to house the masons working on the building of the village church, and it remains a fine example of a once common style of non secular building. After the church had been built the guildhouse became a meeting place and the festivities held here were so great that they were suppressed by the Puritans. Over the years it has also acted as a poorhouse and a village school.

Just a mile to the west of Poundstock lies the Atlantic coast and from the top of the 400 foot cliffs there are views across to Lundy in the north and Trevose Head in the south.

WIDEMOUTH BAY
3 miles S of Bude off the A39

Ever since the 1930s, this little village has been a seaside resort catering to visitors attracted here by the wide curving bay of flat sand. A popular place with families and surfers beyond the two headlands, which define the bay, the shoreline becomes rocky but from **Penhalt Cliff**, at the southern end of Widemouth Sands, there is a wonderful aerial view of the bay.

QUINCEBOROUGH FARM AND COTTAGES,
Widemouth Bay, near Bude,
Cornwall EX23 0NA
Tel: 01288 361236

Set in 120 acres of mixed working farmland and just a short walk away from the sandy, surfing beach at Widemouth Bay, **Quinceborough Farm and Cottages** is splendid place from which to explore the north Cornwall coast and also Bodmin Moor. The farm was originally built in the mid 19th century by the local squire as his riding stables and also a storage for barley and sand. In the 1920s the farm came into the hands of the present owner Guy Rowland's family but, since the decline in
farming in the late 1970s and early 1980s Guy and his wife Pat decided to find other uses for the large Victorian farmhouse and outbuildings. The couple renovated the derelict outbuildings in a sympathetic manner and these now house a variety of local craft workshops including surfboard makers, potters and builders.

At the same time the old hay barn was also converted into three charming holiday cottages for which, in 1982, Guy and Pat won the County Landowners and Cosira Award presented by Prince Charles. Each of these cottages offers superb accommodation in stylish surroundings where many of the building's original features, such as the massive ceiling beams and stone walls, have been retained. Meanwhile, at the large stone farmhouse, there are a further three beautiful guest rooms which are let on a bed and breakfast basis. Quinceborough Farm and Cottages in delightful place to stay that is made special by the imagination of its interesting owners.

Penhalt Cliff, Widemouth Bay

TINTAGEL

The romantic remains of **Tintagel Castle**, set on a wild and windswept headland that juts out into the Atlantic, are, perhaps, many people's image of Cornwall. These ruins were a stronghold of the Earls of Cornwall but the reason that many people clamber up the wooden stairway of some 300 steps to **The Island** is that the castle is best known as the legendary birthplace of King Arthur. Along with Caerleon in Wales and South Cadbury in Somerset, Tintagel also lays claim to being the home of the site of Camelot, the mythical headquarters of the Knights of the Round Table. Fragments of a Celtic monastic house, dating from the 6th century, have been unearthed on the headland and their origins do coincide with the activities of the Welsh military leader on which the Arthurian legends are thought to be based. However, the castle was, in fact, built some 600 years after the time of King Arthur, in the 12th century, by Reginald, Earl of Cornwall, the illegitimate son of Henry I.

Whatever the truth behind the stories, the magic of this site certainly matches that of the tales of chivalry and wizardry. In 1998 the discovery of a 6th century slate bearing the Latin inscription "Artognov" - which translates as the ancient British name for Arthur - renewed the belief that Tintagel was Arthur's home.

According to the legends, which are thought to have been started by Geoffrey of Monmouth in the mid 12th century and which became especially popular during the Romantic era of the 19th century, it was at Tintagel Castle that Uther Pendragon, the High King of Britain, aided by Merlin, the master magician, deceived Igerna, the Duchess of Cornwall. By disguising himself as her husband, Uther Pendragon seduced Igerna

Exit of Merlins Cave, Tintagel

and, later, she gave birth to his son, Arthur. The cave, found at the foot of The Island, is known as **Merlin's Cave** and is still said to be haunted by a ghost.

Tintagel, of course, owes much of its popularity to its Arthurian connections and one of the town's most interesting attractions, **King Arthur's Great Hall**, continues to draw people. These vast halls tell the story of the King and the chivalrous deeds which he and his Knights of the Round Table performed. Visitors can also see 72 stained glass windows which bear the Knights' Coats of Arms and depict some of their adventures.

Also found on the High Street, though this time not connected with King Arthur, is the weather beaten **Old Post Office**. Now owned by the National Trust, this small manor house dates from the 14th century and, inside, can be seen the stone paved medieval hall complete with its ancient fireplace. First

Old Post Office, Tintagel

THE COBWEB INN,

Boscastle, Cornwall PL35 0HE
Tel: 01840 250278 Fax: 01840 250278

Right in the heart of Boscastle lies **The Cobweb Inn**, an interesting old place which is also one of the area's most popular pubs. The premises date back to the early 1700s when they were home to the famous Bowerings Stores. An old wine and spirit merchants, beer was also bottled here and, as well as having a bakery on the site, they also sold coal. Life remained the same here until after World War II when the store became The Cobweb Inn and, in 1969, it was bought by Vera and Ivor Bright.

Recently retired, the couple have handed over the running of the inn to their son Adrian and he now continues to make a success of this well loved local place. Full of character and charm inside,

where many of the building's original features such as the beamed ceilings and flagstone floors remain, this is a wonderfully atmospheric place to come to for a drink from the well stocked bar. Well known for its fine selection of real ales, a tasty range of bar meals and snacks are served in the bar whilst The Cobweb Inn also has a splendid restaurant on the first floor that is highly regarded. Booking is essential at weekends for this à la carte restaurant which is particularly popular on Sundays when a traditional roast lunch is served. Finally, those visiting the area on holiday may be interested to learn that the inn also has a self-catering flat which is available all year round.

HARBOUR RESTAURANT,

The Harbour, Boscastle, Cornwall PL35 0HD
Tel: 01840 250380

Found at Boscastle's harbour, the aptly named **Harbour Restaurant** has an idyllic position with the harbour on one side and the magnificent sight of Bodmin Moor providing a backdrop. This splendid whitewashed stone building dates back over 300 years and, for much of its life, it has been used as a storage area for the harbour. Owners Christine and Christopher Morgan took over the premises in Easter 1998 and, as Christine is the grand-daughter of the original founder of Kelly's Cornish Ice Cream, catering is certainly in the blood. The couple were joined a year later by chef Eddie Fisher and, ever since, the Harbour Restaurant has grown in reputation and it is now one of the most sought after restaurants in the area.

As full of character and charm as its lovely exterior would suggest, Christine and Christopher have taken great care in restoring the interior of the building and presenting it just as it was many years ago. In this atmospheric environment, customers can enjoy a really special meal prepared by Eddie. Specialising in seafood and fish, the menus here are a mouthwatering feast that encompasses tastes and styles from around the world. However, what takes priority here is the use of the very best of fresh local produce and it is not surprising that not only is this a very popular place but also that booking is essential.

becoming a post office in the 19th century, the postmistress's office also lies on the ground floor while, upstairs, there are two bedrooms beneath the heavily beamed roof.

The parish church is set some distance away from the centre of the village on an exposed cliff and its early 15th century tower has long been used as a landmark by sailors. Dedicated to St Materiana, who has been identified as St Madryn a princess from Gwent, this originally Norman building displays some Saxon fragments in its structure and still retains its Norman font.

To the north of the village lies the mile long **Rocky Valley**, a curious rock strewn cleft in the landscape which has a character all of its own.

Bossiney Cove

In the wooded upper reaches can be found the impressive 40 foot waterfall known as **St Nectan's Kieve** - named after the Celtic hermit whose cell is believed to have stood beside the basin, or kieve, at the foot of the cascade. Here too can be seen the **Rocky Valley Carvings**, on a rock face behind a ruined building. Though it is suggested that the carvings date from early Christian times, around the same time St Nectan was living here, it is impossible to be accurate and other suggestions range from 2nd century BC to the 17th century!

AROUND TINTAGEL

BOSSINEY
½ mile N of Tintagel off the B3263

Reached by a short signposted footpath from the village, **Bossiney Haven** is a beautiful, sheltered beach that is surrounded by a semi circle of cliffs. The views from the clifftop are spectacular but only the fit and agile should try to scramble down on to this small and secluded beach.

BOSCASTLE
3 miles NE of Tintagel on the B3263

This ancient and picturesque fishing community stands in a combe at the head of a remarkable S-shaped inlet that is sheltered from the Atlantic Ocean. The straggling village grew up around, and takes its name from, the now demolished Bottreaux castle that the de Botterell family built in Norman times. The picturesque inlet, between the cliffs, is home to the only natural harbour between Hartland Point and Padstow and it is formed by the rivers Valency and Jordan.

Boscastle Harbour

ST CHRISTOPHER'S HOTEL,

High Street, Boscastle, Cornwall PL35 0BD
Tel: 01840 250412
e-mail: stchristophers@hotmail.com

Found in the heart of the older, upper part of this delightful harbour village, **St Christopher's Hotel** is a small and attractive family run hotel. Originally built around 300 years ago, this lovely Georgian building was the home of a wealthy merchant who no doubt had grown rich by trading through this once thriving harbour. Since those days it has also been a village shop before being skillfully converted into the comfortable hotel it is today.

Whilst nothing has been lost of the building's gracious past, the comfort of today's visitors is very much in the minds of owners Ruth and Alan Watson and guests here can expect to be well looked after. Through out the hotel there is an atmosphere of warmth and informality and, in both the lounge and dining room as well as the guest bedrooms, the country style decoration and furnishings make this the ideal place for a relaxing holiday. Guests can enjoy a pre-dinner drink out in the garden whilst making their selections from the tempting menu of traditional and original dishes. After a peaceful night's sleep in one of the nine charming en suite bedrooms and a splendid breakfast, Ruth and Alan are also happy to provide packed lunches for those wishing to spend the day exploring the glorious surrounding countryside.

INNY VALE HOLIDAY VILLAGE,

Davidstow, near Camelford, Cornwall PL32 9XN
Tel: 01840 261248 Fax: 01840 261740
e-mail: jn.c@which.net
Website: www.cornwallinnyvaleholidayvillage.co.uk

Found just five miles from the north Cornwall coast and situated in the sheltered countryside of the River Inny valley, **Inny Vale Holiday Village** is charming holiday location which has with something for everyone. The village's 24 attractive detached bungalows are laid out in a pleasing fashion, with lawns, paths and shrubs, whilst, in a separate woodland location there is a touring and camping side complete with electricity, water and waste disposal hook ups. Each bungalow is fully furnished and equipped to the highest standards and, with four different sizes from which to choose, there is a bungalow to suit every family. Inny Vale Holiday Village is very much a

family run establishment and John and Angela Christopher along with both their daughters and their families have put a lot of effort and hard work into making this place a relaxing location for all. Apart from the glorious setting, there is an outdoor swimming pool, a children's paddling pool and a tennis court for the energetic whilst, at the village's reception office there is also a shop and Knights Bar and Restaurant. An excellent place for a quiet drink or a meal, throughout the season there is also a wide variety of entertainment to be found here for all ages.

The harbour's inner jetty was built by the renowned Elizabethan seafarer, Sir Richard Grenville, in 1584, at a time when the village was prospering as a fishing, grain and slate port. The outer jetty, or breakwater, dates from the 19th century when Boscastle had grown to become a bustling commercial port handling coal, timber, slate and china clay. Because of the dangerous harbour entrance, ships were towed in by rowing boats and a blowhole in the outer harbour sometimes still sends up plumes of spray.

Crackington Haven

Accidentally blown up by a stray mine during World War II, the breakwater has since been repaired.

The spectacular slate headlands on either side of the village provide some excellent, if rather demanding, walking. The Victorian author, Thomas Hardy, was a regular visitor to Boscastle whilst he was working as an architect on the restoration of the church at nearby St Juliot and the village appears as 'Castle Boterel' in his early novel, *A Pair of Blue Eyes*.

ST JULIOT
4 miles NE of Tintagel off the B3266

Found in the wooded valley of the fast flowing River Valency, this hidden hamlet (which appeared as 'Endelstow' in one of Thomas Hardy's novels) is home to the church upon which Thomas Hardy worked and also where, in 1870, he met his future wife, Emma Gifford, the rector's sister-in-law. Emma later professed that the young architect had already appeared to her in a dream and wrote how she was *"immediately arrested by his familiar appearance."* Much of the couple's courtship took place along the wild stretch of coastline between Boscastle and Crackington Haven and, when Emma died, over 40 years later, Hardy returned to St Juliot to erect a memorial to her in the church. Following his death, in 1928, a similar memorial was erected to Hardy himself.

CRACKINGTON HAVEN
7½ miles NE of Tintagel off the B3263

One of the most dramatic places along this remarkable stretch of coastline, the small cove at Crackington Haven is overlooked by towering 400 foot cliffs and jagged rocks which make it Cornwall's highest coastal point. The small and narrow sandy cove is approached, by land, down a steep-sided wooded combe which has a few houses, an inn and a village shop at the bottom, whilst, from the sea it is difficult to see how sizeable vessels once landed here to deliver their cargoes of limestone and Welsh coal.

Some of the most spectacular coastal scenery can be viewed by walking the clifftop path from Crackington Haven to Cambeak but, though impressive, the cliff rock is often loosely packed and care should be taken at all times when close to the cliff edge. Just to the south of Crackington Haven the path leads to **The Strangles**, a remote beach with a rather curious name. Although, at low tide, large patches of sand are revealed amongst the rocks, the undercurrents here are strong and swimming is always unsafe. During one year alone in the 1820s, some 20 ships were said to have come to grief in this cove.

CAMELFORD
4 miles SE of Tintagel on the A39

Situated on the banks of the River Camel, this small and historic old market town lies on the

TRETHIN MANOR HOLIDAY COTTAGES,

Trethin, Advent, near Camelford, Cornwall PL32 9QW
Tel: 01840 213522 Fax: 01840 212898

Set in seven acres of land on the edge of Bodmin Moor between the hamlets of Pencarrow and Tresinney in the parish of Advent, **Trethin Manor Holiday Cottages** are just the place to get away from all the hurly burly of life. The house dates back to the 16th century and it is the splendid mellow stone farm buildings which have been expertly converted to create the comfortable holiday cottages of today. Owned and personally run by Henry and Ruth Hine, who first made this their home in 1996, the superb cottages offer excellent family accommodation.

Beautifully decorated and furnished in a style that befits the buildings' age, the cottages vary in size, from those taking a couple to six adults, and each provides a real home from home for guests. Well appointed inside, the gardens around Trethin Manor Holiday Cottages are equally well kept and the mature plants and shrubs, along with a blaze of colourful flowers in summer, represent the perfect cottage garden. All in all Trethin Manor is a special place that is well worth taking the time to find.

TREWARMETT INN,

Trewarmett, near Tintagel, Cornwall PL34 0ET
Tel: 01840 770460
Fax: 01840 779011

Situated on the main road through this picturesque village, the **Trewarmett Inn** is a delightful old pub which dates back over 300 years. Just a short drive from both the coast and the ancient village of Tintagel, this lovely inn is well worth taking the time to find.

Although owner Edwina Chignell has only been here since May 1999 she has transformed the inn and it is steadily growing a well earned reputation. The interior is true olde worlde, with stone fireplaces, flagstone floors and ancient ceiling beams, and here customers can enjoy a pint of Cornish real ale or Cornish scrumpy from the well stocked bar. Food too is very much a part of the 'new' Trewarmett Inn and all the dishes are freshly prepared and cooked to order by Edwina. Virtually everything on the extensive blackboard menu is home-made - even the breads - and it is the delicious food in these atmospheric surroundings which makes this such a popular place to eat. However, good quality food and drink are not all that Edwina has to offer visitors as there are six charming guest rooms here and children and pets are made most welcome. Lastly, folk music lovers should also make a bee line for the Trewarmett Inn as, every Wednesday and Saturday evenings, folk bands and soloists play here live.

Slaughterbridge, nr Camelford

northern fringes of Bodmin Moor. Building its prosperity on the wool trade, the central small square is lined with 18th and 19th century houses and the early 19th century town hall has a camel for a weathervane. The **North Cornwall Museum and Gallery**, housed in a converted coach house, shows aspects of life in this area throughout the 20th century and includes the reconstruction of a 19th century moorland cottage. A full range of tools used by blacksmiths, cobblers and printers are also on display as well as a large number of domestic appliances and items varying from clothes to vacuum cleaners. Just to the north of this pleasant town is the **British Cycling Museum**.

Close by, on the riverbank at **Slaughterbridge**, lies a 6th century stone slab which is said to mark the place where King Arthur fell at the Battle of Camlann in AD539.

TREWARMETT
1½ miles SE of Tintagel on the B3263

This moorland village like so many places in this area has associations with the legend of King Arthur. Here an ancient rectangular enclosure surrounded by stone slabs is said to be one of the places where King Arthur held court. More recently, in the 19th century, the Prince of Wales slate quarry employed many men around the Trewarmett area. Although the quarry is now flooded, the beam engine house can still be seen.

TREBARWITH
1½ miles S of Tintagel off the B3263

A good surfing beach, **Trebarwith Strand**, some two miles west of this hamlet, is the only easily accessible beach between Polzeath and Crackington Haven. Backed by crumbling cliffs that were once quarried for slate, this sandy stretch of coastline is strewn with rocks and, though popular during the summer, swimmers must be wary of being swept off the rocks.

Rocky Coastline, Trebarwith

DELABOLE
3 miles S of Tintagel on the B3314

Home to the most famous slate quarry in Cornwall, this village is, almost literally, built of slate: it has been used for houses, walls, steps and the church. At one time, most of the buildings in the county incorporated roofing slates or flagstones from Delabole and over 500 people were employed blasting and slicing the stone into attractively named standard sizes, such as Ladies, Countesses, Duchesses, Queens and Imperials. The high quality dark blue slate has been quarried here, without interruption, since Tudor times and it is the oldest continuously worked slate quarry in Europe. However, it is known that, in around 2000 BC, Beaker Folk on Bodmin Moor used slate as baking shelves.

THE OLD COTTAGE,

Westdowns, near Delabole,
Cornwall PL33 9DT
Tel: 01840 212879 Fax: 01840 212879

Originally a carpenter's workshop and at least 200 years old, **The Old Cottage** has been completely refurbished from a derelict state by owners David and Merrilyn Ray. The idea of offering bed and breakfast was suggest to the couple by friends who having stayed here found it the ideal place to relax, explore and escape. The two charming guest rooms are separate from the cottage itself and are housed in the old carpenter's shop. This too has been expertly renovated and throughout the building is beautifully decorated and furnished. The lounge retains the workshop's original open beamed ceiling and, though there is central heating, a corner slate fireplace with a wrought iron wood burner adds to the olde worlde atmosphere here.

The two en suite bedrooms are very comfortable and whilst one lies upstairs on a balcony, the other can be found beyond the lounge. A hearty full cooked breakfast is served to everyone in your cosy lounge. Those looking for more independence will be interested to learn that David and Merrilyn also have two self-catering cottages at nearby Rock. Both have their own private enclosed gardens and, again, the couple have done a splendid refurbishment on these ancient properties. Some of the oldest buildings in the area, one of the cottages was the home of an artisan whilst the other is a converted barn.

The huge crater of **Delabole Slate Quarry** is over half a mile wide and 500 feet deep and it is the largest man-made hole in the country. Although the demand for traditional building materials has declined throughout the 20th century, the quarry is still worked and there are occasional slate splitting demonstrations as well as a range of old slate quarrying tools for visitors to view at the visitors' centre.

Once known as 'the great slate road', the lanes to the west of Delabole used to carry vast quantities of stone to the harbours at Port Gaverne, Port Isaac, Port Quin and Boscastle until the railways took over the transport of the stone in the 1890s.

WESTDOWNS
3½ miles S of Tintagel on the B3314

To the west of the village, lies **Delabole Wind Farm**, the first such farm in Britain and one that produces enough power each year to satisfy over half the annual demands of both Delabole and Camelford. The 10 tall turbines provide an unusual landmark and there is an interesting visitors' centre which explains the process of converting wind power into electricity.

BODMIN MOOR

An Area of Outstanding Natural Beauty, the bleak expanse of Bodmin Moor, which lies between 800 and 1400 feet above sea level and covers around 100 square miles, is the smallest of the three great West Country moors. The granite upland is characterised by saturated moorland and weather beaten tors and from here the rivers Inny, Lynher, Fowey, St Neot and De Lank flow to both the north and south coasts of Cornwall.

Golitha Falls, Bodmin Moor

At 1377 feet, **Brown Willy** is the highest point of the moor and of Cornwall whilst, just to the northwest, lies **Rough Tor** (pronounced 'row tor' to rhyme with 'now tor'), the moor's second highest point. Standing on National Trust-owned land, the Rough Tor is a magnificent viewpoint and also the site of a memorial to the men of the Wessex Regiment who were killed during World War II.

Throughout this wild and beautiful moorland there are the remains left behind by earlier occupiers: there are scattered Bronze Age hut circles and field enclosures, such as Fernacre Stone Circle, and Iron Age hill forts. Many villages grew up around the monastic cells of Celtic missionaries and took the name of a saints whilst others were mining villages where ruined engine houses still stand out against the skyline.

AROUND BODMIN MOOR

BOLVENTOR
Centre of Bodmin Moor off the A30

Situated at the heart of the moor, this scenic village is the location of the former coaching inn which was immortalised in Daphne du Maurier's novel, *Jamaica Inn*. During the 18th and 19th centuries this isolated hostelry,

Jamaica Inn, Bolventor

which lay on the main route across the bleak moorland, provided an ideal meeting point for outlaws and smugglers as well as legitimate travellers between Cornwall and the rest of England.

Daphne du Maurier made her first journey to Cornwall in 1926 when she travelled to Fowey with her mother and sisters. Crossing

Bodmin Moor, she fell in love with the windswept yet romantic landscape and it became the inspiration for many of her novels. Little changed today, **Jamaica Inn** still welcomes visitors who not only come here seeking refreshment and comfortable accommodation during a long journey but also to discover the secrets of the moors and the life and works of du Maurier at **Daphne du Maurier's The Smugglers at Jamaica Inn**. Her stirring tale of smugglers, romance and murder, inspired by a stay at the inn in 1930 is a modern classic and a room here is furnished with her memorabilia that includes her Sheraton writing desk upon which are a dish of Glacier mints, her favourite, and a packet of du Maurier cigarettes, that were named after her famous actor father, Sir Gerald. Other, more colourful characters are remembered at the inn and there is a vast collection of smugglers' relics to be seen.

Also at the inn is **Mr Potter's Museum of Curiosity** where the work of the famous taxidermist, Walter Potter, is celebrated in a display of some 10,000 unique exhibits laid out in a true Victorian fashion.

Just to the south of Bolventor lies the mysterious natural tarn, **Dozmary Pool**, another place that is strongly linked with the legend of King Arthur. According to one tale, King Arthur was brought here following his final battle at Slaughterbridge, near Camelford. As he lay dying at the water's edge, he implored his friend, Sir Bedivere, to throw his sword, Excalibur, into the centre of the lake where it was received by a lady's hand rising up from the water. However, there are several other lakes around the country,

Dozmary Pool, Bolventor

notably Looe Pool at Mount's Bay and both Bosherstone and Llyn Llydaw in Wales, which also lay claim to being home to the Lady of the Lake and the resting place of Excalibur.

This desolate and lonely place is also linked with Jan Tregeagle, the wicked steward of the Earl of Radnor whose many evil deeds include the murder of the parents of a young child whose estate he wanted. As a punishment, so the story goes, Tregeagle was condemned to spend the rest of time emptying the lake using only a leaking limpet shell. His howls of despair are said to be heard here to this day.

This pool, by tradition, is bottomless although it did dry up completely during the prolonged drought of 1869 and it lies close to **Colliford Lake**, the county's largest man-made reservoir. At 1000 feet above sea level, this area is the perfect habitat for long tailed ducks, dippers, grey wagtails and sand martins and the lake also offers some excellent watersports facilities.

ST CLETHER
5 miles NE of Bolventor off the A395

An elaborate holy well can be found a few hundred yards northwest of this tranquil village, standing on its own on a bracken-covered shelf above the River Inney. With its adjacent 15th century chapel, this well is the most enchanting of its kind in the county. The village itself has a part Norman church which was heavily restored by the Victorians; however, a number of earlier features have survived, including the Norman stone pillars and font and the 15th century tower.

WARBSTOW
9 miles N of Bolventor off the A39

This village of old slate cottages is overlooked by **Warbstow Bury Hillfort**; one of the largest Iron Age earthworks in Cornwall and the large mound in the middle is probably now a rabbit warren. There are wonderful views over northern Bodmin Moor from the fort.

NORTH PETHERWIN
10 miles NE of Bolventor off the B3254

Found above the River Ottery, this village is home to the **Tamar Otter Park**, which is a branch of the famous Otter Trust. Dedicated to breeding young otters for release back into

TREDIDON BARTON HOLIDAYS,

Tredidon Barton, St Thomas, near Launceston, Cornwall PL15 8SJ
Tel: 01566 86288/86463 website: www.hidden-valley.com.uk

Tucked away on the eastern edge of Bodmin Moor lies **Tredidon Barton Holidays**, an attractive and select holiday cottage complex that provides the ideal place for a self-catering holiday in quiet and peaceful surroundings. At the centre lies Tredidon House, the home of Catherine Jones who, with the help of her daughter, Allison, personally runs Tredidon Barton Holidays. There are three separate cottages here and the first is a self-contained wing of Tredidon farmhouse which has a beautiful entrance hall and an elegant Georgian staircase. Close by lies the Granary Barn, a stone built house that has been cleverly converted from an old farm building to provide comfortable and interesting

holiday accommodation. Lastly, Sunnyside Cottage, in its picturesque valley setting, is a charming period cottage which, as with the other properties, offers luxury accommodation in spacious and comfortable surroundings.

Near to Tredidon Barton Holidays lies Hidden Valley, a splendid conservation adventure park that is owned by Catherine's son Peter and to which holiday guests have unlimited free access. Apart from the family attractions here there is also coarse fishing on two lakes.

NEW MILLS FARM PARK,

New Mills, St Thomas, near Launceston, Cornwall PL15 8SN
Tel: 01566 777106

Found just a short drive from the centre of Launceston and close to the terminus of the Launceston Steam Railway lies **New Mills Farm Park**, a popular family attraction that has been created by owners, Richard and Sandra Ball. Set in over 40 acres of gently rolling Cornish countryside, New Mills Farm Park has something to offer every member of the family, young and old. There are woodland walks along the trackbed of the old railway, where, in the leafy shade, a whole host of birds and small animals can be spotted by those prepared to tread quietly. Meanwhile, there are large grassed meadows, complete with picnic benches, where families can enjoy the panoramic views and relax while the

children play. Among the many favourite games here is croquet and there is also a safe, secure and imaginative children's adventure play ground and trampolines for those with moundless energy.

A small rural museum provides the ideal opportunity to discover how life was lived in this area through the centuries and there are also numerous farm animals that are sure to delight everyone. Open throughout the season, this pleasant park is a lovely place to visit that not only offers a fun day out but also the chance to enjoy the delightful countryside.

the wild to prevent the species from becoming extinct in lowland England, visitors can watch the otters playing in large natural enclosures, see them in their breeding dens, or holts, and watch the orphans in the rehabilitation centre. The park also includes an area of natural woodland that is home to Muntjac, Fallow and Chinese Water deer whilst, around the Waterfowl lakes, there are peacocks, golden pheasant and wallabies.

EGLOSKERRY
8½ miles NE of Bolventor off the A395

To the north of this granite village lies **Penheale Manor**, an impressive building constructed between 1620 and 1640 although some alterations were made in the 1920s. The home of the influential Speccott family in the 17th century, many of whom are memorialised in the village's part Norman church, the manor house is not open to the public.

LAUNCESTON
10 miles NE of Bolventor on the A388

On the eastern edge of Bodmin Moor and close to the county border with Devon, Launceston (the local pronunciation is Lawnson) is one of Cornwall's most pleasant inland towns and it was a particular favourite of Sir John Betjeman. An important regional capital - the capital of Cornwall until 1838 - which also guarded the main overland route into the county, it was here, shortly after the Norman Conquest, that William I's half-brother, Robert of Mortain, built a massive castle overlooking the River Kensey. A place from which Robert tried to govern the fiercely independent Cornish people, **Launceston Castle** was subsequently the base of the Earls of Cornwall. Visited by the Black Prince and seized by the Cornish rebels of 1549, the castle changed hands twice during the Civil War before becoming an assize court and prison that was famous for imprisoning and executing 'on the nod'. It was here, in 1656, that George Fox, the founder of the Society of Friends, was held for several months. Today,

Launceston Castle

the castle is in ruins and, whilst the outer bailey is a public park, the 12 foot thick outer walls of the round keep and the tower can still be seen.

As well as growing up around the castle, Launceston was also the home of a powerful Augustinian Priory that was founded in 1136 on the northern banks of the river. Though most of the buildings have gone, the priory's chapel of ease, now **St Thomas' Church**, remains. Although this is a small building, it houses, amongst other Norman features, the largest font in Cornwall. The medieval **South Gate** is another reminder of the importance placed on the town as a stronghold as this castellated building has served as both a guardhouse and a gaol.

Elsewhere in Launceston, the streets around the castle are filled with handsome buildings dating from Georgian times and earlier and these include the impressive **Lawrence House**. Built in 1753 and containing some superb plasterwork ceilings, this is home to the **Lawrence House Museum** which dedicates its numerous displays to the history of the area.

To the west of the town, and running through the beautiful **Kensey Valley**, the **Launceston Steam Railway** takes visitors on a journey back in time. Many of the locomotives here are over 100 years old and, travelling in either open or closed carriages, passengers can enjoy a round trip along five miles of track to Newmills and back. Renowned for its station buffet, the steam railway also has a model railway display, workshops open to the public and a transport museum.

LANEAST
5½ miles NE of Bolventor off the A395

The birthplace of John Adams, the astronomer who discovered the planet Neptune, Laneast is also home to one of the many holy wells found in this part of the county. The well is now housed in a 16th century building and, close by, stands a tall Celtic cross and the village's original Norman parish church.

ALTARNUN
4 miles NE of Bolventor off the A30

Situated in a steep-sided valley of Penpont Water, this charming moorland village is home to a splendid, chiefly 15th century, parish church that is often referred to as the

The Gatehouse, Launceston

PENHALLOW MANOR COUNTRY HOUSE HOTEL,

Altarnun, near Launceston, Cornwall PL15 7SJ
Tel: 01566 86206 Fax: 01566 86179
e-mail: stay@penhallow-manor.co.uk website: www.penhallow-manor.co.uk

Dating from 1842, **Penhallow Manor Country House Hotel** is a very special place to visit. As well as being a superb, small, family run hotel set in glorious grounds, this charming early Victorian vicarage has a wealth of history attached to it that will certainly be of interest to visitors. Constructed on a site whose religious associations go back hundreds of years, the hotel lies adjacent to the village's famous church and it still retains its private gateway into the churchyard. Penhallow Manor has also featured in the novels of Daphne du Maurier: a friend of the then vicar of Altarnun, Daphne would spend many hours in the village and the last chapter of her novel, *Jamaica Inn*, are set in the hotel's drawing room. Still displaying many of the building's original features, this wonderful hotel is also fortunate in having

finely proportioned rooms which, thanks to the care and attention of owners, Val and Peter Russell, have been beautifully decorated and furnished in an elegant fashion. Guests can relax in either the drawing room or the well stocked library, before moving through to a splendid freshly prepared dinner in the hotel's charming dining room. Finally, each of the six luxury en suite guest rooms have been individually decorated and furnished, with style and flair, and a further three of these can be found in the recently converted old coach house which also has its own private courtyard and sitting room.

'Cathedral of the Moors'. Dedicated, as is the holy well near by, to St Nonna, the mother of St David of Wales, the church's 108 foot pinnacled tower rises high above the peat stained river whilst, inside the unusually light and airy interior, there are various features from Norman times through to the fine 16th century bench end carvings.

In the churchyard stands a Celtic cross which is thought to date from the same time as that of St Nonna's journey here from Wales in around AD527. There are also fine examples of the work of the Altarnun born sculptor Nevill Northey Bunard, to be found here.

The waters of St Nonna's well were once thought to cure madness and, after being immersed in the waters, lunatics were carried into the church for mass.

MINIONS
6 miles SE of Bolventor off the B3254

Boasting the highest pub in the county, this moorland village was, particularly during Victorian and Edwardian times, a thriving

mining centre with miners and quarrymen extracting granite, copper and lead. This was also the setting for EV Thompson's historical novel, Chase the Wind. Today, a former mine engine house has become the **Minions Heritage Centre** which covers over 4000 years of life on the moorland and includes the story of mining as well as the life and times of much earlier inhabitants of this area.

Close to the village stands the impressive **Hurlers Stone Circle**, a Bronze Age temple comprising three circles - the largest being some 135 feet in diameter. The name comes from the ancient game of hurling (a Celtic form of hockey) and legend has it that the circles were men who were turned to stone for playing the game on the Sabbath.

Also close to the village lies the **Cheesewring**, a natural pile of granite slabs whose appearance is reminiscent of a cheese press. Again numerous legends are attached to this curious monument although the tale of Daniel Gumb, a local stone cutter who was a great reader as well as teaching himself mathematics and astronomy, is undoubtedly true. After marrying a local girl, they made

THE CHEESEWRING HOTEL,

Minions, near Liskeard,
Cornwall PL14 5LE
Tel: 01579 362321

Found in the centre of Minions, on the edge of Bodmin Moor, **The Cheesewring Hotel** is one of Cornwall's highest inns. A large and attractive establishment, with a terrace beer garden to the front, the inn was originally built, in 1840, for the home of the local mine's paymaster general. Its unusual name comes from the spectacular natural granite formation, found nearby on the moors, that is known as the Cheesewring. Legend has it that this peculiar tower was the haunt of a druid who possessed a golden chalice which never ran dry and provided thirsty travellers with an endless supply of water. The story was partially borne out in 1818 when archaeologists excavating a nearby burial chamber discovered a skeleton clutching a golden cup.

Whilst the hotel does not boast such a cup, it is, however, locally famous for serving Cheesewring - a real ale that is locally brewed especially for the inn. The well stocked bar also serves a wide variety of other beers, ales and ciders so that all can enjoy their favourite tipple. Experienced owners, Allan and Rita Witts have also, since arriving here in February 2000, put the inn on the map as a superb place to eat. The regularly changing menu of delicious homecooked food is extensive includes the list of tasty curries which are something of a house speciality. A popular and lively local inn, that welcomes children, The Cheesewring Hotel can also offer visitors excellent accommodation in well appointed room that have panoramic views over Bodmin Moor.

WHEAL TOR HOTEL,

Caradon Hill, Pensilva, near Liskeard, Cornwall PL14 5PJ
Tel: 01579 362281 Fax: 01579 363401
e-mail: pdc@whealtorhotel.freeserve.co.uk website address: www.wheal-tor-hotel.co.uk

The **Wheal Tor Hotel** is not only Cornwall's highest inn but it is also one of the county's most hidden. Found in a remote location on the rugged slopes of Caradon Hill on the eastern fringes of Bodmin Moor, this marvellous hotel is well worth taking the trouble to find. A splendid stone building dating from the 1850s, it was originally built for the captain of the East Caradon Mine and from its woodland setting there are spectacular views across the miles of countryside to Dartmoor in the east and the Cornish coastlines in the west.

A place of peace, solitude and tranquillity, owners Peter and Carol Chapman have, since arriving here in February 1999, completely refurbished the property to provide customers with a comfortable environment in which to enjoy the superb hospitality on offer. Local beer is a feature at the bar whilst many come here to sample the excellent home cooked cuisine in the restaurant. Prepared by Carol, the delicious dishes include many tempting suggestions and the reputation of the Wheal Tor Hotel is spreading rapidly. The accommodation too reaches the same high standards as the rest of the hotel and, with an attractive beer garden and many of Cornwall's attractions within easy reach, this is a great base for a family holiday.

their home in a cave under the Cheesewring and, before the cave collapsed, many of Gumb's intricate carvings could be seen in the granite, including the inscription "D Gumb 1735". A local legend tells that the Cheesewring was the haunt of a druid who possessed a golden chalice which never ran dry and provided thirsty passers-by with an endless supply of water. The discovery, at near by Rillaton Barrow in 1837, of a ribbed cup of beaten gold lying beside a skeleton, does seem to add some credence to the story. Dubbed the Rillaton Cup, it can be seen at the British Museum, London.

UPTON CROSS
7 miles SE of Bolventor on the B3254

A handsome village that is home to Sterts Art Centre, which has one of the few open-air amphitheatres in the country, Upton Cross is also the place to come to for traditional Cornish Yarg Cheese. Made at Netherton in the beautiful Lynher Valley this famous cheese, which comes wrapped in nettle leaves, not only has a distinctive tasty and appearance, but is a local delicacy that has

reached many of the best restaurants and delicatessen counters in the country.

ST CLEER
6½ miles SE of Bolventor off the B3254

A sizeable moorland village in the heart of bleak former mining country, St Cleer is arranged around its 15th century parish church. Just to the northeast of the churchyard lies another 15th century structure: a fine stone building that covers a holy well. One of the many preserved wells to be found in Cornwall, **St Cleer's Holy Well** was thought to have curative powers particularly for those suffering from insanity and, here, the patients were tossed up and down in the waters until they were sane.

Dating from Neolithic times and found a mile east of the village, **Trethevy Quoit** is an impressive enclosed chamber tomb which originally formed the core of a vast earthwork mound. The largest such structure in the county, Trethevy Quoit is believed to be over 5000 years old and, although the rectangular hole cut into the stone blocking the tomb's entrance was thought to allow bodies to be

Trethevy Quoit Dolmen

placed inside, the reason for the hole in the capstone is unknown.

Also close by is **King Doniert's Stone**, a tall stone cross which was erected in memory of King Durngarth, a Cornish king thought to have drowned in the nearby River Fowey in AD875. The Latin inscription on the cross, which is now sadly in two pieces, reads, after translation, "Erected for Doniert for the good of his soul."

Downstream from King Doniert's Stone, the River Fowey descends, for half a mile, through dense broadleaved woodland in a delightful series of cascades known as **Golitha Falls**. This outstanding beauty spot is also a National Nature Reserve.

ST NEOT
6 miles S of Bolventor off the A38

This tranquil village on the edge of Bodmin

Moor once thrived on the woollen industry but, today, it is famous for its splendid 15th century church. Dedicated to St Anietus, this parish church is not only the home of a fine 9th century granite cross but it still retains its fabulous early 16th century stained glass windows. In one, God is depicted measuring out the universe during the Creation whilst, in another, Noah can be seen with his Ark, that takes the shape of a sailing ship of the period.

However, perhaps the most interesting window is that of St Neot, the diminutive saint after whom the village is named. Standing only 15 inches tall, St Neot became famous for his miracles involving animals and one story tells of an exhausted hunted doe who ran to Neot's side. A stern look from the saint sent the pursuing hounds back into the forest whilst the huntsman dropped his bow and became a faithful disciple. Another tale, and the one that can be seen in the church window, tells of an angel giving Neot three fish for his well - saying that, as long as he only eats one fish a day there will always be fish in the well. Unfortunately, when Neot fell ill his servant took two fish from the well, cooked them and gave them to Neot who, horrified, prayed over the meal and ordered the fish to return to the well. As the dead fish touched the water they came alive again.

Outside the church, and tied to the tower, is an oak branch that is replaced each year on Oak Apple Day. The ceremony was started by the Royalists wishing to give thanks for the oak tree where Charles II hid whilst fleeing the country.

Just south of the village are the **Carnglaze Slate Caverns**, where visitors can see a subterranean lake. Slate for use in the building trade was first quarried here in these

RIVERMEAD FARM,

Twowatersfoot, near Liskeard, Cornwall PL14 6HT
Tel: 01208 821464

Set in the glorious countryside on the edge of Bodmin Moor and with the River Fowey flowing along the southern boundary of this large estate, **Rivermead Farm** is not only an attractive place to stay but also well situated for both the north and south coasts of Cornwall. This splendid farm, with its 250 year old stone cottage and 30 acres of mixed woodland and

meadow, is owned by Kathleen and Alan Hunstone and they have created some superb family holiday accommodation in the cottage and the adjacent traditional stone barn. Popular with fishermen and nature lovers, this is also the perfect place for children and, by prior arrangement, the family dog.

vast man-made caverns in the 14th century. The largest chamber is over 300 feet high and was once used by smugglers as a secret rum store. The lichen on the cavern walls is covered with minute droplets of water which reflect the available light in the most magical way. Visitors can see the remains of the tramway which was built to haul the stone to the surface from the lower levels and, at the deepest level, there is a subterranean pool which is filled with the clearest blue-green water.

WARLEGGAN
5 miles S of Bolventor off the A38

The remote location of this hamlet, up a steep wooded lane, has led to its long associations with the supernatural and it has long been acknowledged as a haunt of the Cornish 'piskies'.

However, Warleggan's most eccentric inhabitant was the Reverend Frederick Densham who arrived here in 1931. He immediately began to alienate his parishioners by closing the Sunday School, putting barbed wire around the rectory and patrolling the grounds with a pack of German Shepherd dogs. In response, his congregation stayed away from the church and one record in the parish registry of the time reads, "*No fog. No wind. No rain. No congregation.*" Unperturbed, Densham fashioned his own congregation from cardboard, filled the pews and preached undisturbed. It does appear that the rector did have a kinder nature, however, as his constructed a children's playground in the rectory garden.

CARDINHAM
6½ miles SW of Bolventor off the A30

A small village, on the western slopes of Bodmin Moor, in the churchyard of the 15th century church that is dedicated to St Meubred, a little known hermit, stands a 10th century cross that, though worn, is richly decorated with intricate spirals and rings.

Now a peaceful backwater that is enjoyed by both walkers and cyclists, **Cardinham Woods** was, in medieval times, the location of an important Norman motte and bailey castle. Belonging to the Cardinham family, under-lords of Robert of Mortain of Launceston, the structure was abandoned in the 14th century

and today only an earthwork mound remains on which a few traces of the original keep have been preserved. This attractive and varied woodland was acquired by the Forestry Commission in 1922 and now produces a high quality Douglas fir for the British timber industry. A haven for a wide variety of wildlife, there is also a woodland café, several woodland trails and cycle hire here.

BODMIN
10 miles SW of Bolventor on the A38

Situated mid way between Cornwall's north and south coasts and at the junction of two anicent cross country trade routes, Bodmin has always been an important town and was used by traders between Wales, Ireland and northern France who preferred the overland journey between the Camel and Fowey estuaries rather than the sea voyage around Land's End. Castle Canyke to the southeast of the town was built during the Iron Age to defend this important trade route and a few centuries later the Romans erected a fort on a site here above the River Camel. One of a string they built in the southwest to defend strategic river crossings, the remains of the earthwork can still be made out today. The waymarked footpath, the **Saints' Way**, follows the ancient cross country route.

In the 6th century, St Petroc, one of the most influential of the early Welsh missionary saints, visited Bodmin and, in the 10th century, the monastery he had founded in Padstow moved here as a protection against sea raids by the Vikings. The town's **Parish Church** is dedicated to St Petroc and the 15th century building is certainly one of the most impressive and largest in all Cornwall. Building began on the site of the former Norman church in 1469 and, funded by the towns folk - even the local vicar gave a year's salary - the church was completed in 1472. Though remodelled in the 19th century, it has retained its splendid Norman font, whose immense bowl is supported on five finely carved columns, and the ivory casket that is thought to contain the remains of St Petroc. The town is also renowned for its abundance of holy wells and, in the churchyard, lies **St Goran's Well**, which dates from the 6th century.

The only market town in Cornwall to have appeared in the Domesday Book, Bodmin - the

THE MASONS ARMS,

5/9 Higher Bore Street, Bodmin, Cornwall PL31 1JS
Tel: 01208 72607

Found close to the town centre and in an quiet part of this ancient town, **The Masons Arms** is a splendid traditional old inn that is owned and personally run by Maggie Barter. The inn dates back to the 17th century and it is believed to have held a licence longer than any other inn in the county. An attractive white washed building, bedecked by hanging baskets and window boxes in summer, The Masons Arms is a place well worth seeking out whilst exploring Bodmin. Full of atmosphere inside, the original ceiling beams of the inn are decorated with pump clips from the very many different real ales that have been served here and, along with the flagstone floors and exposed stone walls, stepping in here is like stepping back in time.

As well as serving an excellent selection of drinks from the bar, including at least four real ales, The Masons Arms is also a popular place to eat. A tasty menu of delicious home-made dishes, all prepared by Maggie, are served each lunchtime and there is sure to be something to tempt even the most jaded palate. Warm, friendly and cosy inside, when the weather is fine, customers tend to drift outside into the secluded rear beer garden and, so essential in Bodmin, the inn also has a car park at the back.

HOTEL CASI CASA,

11 Higher Bore Street, Bodmin,
Cornwall PL31 1JS
Tel: 01208 77592 Fax: 01208 75771
e-mail: casi@casa30.fsnet.co.uk

Within a couple of minutes walk from the centre of Bodmin and found next door to The Masons Arms, **Hotel Casi Casa** is a charming and friendly family run establishment that is instantly recognisable by its bright yellow painted front façade. The green and white striped awnings and the flower filled hanging baskets and window boxes add extra splashes of colour to this already attractive hotel. Owners, Peter and Belinda Green, have been here since Easter 1999 and this original Victorian cottage was cleverly converted into this comfortable hotel by Belinda's father in the late 1980s.

Very much a cosy family establishment, where children are made welcome, Hotel Casi Casa has everything guests could want for a perfect stay in this old town. There is an intimate and well stocked bar as well as a well appointed dining room. Here guests are not only treated to a fine breakfast each morning but there is also an extensive homecooked dinner menu, with accompanying wine list, that is sure to please everyone - vegetarians too have plenty of choice. Finally, the hotel's seven en suite guest rooms, four of which are on the ground floor, are not only as well furnished and decorated as the rest of Hotel Casi Casa but they are also the perfect place for a peaceful and refreshing night's sleep.

THE DUKE OF CORNWALL'S LIGHT INFANTRY REGIMENTAL MUSEUM,

The Keep, Bodmin, Cornwall PL31 1EG
Tel: 01208 72810 Fax: 01208 72810 e-mail: dclimus@talk21.com

Housed in The Keep near the General Railway Station in Bodmin this museum covers military history based on the County Regiment of Cornwall, The Duke of Cornwall's Light Infantry. The regiment was formed as marines in 1702 and played a major part in the capture of Gibraltar in 1704.

An important exhibit is General George Washington's bible captured in 1777 during the American War of Independence. and in the same war the Regiment claims to have taken part in the first deliberate night attack carried out by British infantry. Most major wars have exhibitions, Napoleonic wars - including action in

the Peninsula and at Waterloo, the Crimea War, Indian Mutiny, Boer War and the two World Wars. Since 1900 the Regiment has lost 5,000 men killed in action serving the country.

The museum has two main galleries, one a historical gallery telling the story of past battles, and the other holds fascinating displays of uniforms, medals - including eight Victoria Crosses, rifles and pistols. Also on display in the Soldiers' Aisle of St Petroc's Church in Bodmin are the regiment's old colours.

BODMIN AND WENFORD RAILWAY,

Bodmin General Station, Bodmin, Cornwall PL31 1AQ
Tel: 01208 73666 Fax: 01208 77963

Throughout the 1830s and 1840s a great expansion of the railway network in the country took place and Cornwall was no exception. Linking Bodmin, the then county town, with London was a priority and, although the cost of a direct line was too great, a branch line was built linking Bodmin to the main line route running to the south. First opened in 1887, it is this link which is now the Bodmin and Wenford Railway. A further branch line, opened in 1888, running to the north, now also takes the steam and diesel trains of the railway to Boscarne Junction. Set up 100 years after the lines first opened, this railway acquired the then disused lines and, from their headquarters at Bodmin General Station, passengers and railway enthusiasts can relive the days of steam and travel via Colesloggett Halt to Bodmin Parkway Station or, in the other direction, to Boscarne Junction. Lying in peaceful countryside, Colesloggett Halt is the ideal place to stop for a picnic in the glorious Cardinham Woods whilst, at the end of the line, Bodmin Parkway Station is within easy walking distance of Lanhydrock House.

Meanwhile, a steam train ride to Boscarne Junction is an excellent way to link up with the Camel Trail foot and cycle path. Back in the restored splendour of Bodmin General Station visitors also have the chance to see the railway's collection of steam and diesel locomotives and carriages as well as enjoy the homemade refreshments in the buffet and browse through the souvenir shop.   There is a comprehensive timetable and, throughout the year, a series of special events including murder mystery journeys and steam, beer and jazz weekends. All in all this is a fascinating place that will delight all the family.

SILVERSTREAM CORNISH COUNTRY HOLIDAYS,

Hellandbridge, near Bodmin, Cornwall PL30 4QR
Tel: 01208 74408 Fax: 01208 74408
e-mail: Silverstreamhols@hellandbridge.freeserve.co.uk
website: www.Silverstreamcottages.co.uk

Found in its own private six acre nature reserve, **Silverstream Cornish Country Holidays** is the perfect place from which to enjoy peace and tranquillity as well as explore the varied countryside of Cornwall. Owned and personally run by Iain and Ann Cameron, this wonderful establishment has plenty to offer including a range of accommodation that is sure to suit everyone. From their charming old Cornish farmhouse, the couple offer top class bed and breakfast accommodation in a choice of comfortable and well equipped guest rooms. Close by, in fact, two of the cottages adjoin the farmhouse, there are three traditional old cottages which, as well as being a true home from home, offer families and friends the chance to be completely independent. Each has its own patio area and the delightful cottage style gardens are beautifully maintained. Meanwhile,

found in a large meadow down by the River Camel, Iain and Ann also offer self catering accommodation in a choice of superbly constructed cedar wood lodges. As comfortable furnished and decorated as the cottages, these lodges again are the perfect retreat. Back at the farmhouse, Ann and Iain have also opened a lovely restaurant and tea gardens where, not only are they open throughout the day to serve a delicious menu of homemade light meals, snacks and Cornish Cream teas, but also those self catering have a chance to take a well earned break.

TREDETHY HOUSE,

Helland Bridge, near Wadebridge,
Cornwall PL30 4QS
Tel: 01208 841262 Fax: 01208 841707

Overlooking the Camel Valley and situated in its own picturesque grounds, **Tredethy House** is a delightful country house hotel which has retained the atmosphere of a private residence. Dating back, in parts, to Tudor times, this historic building underwent a series of radical alterations at the hands of the owners, the Hext family, in the 1860s which created what is still seen today - an enchanting Victorian country house. Tredethy's most famous owner, however, was its last private resident, Prince of Chula of Thailand who, in the 1930s, made up the ERA motor racing team with his driver cousin Prince Bira. Today's owners, Amanda and David, have also, in the short time that they have been here, made their mark on the house as they are responsible for the tremendous renovation work which has gone to make this one of the most impressive hotel's in the area. Elegant and stylish throughout, Tredethy provides superb hospitality of a standard that is rarely seen outside London. The marvellous guest rooms and suites can be found either in the main house or in the annexe - the house's original stable block which has been expertly converted for the purpose. Another great pleasure here is the hotel's restaurant where gourmet meals are prepared by the chef from the freshest local ingredients. Finally, as both children and dogs are also welcome here, Tredethy House is just the place for a relaxing holiday with the family where every need is taken care of beautifully.

name means the 'house of the monks' - was chiefly an ecclesiastical town until the reign of Henry VIII. However, this does not mean that is was necessarily a quiet place of contemplation and, during Tudor times, there were three uprisings here: against the tin levy in 1496, in support of Perkin Warbeck against Henry VII in 1497 and, in 1549, against the imposition of the English Prayer Book. In the 19th century, the town took over as the seat of the county (from Launceston) but when the Bodmin refused access to the town for the Great Western Railway, forcing the station to be built some distance away, the town failed to flourish as did Truro, now Cornwall's cathedral city.

Of the places and buildings to visit here, **Bodmin Jail**, the former county prison which dates back to 1776, is one of the most interesting. The last hanging took place here in 1909 and visitors have the chance to view the site. This too was the place where, during the Great War, both the Crown Jewels and the Domesday Book were hidden for safe keeping. Meanwhile, **Bodmin Town Museum** provides, through its numerous displays, an insight into the town's past as well as life in and around Bodmin through the centuries.

Just a short distance from the town centre lies **Bodmin Beacon Local Nature Reserve** from which there are splendid views across the town and the moors. On the summit of the beacon stands a 144 foot obelisk, the Gilbert Memorial, which is dedicated to Sir Walter Raleigh Gilbert, a local soldier. Also easily reached from Bodmin is the **Camel Trail**, a walking and cycling path along the River Camel to Padstow which follows the track bed of one of Britain's earliest railways that opened in 1830 linking the town with the Camel Estuary.

BLISLAND
6 miles SW of Bolventor off the A30

Found down a maze of country lanes, at the centre of this moorland village is the tree-lined village green which has stayed faithful to its original Saxon layout - an uncommon sight on this side of the River Tamar. Fine Georgian and Victorian houses, a rectory and an inn complete the picture but it is the

THE BLISLAND INN,

Blisland, near Bodmin, Cornwall PL30 4JF
Tel: 01208 850739

Found opposite Blisland's large village green **The Blisland Inn** is a charming old country inn that is well worth taking the trouble to find. Built on the site of the previous village inn, which burnt down just 100 years ago, this attractive and traditional inn has plenty of outside seating so that customers can not only enjoy the excellent food and drink found here but also the lovely aspect of the inn. Owners, Margaret and Gary Marshall, have certainly worked hard to put this inn on the map of Cornwall and its reputation for superb hospitality is spreading far and wide. The interior, which looks much older than its 100 years, is full of character and there too can be

seen Margaret and Gary's vast collection of memorabilia, including pipes, barometers and Toby jugs. Famous for its real ales, there are at least five from which to choose, The Blisland Inn always serves Blisland Gold, a brew especially produced for the inn by a local micro brewery. Gary has keeps a running total of the different real ales he has served here and, by June 2000, it had reached 1148! However, although drink here is an important aspect of the inn food too draws many to The Blisland Inn. An extensive menu of delicious homecooked meals are served throughout the week, with a marvellous roast lunch on Sundays, and it is advisable to book for both weekends and in the evenings. Add to this the events which Margaret and Gary arrange throughout the year, including the annual Real Ale Festival, and this is an inn that should not be overlooked.

unusually dedicated **Church of St Protus and St Hyacinth** that takes most visitors' attention. A favourite of the Sir John Betjeman, who described it as "dazzling and amazing", the part-Norman building has a bright whitewashed interior, a good wagon roof, an unusual mock-Renaissance altar and two fonts, one Norman and the other dating from the 15th century.

On the moorland to the north of the village are numerous ancient monuments including the 108 foot diameter stone circle of **Blisland Manor Common** and, a couple of miles further away, **Stripple Stone Henge Monument** on Hawkstor Down.

WASHAWAY
10½ miles SW of Bolventor on the A389

Lying just north of the village is one of Cornwall's most attractive manor houses, the lovely **Pencarrow House**. Hidden within a 50 acre wooded estate which encompasses an Iron Age encampment, this historic Georgian house was built in the 1770s by the Molesworth-St Aubyn family and, still living here, they have, over the years, remodelled the house on two separate occasions. Of the many beautiful items to be seen on a visit to this award winning house the series of family portraits, many by eminently fashionable painters of the time, are particularly superb. Excellent furniture and exquisite porcelain is also on show. It was Sir William Molesworth, the Secretary of State for the Colonies, who, during Parliamentary recesses in the mid 19th century, began the ambitious remodelling of the gardens and grounds. Today's visitors benefit from his splendid plans as wandering around this internationally renowned garden there are over 700 different species of rhododendron, camellia, blue hydrangea and conifer to be seen.

2 Southeast Cornwall Coast

In 928 Athelstan used the River Tamar to establish the boundary of his Celtic kingdom and, today, the river still separates Cornwall from its neighbour Devon. Whilst to the north the landscape is dominated by a rugged and rocky coastline and bleak Bodmin Moor, the south coast has numerous coves and inlets as well as tranquil wooded valleys.

Both Saltash, on the south coast, and inland Gunnislake have been gateways into Cornwall for centuries and, whilst, Saltash now has two magnificent bridges - one road, one rail - to carry passengers into the county, Gunnislake is still relying on its 16th century bridge that was constructed by the influential Earls of Edgcumbe.

Along the coast, numerous picturesque ancient fishing villages can be found that not only prospered from pilchard fishing but also from shipping, first, the minerals mined further north on Bodmin Moor and, later, the china clay industry. However, these many sheltered and often lonely beaches also gave rise to a darker and more sinister trade and Fowey, Polperro and many other villages were also alive with smuggling activity. The

Fish Market, Looe

romance of this coastline and its colourful past has led to many writers settling in the area. By far the most famous is Daphne du Maurier who lived just outside Fowey in a house she immortalised in her novel *Rebecca*.

Of the places to see here, apart from the quaint villages and wonderful coastlines and river valleys, there are two superb country houses, Cotehele House and Mount Edgcumbe House, which were both owned by the earls of Edgcumbe. The older, Cotehele, lies in the Tamar Valley and is one of the best preserved late medieval estates in the country whilst 16th century Mount Edgcumbe House has been restored to its original glory after being damaged in a World War II bombing raid. Both too have beautiful gardens, full of exotic plants, that benefit from the mild climate that Cornwall enjoys courtesy of the Gulf Stream.

Rocky Coastline, Polperro

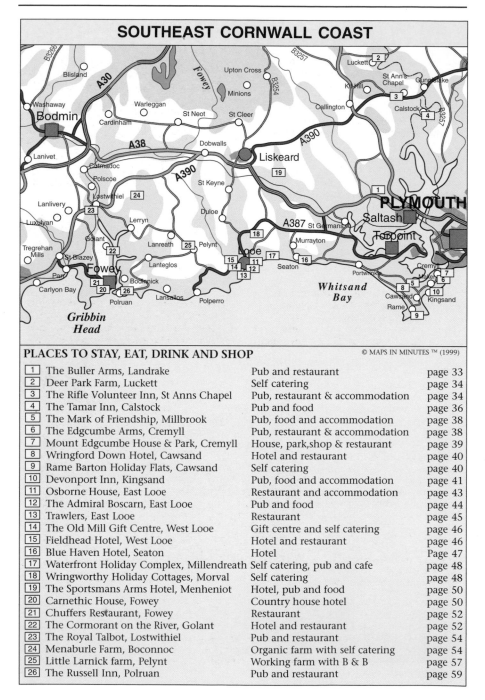

SOUTHEAST CORNWALL COAST

© MAPS IN MINUTES ™ (1999)

PLACES TO STAY, EAT, DRINK AND SHOP

SALTASH

A small medieval port on the River Tamar, and once the base for the largest river steamer fleet in the southwest, the narrow streets of Saltash's old town rise up steeply from the riverbank. It is still very much the "Gateway to Cornwall" for many holidaymakers, who cross the Tamar River into Cornwall at this point via one of the town's mighty bridges. Designed by Isambard Kingdom Brunel in 1859, the iron-built **Royal Albert Bridge** carries the railway whilst, alongside, is the much more slender **Tamar Bridge** that was opened in 1961. This modern suspension road bridge replaced the ferry service which had been in use since the 13th century.

Though older than Plymouth, on the other side of the Sound, Saltash, particularly with the construction of the road bridge, is now becoming a suburb of the large town. However, though heavily influenced by its neighbour, Saltash has retained much of its charm and Cornish individuality. From the old quayside, there are river trips up stream to Calstock and there are also several interesting

Brunel Bridge, Saltash

buildings to discover. The mainly 17th century **Guildhouse** stands on granite pillars and close by is **Mary Newman's Cottage**, a quaint old building that was the home of Sir Francis Drake's first wife. Dating from the 15th century, the cottage and gardens are occasionally open to the public.

Just a short distance from the town centre lies **Trematon Castle**, the home of the Lord Caradon. Only a few remains of the Norman keep, which had associations with the Black

THE BULLER ARMS,

The Square, Landrake, nr Saltash,
Cornwall PL12 5DY
Tel: 01752 851283

Dating back to the early 18th century, **The Buller Arms** is an old coaching and post inn that is named after the Buller family who owned much of the land around the village of Landrake. Still very much the village inn, The Buller Arms lies close to the church and it is, quite literally, the centre of Landrake. Although landlords, Laura and Leroy, have only been here since early 2000 they have certainly turned the fortunes of the inn around and it is now a popular place with plenty to offer both locals and visitors alike. In

the olde worlde atmosphere of the bar, customers can enjoy a wide range of drinks, including at least two real ales, whilst, during the August Bank Holiday weekend, the inn holds a beer festival when over 30 real ales can be sampled. With over 15 years in the catering industry, Leroy has vast experience and the success of the food at the inn is down to his hard work. The restaurant here specialises in fish and vegetarian dishes and such is its popularity that booking is essential. However, there is also a takeaway services along with a picnic hamper service which have both proved to be part of the inn's winning combination. Live music on Saturday evenings draws people to The Buller Arms as do the summer barbecues outside in the inn's large and attractive beer garden. All in all this is a delightful place where a warm welcome is assured.

DEER PARK FARM,

Luckett, near Callington, Cornwall PL17 8NW
Tel: 01579 370292 Fax: 01579 370292 e-mail: deer.park.farm@btclick.com

Found in the tranquil surroundings of the unspoilt Tamar Valley and with views overlooking Dartmoor, **Deer Park Farm** covers some 280 acres and was, until recently, owned and farmed by HRH Prince Charles, Duke of Cornwall. However, this area's associations with the monarchy go back many centuries and, in the 14th century, the surrounding countryside was an ancient Royal Deer Park. In 1985, Brian and Edna bought the property and, as well as continuing the mixed farming, they have also restored one of the farm's old barns into three luxury self-catering cottages.

These attractive stone buildings provide superb holiday accommodation for up to five and, as well as having all the latest modern equipment, they have been sympathetically converted to retain the old building's original features. Added attractions at the Deer Park Farm are the guests' recreation room and the private lake that can be fished for carp. Plans are underway to create a nature and heritage trail around the farmland and holidaymakers are welcome to see many of the farming activities throughout the year from lambing in spring to the haymaking in late summer.

THE RIFLE VOLUNTEER INN,

St Anns Chapel, Tamar Valley,
Cornwall PL18 9HL
Tel: 01822 832508 Fax: 01822 834230

With panoramic views down the River Tamar to the south and Dartmoor to the east, **The Rifle Volunteer Inn** is both a superb place to stay and an ideal base to explore the southwest. Dating back to the 1800s, this was originally a mine captain's house before becoming a coaching inn in the mid 19th century and it is named after the volunteer corps that was formed to defend England from a possible invasion by the French

between the 1850s and the 1880s. The traditional lounge bar is very much the village local and is an ideal place to relax and, like the distinctive Chapel bar, it has been furnished and decorated with items from an old Methodist chapel.

Assured of a warm friendly welcome from owners Frank and Lynda Hilldrup, customers will appreciate the excellent value of meals cooked on the premises and served in one of the most beautiful restaurants in the southwest. Fresh meat, fish, vegetarian, pastas or curries with a range of sauces cater for all tastes. The bar is stocked with the largest range in the area of wines, spirits and beers including local real ales. Finally this first class inn also offers superb accommodation in a choice of luxury en suite guest rooms that provide the same high level of comfort in stylish surroundings as the rest of the establishment.

Prince, can still be seen and they are now combined with the Georgian mansion house. The castle is not open to the public.

AROUND SALTASH

KIT HILL
8 miles N of Saltash off the B3257

On the summit of this 1096 foot peak is a reminder of the area's old industry in the form of a 80 foot chimney stack that was built in 1858 to serve one of the area's mines. Providing a dramatic outline for many miles, this 500 acre site was donated to the county of Cornwall by Prince Charles in 1985 and it has recently been designated a country park that is also rich in old industrial remains. From the summit there are outstanding views across southeast Cornwall to Plymouth Sound.

CALLINGTON
7½ miles N of Saltash on the A388

This old market town, which lies at the foot of Kit Hill (to the north), is situated on the fertile land between the Rivers Tamar and Lynher and which is rich fruit growing country. However, during the 19th century, the countryside around Callington, from Dartmoor in the east to Bodmin Moor in the west, prospered from frantic mining activity. The area's heritage, landscape and character can be seen by wandering around Callington as, through the interesting and unusual **Mural Project**, local scenes have been painted on the walls of the town's buildings.

Overlooking the River Lynher, to the southwest of the town, lies **Cadsonbury Hillfort** - a massive Iron Age bank and ditch encompassing a hill that are thought to be the remains of the home of a local chief.

Meanwhile, to the east of Callington, lies the attractive early 16th century granite **Dupath Chapel** that houses **Dupath Well**. The waters of this holy well were though to cure whooping cough and the charming chapel was used for baptisms.

ST ANN'S CHAPEL
7½ miles N of Saltash on the A390

Found close to the Cornwall-Devon border,

and in the heart of glorious countryside, the **Tamar Valley Donkey Park** is just the place for a family day out. A friendly establishment offering a fun-packed day, as well as the donkeys and donkey rides, there are a whole host of other animals to watch, a children's adventure play ground and a café.

GUNNISLAKE
8 miles N of Saltash on the A390

Often referred to as the first village in Cornwall, Gunnislake is a charming community that is set in the beautiful wooded valley of the River Tamar. In the 1520s, Sir Piers Edgcumbe of Cotehele House built the **New Bridge**, a striking 180 foot long, seven-arched granite structure which continues to serve as one of the major gateways into the county. In fact, this remained the lowest crossing of the river by road until the 1960s when the massive suspension bridge linking Plymouth with Saltash was opened. The river

New Bridge over the Tamar

crossing at Gunnislake meant that the village was a place of strategic importance, a feature which made it the centre of bitter fighting during the Civil War.

Like many other villages of the Tamar Valley Gunnislake, during the 18th and 19th centuries, was alive with mining although one of the first mines here had been worked from the 14th century. The mines have now closed and many of their buildings have been left to be reclaimed by nature. One of Turner's great paintings, *Crossing the Brook*, takes in a view of Gunnislake and the surrounding valley and, as well as the beauty of the countryside, a miners' lodging house is also immortalised.

THE TAMAR INN,

The Quay, Calstock,
Cornwall PL18 9QA
Tel: 01822 832487

Overlooking the River Tamar and found in the heart of this picturesque village on the county border, **The Tamar Inn** is a place well worth taking the time to discover. Dating back to the 17th century, this inn has, during its long history, been a meeting place for both smugglers and highwayman and, not unlike other inns, where there is a cool cellar, it has also been used as a morgue. Fortunately, today, landlords Helen and Jim, along with mum, Julie, welcome an altogether less gruesome group regular and new customers.

A wonderfully atmospheric inn, which has retained much of its character and charm down the years, The Tamar Inn is just to place to come to for good food and drink. The bar is well stocked, with at least five real ales available along with the usual beers, lagers, ciders and spirits. Meanwhile, an extensive menu of tasty home-cooked dishes are served that are sure to satisfy all the family. The inn's traditional Sunday lunches are generally served to the soothing music provided by a live pianist or violinist whilst, on Saturday evenings, there is further live entertainment. Whether eating, drinking and chatting in the cosy, olde worlde interior or outside in the secluded rear beer garden, it is easy to see why The Tamar Inn is fast becoming a popular and well known place indeed.

CALSTOCK
6 miles NE of Saltash off the A390

Well known for its splendid views of the Tamar valley, this village was an important river port in the 19th century when vast quantities of tin, granite and copper ore were brought here for loading on to barges to be transported down the Tamar to the coast and beyond. In the countryside surrounding Calstock the remains of old mine workings, along with the spoil heaps, can still be seen along with the remains of the village's boat-building industry. Earlier, in the 18th century, the Tamar Valley was renowned for its fruit growing and, in particular, its cherries. Today the springtime blossom is still a beautiful sight though not as spectacular as it once was.

The decline of the town as a port came with the construction of the huge **Railway Viaduct** which carries the Tamar Valley Line southwards to Plymouth. Completed in 1908 the giant 12-arched viaduct, the first in the country to be constructed of concrete blocks, stands 120 feet above the River Tamar. Probably one of Britain's most picturesque branch lines, the **Tamar Valley Line** can still be taken down to the coast and, though the river has lost most of its commercial traffic, it is a starting point for Tamar River canoe expeditions.

Found just to the southwest of Calstock and set on the steep wooded slopes of the Tamar

Railway Viaduct over Tamar River

Cotehele House

Valley is **Cotehele House**, one of the best preserved late medieval estates in the southwest of England. Largely built in the late 15th and early 16th centuries by Sir Piers Edgcumbe and his son Richard, this low granite fortified manor house is surrounded by, first, grounds that contain exotic and tender plants that thrive in the mild valley climate and, then, an estate that has retained its ancient network of paths which allow exploration of the valley.

In the 1550s, the Edgcumbe family moved their main residence from here southwards to Mount Edgcumbe overlooking Plymouth Sound and, since then, Cotehele has remained relatively untouched save for some additions to the northwest tower in 1627. There are many remnants of earlier ages to be seen here including the Great Tudor Hall, exceptional tapestries, period furniture and, outside, there is a medieval stewpond and a domed dovecote. The house also incorporates some charming individual features such as a secret

spy-hole to the Great Hall, a private chapel and a tower clock with a bell but no face or hands that is believed to be the oldest working example of its kind in the country.

Elsewhere, in the grounds, at the foot of a combe stands a tiny chapel situated on a promontory 70 feet above the river's edge. This was built in the 15th century by Sir Richard Edgcumbe, a Lancastrian, to show thanks for his escape from the Yorkist forces of Richard III who had been pursuing him through Cotehele Woods. Edgcumbe avoided capture by placing a stone in his cap and throwing it into the fast-flowing River Tamar, a clever ploy which made his pursuers think that he had jumped into the torrent and drowned.

Also along the river, and close to the estate's old cider house and mill, lies **Cotehele Quay**. A significant port in Victorian times, today's visitors will find a fascinating Museum that is devoted to telling the story of the River Tamar's vital role in the local economy.

Shamrock Tamar River Barge

Visitors can also see the *Shamrock*, a restored Tamar sailing barge moored outside the museum. Cotehele House and the surrounding estate are owned by the National Trust.

Upstream, beyond Calstock, lies **Morwellham Quay**, another important 19th century river port from which the ore and minerals extracted from the local mines were transported to the coast.

Cotehele Quay

THE MARK OF FRIENDSHIP,

5 New Street, Millbrook, near Torpoint,
Cornwall PL10 1BY
Tel: 01752 822253

Dating back over 200 years, **The Mark of Friendship** is a friendly and inviting inn found close to the sea down a quiet street in this picturesque village. Formerly three cottages and originally called the Commercial Arms until the 1940s, this delightful and attractive inn is a popular place with walkers, locals and visitors. Landlords, Iris and John Elliott, have been here since 1997 and this charming couple have certainly created a splendid place to enjoy superb hospitality. The food on offer here is wonderful homecooked fare which makes excellent use of the wealth of fresh local ingredients available. Sea food and fish is the house speciality and Surf and turf is one of the most popular dishes. However, the extensive menu, which is supplemented by an ever changing specials board, includes many other delights and ranges from tasty fresh filled sandwiches to succulent steaks. From the bar an equally extensive range of drinks are served, including several real ales, so that everyone can wash down their meal with their favourite tipple. Popular too are the various live music evenings on Saturday and Sunday and there is live jazz on Tuesdays. A splendid place to bring the whole family as children are especially made welcome, Iris and John also offer excellent bed and breakfast accommodation in a choice of two comfortable en suite guest rooms.

THE EDGCUMBE ARMS,

Cremyll, near Torpoint,
Cornwall PL10 1HX
Tel: 01752 822294 Fax: 01752 822014

The Edgcumbe Arms stands in a magnificent position with views over Plymouth Sound to Drake's Island to the front and Mouth Edgcumbe House and Country Park standing behind it. A large and attractive inn, the building seen today dates from 1995 and it replaces the previous inn which had stood here since the early 15th century before being destroyed by fire. However, though a new inn The Edgcumbe Arms is very traditional, both inside and out. With flagstone floors, wood panelled walls and beamed ceilings, this inn certainly gives the impression that it has been here for centuries and, the roaring log fires in winter, all add to the olde worlde atmosphere found here. Well known for its quality real ales, including brews with names such as Daylight Robbery and Celtic Smooth, this excellent inn is also highly regarded locally for its superb meals. There is plenty of choice and, whilst the meals and snacks can be taken in the bar or outside in the delightful surroundings of the lovely beer garden, there is also a splendid carvery served in the inn's first floor restaurant. The same blend of traditional decoration and furnishings and modern needs have been used in the inn's six superb en suite guest rooms which, are not only ideal for families, but also have their own private entrance.

TORPOINT
3 miles SE of Saltash on the A374

This small town grew up around the ferry service that began running across the **Hamoaze** (as the Tamar estuary is called at this point) between here and Devonport in the 18th century. Now it is more a dormitory town for Plymouth, though some small industrial boat-building remains. From its position on the northern arm of the Rame peninsula, Torpoint offers some excellent views across the river to the Royal Navy Dockyards, the *HMS Raleigh* and to the naval training centre.

Lying a mile north of Torpoint is **Anthony House**, a superb example of an early 18th century mansion that is now in the hands of the National Trust. Although this estate has been the home of the influential Cornish Carew family for nearly 600 years, this superb pale silver-grey stone building was constructed between 1718 and 1729 in a neo-classical style that consists of a forecourt enclosed by brick colonnades with both the east and west wings fashioned in red brick. Inside there is a wealth of paintings, tapestries

and furniture to be seen whilst, outside, the house is surrounded by glorious grounds.

Landscaped by Humphry Repton in the late 18th century, the superb **Anthony Woodland Gardens**, which overlook the River Lynher, are at their best in the spring when the rhododendrons, magnolias, camellias and azaleas are in full bloom and in autumn when the exotic and indigenous species of trees provide a vivid and colourful display.

CREMYLL
4 miles SE of Saltash on the B3247

This village, which is linked to Plymouth by a foot ferry, is an excellent place from which to explore **Mount Edgcumbe House**, the 16th century home of the Earls of Edgcumbe who moved here from Cotehele House, near Calstock. After marrying Jean Durnford, the heiress to considerable estates on both sides of the Tamar estuary as well as the Cremyll ferry, Piers Edgcumbe received a royal licence to enclose the wooded grounds of the estate on the Rame peninsula and, following his death, his son, Richard, had the splendid Tudor mansion built between 1547 and 1554.

MOUNT EDGCUMBE HOUSE
AND COUNTRY PARK,
Cremyll, near Torpoint, Cornwall PL10 1HZ
Tel: 01752 822236 Fax: 01752 822199

Dating back to the mid 16th century, **Mount Edgcumbe House** was built by Sir Richard Edgcumbe of Cotehele in his deer park. A magnificent red sandstone building, of a typical Tudor style, the house has survived today very much intact, despite receiving a direct hit during an air raid in 1941. Beautifully restored between 1958 and 1964 by the Earl of Mount Edgcumbe, there are many treasures to see within its splendid rooms including paintings by Sir Joshua

Reynolds, 16th century tapestries and 18th century Chinese and Plymouth porcelain. Whilst the house is certainly a remarkable place the extensive grounds, including the 800 acre Country Park, draw many to this historic estate. Close to the house is the Earl's Garden which was created in the 18th century and where a whole host of rare and ancient trees can be seen. To the south, and overlooking Plymouth Sound, are the Formal Gardens. Again laid out in the 18th century, over an original 17th century wilderness garden, this is a series of gardens of contrast where the formal beds of the Italian and French Gardens give way to the irregular pattern of lawns of the English. There is also the modern addition of a New Zealand garden complete with a geyser. Beyond, to the north and continuing around the coastline, there is the extensive Country Park which was created in 1971. Visitors are guided through woodland and large lawns beside shingle beaches and there are numerous historic forts and follies to discover. The house is open from April to the end of September and, as well as the marvellous sights there is also an information centre, shop and restaurant within the Formal Gardens.

WRINGFORD DOWN HOTEL,

Wringford Down, near Cawsand,
Cornwall PL10 1LE
Tel: 01752 822287 Fax: 01752 823859
e-mail: ramehols@aol.com

Found on the Rame peninsula, one of Cornwall's
secret corners, **Wringford Down Hotel** is based
on one of the area's key properties. Built on the
site of an 11th century dwelling, this old Cornish
farmhouse dates from the 16th century and it
was also the site of a picket post during the Civil
War - the musketry lines can still be seen in the
two of the walls surrounding the hotel. Now a
splendid hotel, but still retaining its original

farmhouse appeal, Wringford Down has been owned and personally run by
Andrea and Harvey Jay since 1982 and, during this time, they have
established an excellent reputation for all round hospitality. Each of the 15
en suite guest rooms - some of which are suites - are superbly decorated and
furnished and children of all ages are welcome. The hotel's restaurant is
highly regarded throughout east Cornwall and here guests are treated to a
menu of home cooked food that is inspired by world cuisine. The wine list
too is extensive and there is sure to be a vintage to suit every dish and
palate. However, what makes the Wringford Down Hotel special are the
additional features. There is a tennis court, a heated indoor swimming
pool and a games room so that both children and adults can take some exercise, the menagerie of farm
animals will keep all amused and, so allow adults time on their own, the hotel also has both a nursery
and a children's club where they will be safely looked after by trained professionals.

RAME BARTON HOLIDAY FLATS,

Rame Barton, Rame, Cawsand, near Torpoint, Cornwall PL10 1LG
Tel: 01752 822789

Found on the beautiful Rame peninsula and surrounded by its own extensive grounds, which are also a
conservation area, Rame Barton Holiday Flats make an idyllic place for a break. This large white painted
building dates back, in parts, to 840 and it was mentioned in the Domesday book. First modernised in
1740 as a gentleman's residence, it later became a farm house and remained so until the 1970s when it
was converted to a guest house. Today's owners, Jean and Arthur Fidler, took over this charming old
property in the mid 1980s and continued it as a guest house until the mid 1990s when they expertly
converted the first floor to create two self-contained holiday flats. Now fully furnished with all of the
latest modern conveniences and stylishly decorated, the flats are both comfortable and pleasing. Each
is easily capable of accom-
modating a family and, as well as
children being very welcome
here, the family dog can also
enjoy the fun to be had here.

Ideally situated for many of
the local places of interest -
Mount Edgcumbe House, Park
and Gardens are close by - Rame
Barton Holiday Flats are also
surrounded by some of the most
beautiful and also least
discovered of south Cornwall's
coastline and a holiday here is
sure to be a real escape from the
crowds.

Today, the house has been restored to its original 16th century glory, both inside and out, after being destroyed by bombs in 1941.

The extensive and magnificent grounds, which incorporate land from Cremyll westwards along the peninsula to Tregonhawke, include the historic 18th century gardens that contain an orangery and the Italian Garden. Together with Mount Edgcumbe Country Park, that takes in a stretch of heritage coast line and has freely roaming fallow deer, numerous follies and over 600 species of camellia, this is one of Cornwall's greatest gardens and country parks.

MAKER
5 miles S of Saltash off the 3247

Dating from the 15th century and retaining much of its original charm, Maker church, whose name is derived from a Cornish word meaning 'ruin', was comprehensively restored in the 19th century. Inside the church is a copy of a portrait of the early 18th century vicar here, Thomas Smart. It is not the subject but the artist which makes this work particularly special: at aged 12, the young Sir

Joshua Reynolds made drawings of the vicar on the back of his hymn book during a service and then, back at a Cremyll boatyard, painted the original portrait on to canvas.

Just north of the church, surrounded by woodland and hidden within an oratory, lies **St Julian's Well** which is dedicated to the 5th century Cornish saint who is, aptly for this area, the patron saint of ferrymen.

CAWSAND AND KINGSAND
5½ miles S of Saltash off the B3247

It is hard to believe that these two small and attractive neighbouring villages once operated one of the largest smuggling fleets in Cornwall. The landing place of the future Henry VII after the battle of Bosworth, it was not long afterwards that **Cawsand Bay** and the narrow streets of the two villages began to see the illegal night-time activities that were to peak in the late 18th and early 19th centuries. Thousands of barrels of brandy, silk and other contraband were landed here in secret and transported through the sleeping villages to avoid the attentions of the revenue men.

DEVONPORT INN

The Cleave, Kingsand, Cornwall PL10 1NF
Tel: 01752 822869

Dating back to 1740 and situated right on the seafront at Kingsand, the **Devonport Inn** is a place that is hard to miss as its front façade is painted a gentle, yet eyecatching, pale yellow with dark oxford blue. A wonderful old building from the outside, the interior of this charming inn is equally pleasant with a traditional dark wood bar, low ceilings and a well polished wooden floor.

Owned and personally run by James and Vanda since 1994, this well liked pub is highly regarded for the excellent range of real ales, there are always four on tap, as well as for its extensive choice of beers, lagers, ciders and spirits. Food too is served here and the delicious menu of tasty homecooked dishes are all prepared by Vanda. The house speciality, during the summer, is fish and the menu changes regularly according to local availability.

A popular place in the heart of this delightful community, James' 60s and 70s discos on a Sunday evening are a weekly highlight that are

thoroughly enjoyed by all. Finally, this charming old inn also has two lovely en suite guest rooms which, with rooms overlooking the sea, make a wonderful choice for a seaside break.

Today activities in the twin villages - which for centuries some administrative quirk placed in different counties (Cawsand in Cornwall and Kingsand in Devon) - are quieter and from here the Royal Navy can be seen sailing in and out of **Plymouth Sound**. Before the **Plymouth Breakwater** was completed in 1841, the Royal Navy fleet used to shelter from southwesterly gales by anchoring in the sheltered Cawsand Bay, a common occurrence in those days which has left the villages with a surprising number of inns that are welcomed by locals and holidaymakers alike. Taking some 30 years to construct, from several tons of local limestone, the Breakwater was designed and engineered by John Rennie. At either end, some 5000 feet apart, are beacon lights and, at the eastern end, lies a large lobster-pot on top of a 24 foot pole which acts as a refuge to shipwrecked mariners.

RAME
6 miles S of Saltash off the B3247

Positioned at the southeastern end of Whitsand Bay and the southernmost point of Mount Edgcumbe Country Park, spectacular **Rame Head**, just southeast of the village, guards the entrance to Plymouth Sound. There are, naturally, superb views from the 400 foot cliffs but this beautiful headland has its own special feature - the ruined 14th century St Michael's Chapel from which a blazing beacon told of the coming of the Armada. Back in the little hamlet of Rame is the older, 13th century Church of St Germanus that is still lit by candles and whose west tower and spire, for centuries, acted as a landmark for sailors.

The **Eddystone Lighthouse**, which can be seen on a clear day, lies 10 miles offshore from Rame Head and it was from this point, in July 1588, that the English fleet had their first encounter with the Spanish Armada.

WHITSAND BAY
5 miles S of Saltash off the B3247

Running between the hamlet of Portwrinkle and Rame Head, this impressive stretch of beach is more a series of coves than one continuous expanse of sand. There are various paths leading down the slate cliffs - some of which are over 250 feet high - to the

gently curving bay which, though peaceful, has notoriously strong cross currents of which bathers should be wary.

PORTWRINKLE
5 miles SW of Saltash on the B3247

This small seaside village on Whitsand Bay developed around its medieval harbour. Now a tiny resort it boasts a large Victorian hotel that was moved here from Torpoint at the turn of the 20th century.

ST GERMANS
4 miles W of Saltash on the B3249

Situated on a tributary of the River Lynher, this rural village was, for half a century before the Anglo-Saxon diocese of Cornwall was incorporated with Exeter in 1043, a cathedral city. The present **St Germans' Church** stands on the site of the Saxon cathedral and it was the largest church in the county until the construction of Truro cathedral in 1910. Dating from Norman times, it was built as the great church for an Augustinian priory founded here in 1162 and, as well as having a particularly fine west front, it has two curiously dissimilar towers that date from the 13th and the 15th centuries.

Inside the church are several striking monuments but perhaps the most impressive is that to Edward Eliot. The Eliot family acquired the priory shortly after Henry VIII's Dissolution of the Monasteries in the 16th century and renamed their new estate Port Eliot. The present house, with its Gothic style turrets, is largely 19th century, although it does include fragments of the ancient monastic buildings but the grounds date from the late 18th century when they were laid out by Humphry Repton. Port Eliot is not open to the public.

Meanwhile, back in the church is an old chair that has a series of carvings depicting the story of Dando, a 14th century priest from the priory. According to local stories, one Sunday Dando left his devotions to go out hunting with a wild group of friends. At the end of the chase, Dando called for a drink and a stranger, riding a black horse, presented him with a richly decorated drinking horn. Dando quenched his thirst and saw that the horseman was stealing his game. Despite the priest's curses, the stranger refused to return the game and, in a drunken frenzy, Dando swore that he would follow the stranger to Hell in order to retrieve his prizes. The horseman then pulled Dando up on to his horse and rode off in the direction of the River Lynher where both the horse and the two riders were seen to disappear under the water with a hiss of steam.

Another of St Germans' exceptional buildings, the **Sir William Moyle's Almshouses**, were built in 1583 to an unusual design - the row has prominent gables and a long first floor balcony which is reached by a sturdy external staircase. Surrounded by neatly kept stone cottages set in flower filled gardens the almshouses were restored in 1967.

LOOE

The two Looe rivers, the East Looe and the West Looe, create a tidal harbour which has been a fishing and seafaring port from the time of the Middle Ages through to the 19th century when stone and copper from the quarries and mines in the north were shipped from here. Originally two separate towns

Looe River and Bridge

facing each other across the narrow estuary, East and West Looe were first connected by a bridge in the early 15th century and were, finally, officially incorporated in 1883. For many years, these two small communities each dutifully elected their own MP; a practice that eventually ceased in 1832. The present day seven-arched bridge dates from the 19th century and, not only does it link the two towns, but it also carries the main road.

In common with many other Cornish coastal settlements which have had to scratch a living by whatever means available, Looe

OSBORNE HOUSE,

Lower Chapel Street, East Looe, Cornwall PL13 1AT
Tel: 01503 262970

Found right in the heart of historic East Looe, **Osborne House** is an attractive and delightful old building which lies down one of the town's tiny meandering streets. Dating back some 360 years, the house was, originally, two fisherman's cottages and it has, today, retained much of its character and charm. Owners, Richard and Wilma Hatcher brought the building in 1988 and, over the years, they have totally refurbished the cottages to create the marvellous Osborne House. The ground floor of this splendid place is a small and intimate restaurant which has gained an enviable reputation far and wide for its wonderful cuisine. Dining in the low beamed ceiling restaurant and surrounded by a mass of old artefacts and memorabilia, customers can enjoy a splendid menu of delicious dishes which are all prepared to order from the very best local produce. Naturally, fish appears on the menu and the freshness is guaranteed as it comes from Looe's quayside.

Visitors to the area also have the opportunity of staying in the lovely house as, on the upper floors, there are three excellent en suite guest rooms which Richard and Wilma let on a bed and breakfast basis. Though

not suitable for children, this delightful house, which is full of olde worlde charm, is a fabulous place to stay a while and enjoy superb hospitality.

THE ADMIRAL BOSCARN,

Church End, East Looe, Cornwall PL13 1BU
Tel: 01503 262923

Found down East Looe's small and winding streets and overlooking the beach, **The Admiral Boscarn** is one of the town's most attractive inns. Originally a large town house, the building has been transformed into this splendid pub and, now owned and personally run by Allan and Mandy, this is a superb establishment that is very popular with both locals and visitors to Looe alike. Although Allan and Mandy only came here in 1997, they gained their experience by running a local holiday complex for many years and their ability to make people feel relaxed and to provide a pleasant and comfortable environment is easy to see.

The ground floor of the inn is taken up with a large lounge bar that is the perfect place to enjoy the wealth of real ales, lagers and ciders, and all the usual drinks served here. Food too is very much a feature of the Admiral Boscarn and the menu includes many favourites such as Curry, Chilli con Carne, and Spaghetti Bolognaise, which are all home-made, as well as a wide range of freshly filled sandwiches, salads and jacket potatoes.

However, the house speciality here has to be the All Day Breakfast, a wonderful feast that is served through until 3pm A place for all the family, to the rear of the inn and on a higher level, is the fabulous award winning beer garden that has plenty of space to accommodate the large clientele in comfort. Not only can the splendid food and drink be served here and be enjoyed out in the garden but there is a bird's eye view over Looe harbour and to the sea beyond. Whilst it would appear that The Admiral Boscarn has plenty to offer the whole family, whether visitors or locals, Allan and Mandy do not rest on their laurels as, throughout the season, there is live entertainment at the inn every evening. Add to this the friendly nightclub, to which all are welcome, which runs from Wednesday through to Saturday, and the obvious high regard of the locals and The Admiral Boscarn is an inn not to be missed.

Old Houses in East Looe

has always been something of a jack-of-all-trades. As well as having a long established pilchard fishing fleet, it has also served the mineral extractors of Bodmin Moor and been a place popular with smugglers. The fishing industry is all that remains of the town's colourful past and it is still Cornwall's second most important port with fish auctions taking place at East Looe's bustling quayside market on the famous **Banjo Pier**.

Of the two distinct parts of the town, East Looe is the most famous and also the oldest with its narrow cobbled streets and twisting alleyways. Housed in one of the town's several 16th century buildings is the **Old Guildhall Museum** which details much of Looe's history along with that of the surrounding area. The building's old magistrates' bench can still be seen here as well as with the original cells. As early as 1800, a bathing machine was constructed overlooking East Looe's sandy beach and, after the opening of the Looe Valley Line (a railway branch line to replace the Liskeard and Looe Canal) to passengers in 1879, the development of the two towns as a holiday resort began in earnest. Fortunately, the

TRAWLERS,

Buller Quay, East Looe, Cornwall PL13 1AH
Tel: 01503 263593

Trawlers, one of the best fish and seafood restaurants in Cornwall, is a place well worth finding as, not only is the food excellent, but its situation, on the quay overlooking the harbour, is idyllic. The town's many trawlers boats pass to and fro throughout the day and, as many also moor outside the restaurant, the fish and seafood is the freshest possible. Housed in a 16th century building, owners Roger and Cathy, who live above the restaurant with their son Jack, came here for a meal in 1998 and fell in love with the place. They bought the business and, with top chef, Todd Vernedoe, in the kitchen, Roger and Cathy have created one of the West Country's premier restaurants.

In the intimate and cosy surroundings of this small restaurant customers can experience some of the best produce that Looe has to offer. The range is extensive and, depending on availability and quality, the selection includes monk fish, sea bass, turbot, brill and shark along with crab, lobster and oysters. Todd, who grew up in Louisiana, USA, not only cooks the fish to perfection but also provides an interesting menu that combines traditional English and European flavours with those of his native Louisiana. Vegetarians and meat lovers are also well catered for and the wine list complements beautifully the menu on offer.

THE OLD MILL GIFT CENTRE,

West Looe, Cornwall PL13 2AE
Tel: 01503 262104 Fax: 01503 265877

Housed within an old mill building, which dates back to 1554, **The Old Mill Gift Centre** can be found in the heart of West Looe, overlooking the River Looe. Nigel Pearn, the owner since the 1970s, was born and bred in the town and, for many years, he was a boat builder here working alongside his father and brother. Today, in his studio on the ground floor of this lovely building, Nigel creates wonderful and unusual tables made from Californian wood. Each piece is unique and takes around six weeks to complete and these splendid pieces of furniture can be found on display at the Gift Centre. Along with Nigel's tables, the centre has an outstanding selection of gifts from around the world and, whilst being a delightful place to wander around and browse, a present brought here for a friend or family member is sure to be treasured for years. There is pottery from Italy, Stieff teddy bears,

Devon ceramics and much, much more. Along with all this the Old Mill is one of the West Country's leading stockists of the famous "Flower Fairies", carrying three separate ranges of these lovely little figures. Those who also enjoy ice cream will find that, within the centre, they can buy real Cornish ice cream - a treat well worth trying. Situated on the sea front of East Looe are Nigel's two charming cottages both with their own private parking space. **Albatross Cottages** provide all that is needed for a family self catering holiday in one of Cornwalls most attractive old fishing villages. As well as having all the latest conveniences, both cottages have been decorated and furnished to the highest standards.

FIELDHEAD HOTEL,

Portuan Road, Hannafore, West Looe, Cornwall PL13 2DR
Tel: 01503 262689 Fax: 01503 264114
e-mail: field.head@virgin.net websites: www.fieldheadhotel.co.uk; www.chycor.co.uk/fieldhead

Occupying an elevated position overlooking the sea front and Looe harbour, **Fieldhead Hotel** is a

wonderful place that certainly is a country house by the sea. Surrounded by substantial gardens and terraces, from where there are glorious views out to sea that take in the famous Eddystone Lighthouse, lazy summer days can be whiled away by the heated swimming pool, by reading in the shade of luxurious palm tree or enjoying a drink on the terrace. This splendid and attractive hotel was originally built, in 1896, as a grand private house for the same civil engineer that also constructed the town's Banjo Pier. Successfully converted into a comfortable family hotel, resident owners Barrie and Gill Pipkin have created elegant and relaxing public rooms and comfortable and stylish guest bedrooms that provide visitors with the perfect environment for a wonderful holiday.

However, not only do residents of the Fieldhead Hotel have the opportunity to dine in luxury as the hotel's restaurant is also open to non residents. A highly regarded restaurant with a fast growing reputation, the mainly French and English influenced menus are prepared by experienced chef Peter Wright. The interesting and tempting menus, obviously, make excellent use of the fresh fish and seafood landed daily at Looe, but the vast range of other local fresh produce is also featured. An extensive wine list complements any meal taken here.

character, particularly of the older East Looe, has been retained. West Looe remains essentially a residential area with many Victorian and Edwardian buildings.

More recently, Looe has established itself as Britain's major shark fishing centre, regularly hosting an International Sea Angling Festival, and there is an **Aquarium** where both fish and other curious creatures from the deep can be seen. Meanwhile, just a short distance from the coast, lies **Looe Island** (sometimes known as **St George's Island**), which is now home to a bird sanctuary. Made famous by the Atkins sisters who featured the island in their books, *We Bought an Island* and *Tales from our Cornish Island*, Looe Island can be reached, throughout the summer, by boarding one of the many pleasure boats offering trips to the island and along the coast. Looe Island has also been the refuge for one of the Cornish coast's many notorious pirates and smugglers, Black Joan, who, along with her brother Fyn, terrorised the population of this lonely stretch of coast.

For an all round view of the area's fauna and flora, the **South East Cornwall Discovery Centre** is ideal. Situated in West Looe, through displays and video presentations, visitors to the centre are introduced to the wealth of wildlife, plant life and the splendid scenery of southeast Cornwall.

AROUND LOOE

SEATON
3 miles E of Looe on the B3247

Once a favourite place with smugglers, who would land their contraband on the sandy beach, this village, at the mouth the River Seaton, offers some excellent cliff top walking to today's visitors.

MURRAYTON
2 miles E of Looe off the B3247

Established in 1964 in this sheltered, wooded valley is the famous **Monkey Sanctuary** - the world's first protected colony of Amazonian Woolly monkeys. Set up to provide a safe environment for monkeys rescued from lives

BLUE HAVEN HOTEL,

Looe Hill, Seaton, near Torpoint, Cornwall PL11 3JQ
Tel: 01503 250310
e-mail: bluehaven@btinternet.com website: www.smoothhound.co.uk/hotels/bluehave.html

Built in the 1950s, **Blue Haven Hotel** is a small and friendly establishment personally run by Pat and David Rowlandson. The couple have been here since 1997 and, in this short period, they have created a delightful and relaxing hotel that has a real family feel. Throughout, the hotel is well furnished and decorated in a style that is both comfortable and relaxing and each of the four double en suite guest rooms provides all that is necessary for a refreshing night's sleep. Accommodation is on a bed and breakfast basis and this meal is a hearty feast that will set everyone up for a day out discovering the

many local places of interest, or just lazing around on the beach.

However, what really makes the Blue Haven Hotel special is the fabulous panoramic views over the sea. The hotel is situated on top of a cliff and, from both the beautiful terraced gardens and the south facing windows, guests can not only watch the changing moods of the sea and spot surfers and dolphins playing, but also enjoy some marvellous sun sets and sun rises. An ideal place for those who enjoy the south Cornwall coastline, Blue Haven Hotel is an excellent choice for families with children as they are made most welcome.

The Waterfront Holiday and Leisure Complex,

Millendreath, near Looe, Cornwall PL13 1NY
Tel: 01503 263281 Fax: 01503 264467

Occupying a splendid situation on a gently sloping 70 acres site, The **Waterfront Holiday and Leisure Complex** provides everything for a perfect family holiday. Overlooking a sandy beach, which is part of the complex, the position of the complex allows all the superb bungalows and villas to have a view, either over the sea or across a tree lined valley. Designed with both adults and children in mind, this is just the place to enjoy a wide range of activities but it is also within easy reach of many of Cornwall's best attractions.

From the private beach a wide range of watersports can be tried and experienced but, for those who just wish to soak up the sun, there are traditional deck chairs in which to relax. Away from the attraction of the sea, the complex has an excellent indoor swimming pool, where children can be supervised so that the adults can go off an enjoy the complex's pub, The Tavern. A charming pub during the day, this is the centre of the complex's nightlife. Meanwhile, there is also the café, which opens for breakfast and continues to serve a wide range of dishes throughout the day, though the house specialities to watch out for are fish and the Cornish cream teas. In fact, there is so much going on here, from morning right through to the nightlife that many find there is no time left to leave The Waterfront at all.

Wringworthy Holiday Cottages,

Morval, near Looe, Cornwall PL13 1PR
Tel: 01503 240685 Fax: 01503 240830
e-mail: wringholcot@aol.com website: www.cornwallwringworthycottages.co.uk

Found in the heart of farmland, yet just five minutes drive from Looe, **Wringworthy Holiday Cottages** is a charming establishment with the feel of a tiny hamlet. The eight character cottages which make up Wringworthy have all been converted from the original barns of the farm which were built around 200 years ago from local stone. Whilst the cottages are all different, each also attains the same high standard of furnishings, decoration and facilities which makes them a real home from home. The facilities on this site make it an ideal place for a family holiday or a relaxing short break. The large lawns allow plenty of space for games and barbecues, with safe play areas, swings and sandpit, and the heated

outdoor swimming pool is open from mid May to September. There is a large games barn for indoor play with snooker and pool tables, and play castle for smaller children, but the main attraction for most visitors seems to be the two donkeys, Zak and Pepe, and the chickens, ducks and rabbits. Just a mile away is Looe's superb golf course, which overlooks Looe Bay, and the owners have arranged discounted green fees for Wringworthy visitors. For those who enjoy walking there are wonderful coastal walks and the moors are a short drive away. The exciting new Eden Project and Heligan Gardens are within a 30 minute drive.

of isolation in zoos and as pets, the monkeys roam freely in the gardens of the outdoor enclosures. Talks and indoor displays explain more about the monkeys' life and their natural habitat in the Amazonian rainforest and, as well as the monkeys, there are other birds and animals to view at close quarters.

DULOE
3½ miles N of Looe on the B3254

This charming Cornish village of stone cottages surrounding its medieval church, which is dedicated to St Cuby and St Leonard, is also the location of a **Stone Circle**. Some 38 feet in diameter and with eight standing quartz stones, this circle is said to be older than Stonehenge.

ST KEYNE
5 miles N of Looe on the B3254

This small village is named after one of the daughters of a Welsh king, St Keyne, who settled here during the 5th century, and her famous holy well, **St Keyne's Well**, lies a mile southeast of the village. Found beneath a great tree - which is said to bear the leaves of

St Keynes Holy Well

four different species - according to local legend the first member of a newly married couple to drink from her well will be the one to wear the trousers in the marriage. This notion captured the imagination of the Victorians and brought newly-weds here in their thousands. It is still customary for a newly married couple to rush here from the church to see who drinks the waters first.

One of the more curious episodes in St Keyne's history took place during the reign of Catholic Mary Tudor, when the local rector and his wife (who had married during the reign of Protestant Edward VI) were dragged from their bed in the middle of the night and placed in the village stocks.

The attraction at St Keyne which brings most visitors here today is **Paul Corin's Magnificent Music Machines**, a fantastic display of mechanical instruments that first opened in 1967. Paul Corin was the last miller in the village and, still housed in the lovely old mill close to the bridge over the East Looe River, his son, also Paul, now looks after this amazing collection. There are continuous tours throughout the day and visitors can view and listen to a wide range of sounds and music from the AMPICO Player Pianos with rolls of great pianists such as Rachmaninov to a 1908 piano-playing machine what was owned by the real life 'Model of a Modern Major-General' in Gilbert and Sullivan's opera *The Pirates of Penzance*. This collection has featured in numerous television and radio programmes though the family is no stranger to media fame as Paul's grandfather, Bransby Williams, was the only great Music Hall star to have had his own BBC television show in the early 1950s.

DOBWALLS
8 miles N of Looe on the A38

Just to the north of this large modern village lies **Dobwalls Family Adventure Park**, a popular theme park which offers something for all the family. There is a charming Edwardian countryside museum, with a permanent exhibition on the life and work of English wildlife artist, Archibald Thorburn; a miniature stream railway, based on an old North American railroad, that runs for two miles around the park's grounds; woodland play areas; indoor attractions and a restaurant and café.

THE SPORTSMANS ARMS HOTEL,

Lower Clicker Road, Menheniot, near Liskeard, Cornwall PL14 3PJ
Tel: 01503 240249

Found opposite Menheniot's railway station, **The Sportsmans Arms Hotel** is an attractive and pleasant hotel that is well known in the area for the high standard of its food, drink and accommodation. A quiet and peaceful place today, in the early 1890s, the hotel played a part in the worst disaster that south east Cornwall has ever seen. Whilst reconstructing the Coldrenick Viaduct, which had originally been built by IK Brunel, 12 local men fell to their deaths and the inquest into this tragic event was held at The Sportsmans.

Owner Michael, along with his partner Rosa, has had a long association with the inn as he owned the hotel for a few years in the 1980s before purchasing it again in 1992. A former racehorse owner and breeder, visitors will not be surprised to see that the hotel's pub sign is that of a racehorse in full flight over a fence. A splendid place to come to for a good pint of real ale, there are several from which to choose and always some local brews, The Sportsman is also a popular place to eat. The menu ranges from freshly filled sandwiches and other light snacks through to full gourmet meals, served in the cosy restaurant, and the traditional Sunday lunch draws people from near and far. Finally, the superb guest accommodation, makes this delightful country hotel an excellent choice for a family break.

CARNETHIC HOUSE,

Lambs Barn, Fowey, Cornwall PL23 1HQ
Tel: 01726 833336 Fax: 01726 833296
e-mail: carnethic@btinternet.com
website: www.cresom.co.uk/carnethic

Close to Fowey and set within its own mature grounds, **Carnethic House** is a large and attractive Georgian country estate house that makes the perfect holiday location. Refurbished and decorated to a very high standard, this lovely house has lost none of its elegant appeal over the years and, today, it is a superb blend of modern day comforts with old fashioned hospitality. A stay here is just like a visit to an English country house and hosts, the hotel's owners, David and Trisha Hogg, play their role to perfection. Carnethic House's eight en suite guest rooms, some of which have a garden and sea view, have been specially designed to create the perfect environment for a relaxing night's sleep.

A four course dinner is served in the elegant dining room each evening and here the emphasis is on presenting guests with the very best in home-cooked dishes and locally caught fish is the speciality here. A well stocked bar and good wine cellar add further enjoyment to an evening meal here. As well as the heated outdoor swimming pool and other activities available at the hotel, David and Trisha are happy to help arrange other trips for guests and, in particular, visits to the Eden Project and the Lost Gardens of Heligan which are both close by.

LISKEARD
7 miles N of Looe on the B3254

A picturesque and lively market town, situated on undulating ground between the valleys of the East Looe and Seaton Rivers, Liskeard was one of Cornwall's five medieval stannary towns - the others being Bodmin, Lostwithiel, Truro and Helston. The name comes from the Latin word for tin, 'stannum', and these five towns were the only places licensed to weigh and stamp the metal. However, before this right was granted, the town was an agricultural centre with its first Royal Charter being given to hold a market in 1240.

The town has a long history as a centre for mineral extraction and, for centuries, the medieval Cornish tinners brought their smelted tin down from Bodmin Moor for weighing, stamping and taxing. The construction of a canal, linking the town with Looe, saw, by the 19th century, great quantities of both copper ore and granite also passing through Liskeard bound for the coast and beyond. In the 1850s, the canal was replaced by the Looe Valley branch of the Great Western Railway and a scenic stretch of the line is still open today though the industrial cargoes have long since been replaced by passenger carriages.

Though a small town, Liskeard does boast two sets of public buildings which are a reminder of its past importance and prosperity. **The Guildhall** was constructed in 1859 whilst the **Public Hall** opened in 1890. Still used as the office of the town council, the hall is also home to the local Museum. Adjacent to the Passmore-Edwards Public Library stands **Stuart House**, a handsome Jacobean residence where Charles I stayed in 1644 whilst engaged in a campaign against the Parliamentarian forces at nearby Lostwithiel. The **Church of St Martin** is also worthy of a mention as, not only is it the second largest parish church in Cornwall, but this mainly 15th century building stands on Norman foundations. Finally, one of Liskeard's most curious features can be found in Well Lane, where an arched grotto marks the site of **Pipe Well**, a medieval spring that is reputed to have curative powers.

FOWEY

A lovely old port and historic seafaring town, Fowey (pronounced Foy) guards the entrance to the river from which it takes its name. An attractive place, with steep, narrow streets and alleyways that lead down to one of the best natural harbours along the south coast, Fowey exhibits a pleasant mixture of architectural styles that range from Elizabethan to Edwardian. An important port in the Middle Ages, though it is known to have been previously used by the Romans, the town lay on the trade route between Ireland and continental Europe which crossed Cornwall via the Camel Estuary.

As a busy trading port, Fowey also attracted pirates and it was home to the "Fowey Gallants" who, not only preyed on ships in the Channel but also raided the French coast. Recruited during the Hundred Years War, these local mariners were brought together to fight the French but, after the hostilities were

Fowey

CHUFFERS RESTAURANT,

34 Station Road, Fowey,
Cornwall PL23 1DF
Tel: 01726 833822

Close to the town's old railway station and housed in a building that dates back to 1896, **Chuffers Restaurant** is not only one of Fowey's best establishments but has a reputation that extends much further afield. The typical railway style awning along the front of the building, which provides shade for the outside seating is the first indication that this restaurant has a railway theme and, inside, there is a large collection of memorabilia on display that depicts the great age of steam.

Owned and personally run by Mike and Marcia Rudd since 1997, Chuffers Restaurant is not only dedicated to steam engine fans but is also an excellent restaurant with a justly deserved following. Open from lunchtimes into the evening (except Sunday evening and all day Monday) a selection of menus caters to customers requirements. A tasty list of light meals and snacks and including home-made cakes and the restaurant's traditional cream teas provides a good choice of refreshment throughout the day. The mood changes in the evenings and the delicious menu of tempting dishes reflects not only the abundance of fresh local fish and seafood but also the imagination of the chef. Prepared with flair and stylishly presented, customers can enjoy a wide variety of dishes that include such delights as Smoked chicken and apple salad, Lamb Tagine, Peppered Salmon Fillet and succulent fillet steaks. The comprehensive wine list and the wonderful dessert menu are sure to add further to the enjoyment of a meal here.

THE CORMORANT ON THE RIVER,

Golant by Fowey, Cornwall PL23 1LL
Tel: 01726 833426 Fax: 01726 833574
e-mail: relax@cormoranthotels.co.uk
website: www.cormoranthotels.co.uk

Renowned as one of the best hotels in the area, **The Cormorant on the River** is a wonderful establishment which has a fantastic setting. Found on the edge of this attractive fishing village, the hotel overlooks the River Fowey and the views from its windows and the charming garden are unrivalled. Originally built as a private residence in the 1930s, The Cormorant became a hotel in the late 1960s and, since early 2000, it has been owned and personally run by Carrie and Colin King.

This small luxury hotel certainly has a great deal to offer its visitors and, apart from the glorious views, the high standard of friendly hospitality in these relaxing surroundings are sure to make for a very peaceful and restful holiday. Well known for the high standard of cuisine in its restaurant, where only the freshest local produce is used, guests here also have the chance to work off the excellent cuisine in the hotel's heated swimming pool. The 11 comfortable and elegant guest rooms too provide the perfect environment for an excellent night's sleep and each has a large picture window through which the everchanging scene of the River Fowey can be watched. In addition to the wonderful local scenery, ideal for walking, the hotel is just a few minutes drive from the Eden Project.

Harbour at Fowey

over, they did not disband but continued to terrorise shipping along this stretch of coast and beyond. A devastating raid by the French on the town in 1457, in retaliation for attacks made by the Fowey Gallants, saw much of Fowey burnt to the ground. The maritime tradition here continued into the 19th century when Fowey became a china clay port and, today, the harbour is still a busy place with huge ships calling at this deep water harbour along with both fishing boats and pleasure craft.

For the last 700 years, this now peaceful community has been connected to Bodinnick by a car ferry which has, for many years, been known locally as **The Passage**. Around the town's main square, bordering the Town Quay, are several interesting old buildings, including the **King of Prussia** - an inn named after an 18th century smuggler. Other buildings to look out for are the **Toll Bar House**, which dates from the 14th, 15th and 16th centuries, and the **Ship Inn**, which stands on the opposite side of the street. The inn was originally a town house built by the influential Rashleigh family in the 15th century and inside can still be seen the carved ceilings and, above a fireplace, the inscription: "John Rashleigh - Ales Rashleigh 1570", which remembers a family wedding.

Seen rising above trees is the tower of **St Nicholas Church** which was built on the site of a 7th century chapel to St Goran. Dedicated in the 1330s, the church was set on fire by the French in the 15th century during their devastating raid on Fowey. The church's font is a legacy of the deeds of the Gallants as it was made from panelling seized by them from a Spanish galleon in 1601. The town's **Museum** is an excellent place to discover Fowey's colourful history, from the days of piracy and smuggling to the rise of the town's harbour and the china clay industry.

To the south of Fowey lies **Readymoney Cove**, whose expanse of sand acts as the town's beach, and, further along the coast, lies **St Catherine's Castle**. Part of a chain of fortifications along the south coast, this small fort was built by Henry VIII to protect the harbour and, now in the hands of English Heritage, it is just the place to come to for fine views over the river estuary and over the surrounding coastline.

To the west of Fowey lies the **Tristan Stone** which, although not thought to be in its original location, is a 6th century monument bearing the inscription (in translation): "Drustanus lies here, son of Conomorus." Drustanus is an alternative version of Tristan and it is believed that this is the same Tristan who was a knight of King Arthur. The son of King Mark, Tristan fell in love with Iseult, his father's young bride, after they had both drunk the love potion prepared for Mark's wedding night.

Finally, Fowey has two literary connections: with Daphne du Maurier, who lived at Gribbin Head; and with Sir Arthur Quiller-Couch, who lived for over 50 years at **The Haven**, on the Esplanade, and made 'Troy Town' his fictional Fowey.

AROUND FOWEY

GOLANT
2 miles N of Fowey off the B3269

This delightful waterside village has a landmark church that still, chiefly, dates from

The Royal Talbot,

Duke Street, Lostwithiel, Cornwall PL22 0AG
Tel: 01208 872498 Fax: 01208 872498

Although **The Royal Talbot**, in the heart of this historic town, dates back to the days of stagecoach travel it has not always occupied this particular site. In 1937, whilst the main road through the town was being widened, the inn, which lay on the opposite side of the road from today, was knocked down and then rebuilt after the road works had finished. A large and impressive building, this popular and well known inn is run by landlords, Pamela and Stephen Fisher - a charming couple with a great deal of experience in the licensing trade. An inviting and friendly inn, where the whole family is welcome, The Royal Talbot is highly regarded for its high standards of food and drink. From the bar there is an excellent selection of all the usual beers, lagers and spirits as well as real ales, including a local brew called Daylight Robbery.

The menu, served here throughout the day in the season, is supplemented by the ever-changing list of blackboard dishes and almost everything on offer is home-made. Eaten in either the bar or the separate restaurant, the extensive range of dishes on offer ensures that everyone will find a favourite. Add to this the occasional live music which Pamela and Stephen lay on at the weekends and it is easy to see why The Royal Talbot is so popular.

Menaburle Farm,

Boconnoc, near Lostwithiel, Cornwall PL22 0RT
Tel: 01208 873703 Fax: 01208 873703 e-mail: vicki_alderman@yahoo.com

Very much off the beaten track, Menaburle Farm lies in a sheltered position amidst fields and woodland just to the south of Bodmin Moor. A short distance from the south coast, Lostwithiel and Fowey, this attractive and peaceful working farm is an ideal place to stay for those looking to really get away from it all. Chris and Vicki Alderman have been working this organic farm since 1990 as well as offering self-catering holidays in three distinctive properties. All lie around the central farmyard and each has been individually restored, decorated and furnished to complement the style of the original buildings.

The west wing of the charming old farm house is completely self-contained and can comfortably sleep four adults. Meanwhile, there is the lovely Apple Loft where once not only apples were stored but there was also a cider press. Ideal for a couple or small family, as well as being well equipped like the other properties, the Loft has a character all its own. Finally, there is the Mill House, a splendid old barn that has been stylishly converted to accommodate eight adults. Stabling and grazing can also be arranged for those wishing to bring their horses and, of course, dogs are welcome.

the early 16th century and is home to another of Cornwall's many holy wells. This particular source of curative water can be found in the church porch. Near to the village can also be found the **Castle Dore Earthworks**. An Iron Age lookout point, the densely overgrown site is thought to be the site of King Mark's castle and, so, it is linked with the legend of Tristan and Iseult.

LOSTWITHIEL
5 miles N of Fowey on the A390

This attractive small market town's name means, literally, 'lost in the hills', which perfectly describes its location - nestling in the valley of the River Fowey and surrounded by wooded hills. The capital of Cornwall in the 13th century and one of the Stannary towns, Lostwithiel's history is very much governed by its riverside position. For centuries, tin and other raw materials were brought here for assaying and onward transportation until the upstream mining activity caused the quay here to silt up and forced the port to move further down river.

Lostwithiel was a major crossing place on the River Fowey and the original medieval timber bridge was replaced and then gradually altered until Tudor times when the bridge seen today was completed. Alongside the banks of the River Fowey and downstream from the bridge lies the tranquil **Coulson Park**. Opened in 1907, the park was named after the American millionaire, Nathaniel Coulson, who not only put up the money for the park's construction but who had also grown up in the town. Across the river from the town lies the **Bonconnoc Estate**, the home of the Pitt family who gave Britain two great Prime Ministers: William Pitt the Elder and his son William Pitt the Younger.

Throughout Lostwithiel there are reminders, in the buildings, of the once importance of this pleasant and picturesque place. The remains of the 13th century **Great Hall**, which served as the treasury and stannary offices, can still be seen whilst, in Fore Street, there is a fine example of an early 18th century arcaded **Guildhall**. built in 1740, by Richard, Lord Edgcumbe, the ground floor was originally an open Corn Market with the town lock-up behind and the guildhall on the first floor. Today, the building is home to the **Lostwithiel Museum**

and it provides the perfect atmosphere in which to not only tell the story of this interesting town but also display photographs documenting everyday life in Lostwithiel from the late 19th century to the present day. Meanwhile, 16th century **Taprell House** is worth finding for its unusual plaque which declares "Walter Kendal founded this house and hath a lease for 3000 years beginning 29 September 1652."

The striking **Church of St Bartholomew** has an distinctive octagonal spire and its Breton style design is a reminder of the close links there have been between the Celts of Cornwall and those of northern France. Dedicated to the patron saint of the sick and of tanners (tanning was another industry of medieval Lostwithiel), the church, like other parts of the town, still bears some scars from the Civil War. The area became a battleground between the opposing forces and **Braddock Down**, to the east, was the site of a Royalist victory

POLSCOE
5½ miles N of Fowey off the A390

Lostwithiel's strategic position, as a riverside port and important crossing point, led to the building of **Restormel Castle** which stands perched on a high mound overlooking the wooded valley of the River Fowey. The magnificent Norman keep of local slate and shale rock was built in the early 12th century by Edmund, Earl of Cornwall. With walls that are over 300 feet thick in places and a deep moat surrounding the whole fortress this was certainly a stronghold worthy of the earls of Cornwall and Edward, the Black Prince. In use until just after the Civil War, this splendid

Restormel Castle

castle, which survives in remarkably good condition, is now a peaceful and attractive place - particularly in spring when the banks of daffodils and bluebells are out - it is now in the hands of English Heritage.

CUTMADOC
7 miles N of Fowey off the A38

To the west of the village lies the spectacular National Trust-owned estate of **Lanhydrock House**. Prior to the Dissolution of the Monasteries, this large estate belonged to Bodmin's Augustinian priory of St Petroc, then, in 1620, it was bought by Sir Richard Robarts, who accumulated his fortune in tin

Lanhydrock House

Lanhydrock Gardens

and wool, and the family lived here until it passed into the hands of the National Trust in 1953. Probably the grandest house in Cornwall, set in a superb position in the Fowey Valley, the surrounding estate includes formal and woodland gardens, woods and parkland. The magnificent house dates from the mid 17th century and it was constructed symmetrically around a central courtyard. However, a fire in 1881 destroyed most of the building, except the entrance and north wing, but after four years of hard work, the house was returned to its original splendour whilst the interior was modernised to include the very latest Victorian amenities, such as central heating, plumbed bathrooms and modern kitchens.

Many of the rooms are open to the public and as well as seeing the magnificent plaster ceiling in the Long Gallery - one of the rooms that escaped the fire - visitors can also see the kitchen complex, the nursery where the Agar-Robartes children lived and the grand dining room.

The grounds too are a pleasure to wander around and here there are fabulous displays of rhododendrons, magnolias and camellias in the spring, a famous avenue of ancient beech and sycamore trees and a photogenic formal garden that is overlooked by the small estate church of St Hyderoc.

LERRYN
3½ miles NE of Fowey off the A390

A quiet and peaceful village found in a sleepy creek, it is hard to imagine that Lerryn was once a busy riverside port. Those familiar with Kenneth Grahame's novel *The Wind in the Willows* may find the thickly wooded slopes of **Lerryn Creek** familiar as they are thought to have been the inspiration for the setting of this ever popular children's story.

LANREATH
4½ miles NE of Fowey off the B3359

This pretty village, with traditional cob cottages at its centre, is home to the **Lanreath Folk and Farm Museum**, which can be found in Lanreath's old tithe barn. There are numerous vintage exhibits here, many of which can be touched, including old agricultural implements, mill workings, engines, tractors, a traditional farmhouse kitchen and a bric-a-brac shop. Craft workshops and a pets' corner complete the museum.

PELYNT
5 miles NE of Fowey on the B3359

The church in this large and rather exposed village not only has an unusual classical aisle (dated 1680) but it is also associated with Bishop Trelawny (1650-1721). Hawker's famous song *Sons of the Western Men*, which is perhaps better known today as the Cornish rugby battle hymn, recounts the story of Bishop Sir Jonathan Trelawny's incarceration in the Tower of London. As well as seeing the chair put inside this 14th century church in his memory there is also a fragment of the bishop's coffin and his pastoral staff.

LANTEGLOS-BY-FOWEY
2 miles NE of Fowey off the A3082

Here can be found a lonely church whose isolated position can be attributed to its being built to serve Polruan as well as several other scattered hamlets in this area. Though some remnants of the original Norman building exist, the church is chiefly 14th century and, fortunately, was not over zealously restored in the 19th century. Its unusual dedication is to St Wyllow, a Christian hermit who lived in area well before St Augustine landed in Kent in the 6th century. St Wyllow is thought to have died a martyr after being killed close to the creek.

POLPERRO
5½ miles E of Fowey off the A387

This lovely old fishing community is many people's ideal of the typical Cornish fishing. It stands at the point where a steep-sided wooded combe converges with a narrow tidal inlet from the sea and the village's steep narrow streets and alleyways, some only six feet wide, are piled high with white painted fisherman's cottages. All routes in Polperro seem to lead down to its beautiful **Harbour** which is still a busy fishing port and there are normally an assortment of colourful boats to be seen.

Whilst, for centuries, the village was dependent on pilchard fishing for its survival, Polperro also has a long association with smuggling and the practice here was so rife in the 18th century that many of the village's inhabitants were involved in shipping, storing or transporting contraband goods. To combat what was such a widespread problem, HM Customs and Excise established the first 'preventive station' in Cornwall at Polperro in the 1800s. At the **Museum of Smuggling** a whole range of artefacts and memorabilia from around the 18th century are used to illustrate the myths, legends and larger-than-life characters who dodged the government taxes on luxury goods. A model of *Lady Beatrice*, a traditional large, gaff-rigged fishing boat that is typical of Polperro, can also be seen.

Polperro Village Centre

Around the rest of the village there are numerous interesting buildings to be seen, including the **House on Props** and **Couch's House**, the 16th century house where Dr Jonathan Couch, the naturalist and grandfather of author Sir Arthur Quiller-Couch, lived. Found within beautiful formal gardens, the **Model Village** is a perfect miniature replica of old Polperro that is well worth visiting.

Just west of Polperro harbour lies **Chapel Hill** from which there are superb panoramic views both inland and out to sea. At the bottom of the hills lies a cavern that is known as **Willy Willcock's Hole**. Willy was a fisherman who, walking here one day, decided to explore the cave. Unfortunately he lost his way in the maze of underground tunnels and was never seen again and, so the story goes, his lost soul can still be heard crying out for help. A two mile cliff top walk eastwards from Polperro leads to **Talland Bay**, a sheltered shingle cove that is overlooked by the 13th century Church of St Tallan.

BODINNICK
½ mile E of Fowey off the A3082

This pretty hamlet runs uphill away from the **ferry** slipway which provides a car and passenger service across the river to Fowey. Close to the slipway stands the house in which Daphne du Maurier lived before her marriage and where she wrote her first novel, *The Loving Spirit*. Another writer, Leo Walmsey, lived further along the river in a hut and here he wrote his romantic story, *Love in*

Polperro Harbour

Bodinnick Ferry

the centre of this small village, there is a path which follow a tree-lined stream down to the

Lantivet Bay

the Sun. Yet another writer to be acknowledged at Bodinnick is Sir Arthur Quiller-Couch who is remembered by a monolithic memorial which stands on the coast facing Fowey. It was also close to the site of this monument that in 1644, during the Civil War, Charles I narrowly escaped death from a sniper's bullet whilst he was making a survey of the Parliamentary forces occupying Fowey.

coast and sheltered Lantivet Bay. Here also lies the small shingle beach of Lansallos Cove.

POLRUAN
1 mile S of Fowey off the A3082

Facing St Catherine's Castle across the mouth of the River Fowey, Polruan is a pretty village of cottages stacked high above the waterfront that can also be reached by ferry from Fowey. Beside the harbour, which is still busy with

LANSALLOS
3 miles E of Fowey off the A387

From the 14th century St Ildierna's Church, in

THE RUSSELL INN,

West Street, Polruan, Cornwall PL21 1PJ
Tel: 01726 870292

Found tucked away in the narrow lanes of this ancient village, **The Russell Inn** is a charming and attractive pub which lies just a few yards from Polruan's quayside. Although the building, like most of those found in this quaint place, is centuries old it first opened as an inn in 1836 and ever since it has been a popular and well frequented drinking hole. Today's landlords, Eric and Andrea Tomlin, carry on the tradition of serving excellent food and drink and The Russell Inn is certainly a place to make for

when exploring Polruan. There is a superb selection of drinks from the bar which also includes at least four real ales and cider so everyone can enjoy their favourite tipple.

The Russell Inn has an enviable reputation for its food which is served in the inn's comfortable restaurant. A popular place at weekends, when it is advisable to book, customers can choose from either the menu or the daily changing specials board. Many of the dishes are home-cooked by Andrea from the freshest local produce and this, along with Andrea's flair and imagination, is what draws people to eat here.

View across to Polruan

pleasure craft and china clay vessels, lies the
late 15th century **Polruan Blockhouse**. One
of a pair of artillery buildings that was
constructed to control the entrance to Fowey,
it was from here that, during the Hundred
Years War, heavy linked chains were stretched
between the two to prevent a sea invasion by
the French. The grooves made by the chains
can still be seen carved into the rock.

GRIBBIN HEAD
2 miles SW of Fowey off the A3082

The beacon on Gribbin Head, Mariner's Mark,
was built here in 1832 to help seafarers find
the approaches to Fowey harbour. However,
this craggy headland is best known as being
the home of Daphne du Maurier who lived at
the still private house of **Menabilly**.
Originally the country retreat of the wealthy
local Rashleigh family, it was her home for
many years and featured as 'Manderley' in her
most famous novel, *Rebecca*, as well as making
an appearance in *The King's General*.

3 Padstow, Wadebridge and the Camel Estuary

This area, around the River Camel and its estuary, centres around the two towns of Wadebridge and Padstow. The former, found inland, was once a busy riverport and, following the building of the 'Bridge on Wool' the historic lowest crossing place. An ancient and now quiet town, from which the Camel Trail heads off towards the foothills of Bodmin Moor, Wadebridge not only clings on to its trading past by being the home of the Royal Cornwall Agricultural Show but is also home to the John Betjeman Centre.

The Poet Laureate was introduced to the villages around the Camel estuary during boyhood holidays and this began a life long romance with the area. He died, in 1984, at his second home, at Trebetherick and he is buried, along with his parents, in the graveyard of the ancient Church of St Enodoc which stands amongst the sand dunes over-looking Padstow Bay. Those familiar with the great poet's verse will discover many of the places of which he wrote and, though time has march on, they remain little changed today.

House on the Rocks, Bedruthan Steps

Closer to the mouth of the River Camel, which is guarded now by Doom Bar, lies Padstow, a small fishing town that is synonymous with fish, seafood and the restaurateur Rick Stein. Another old port, which is named after St Petroc who landed here at the beginning of his missionary work in the West Country, Padstow has seen many visitors over the years, including Sir Walter Raleigh, the 16th century explorer, who lived here for a time as Warden of Cornwall.

Nearby Prideaux Place, which also dates from the first Elizabethan age, is a marvellous mansion house that was built on the site of St Petroc's monastery. This family residence - the ancient Prideaux-Brune family have lived here for over 400 years - not only contains many treasures but it is also surrounded by beautiful parkland and gardens.

PADSTOW, WADEBRIDGE AND THE CAMEL ESTUARY

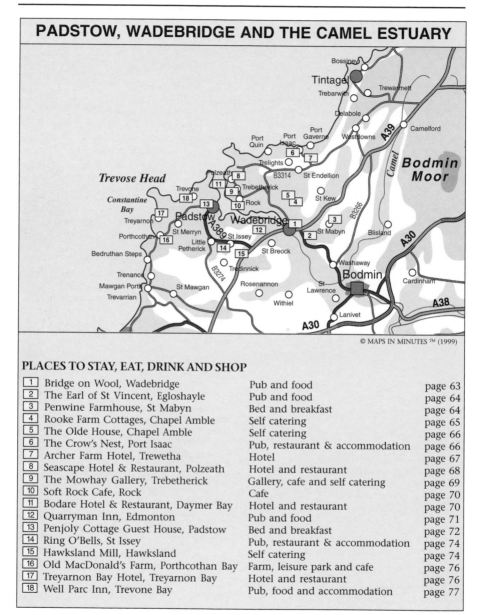

© MAPS IN MINUTES ™ (1999)

PLACES TO STAY, EAT, DRINK AND SHOP

WADEBRIDGE

Standing at the historic lowest bridging point on the River Camel, this ancient port and busy market town is a popular holiday town that is not only attractive but also is renowned for its craftware. Linking the North and South coasts of Cornwall and the moorland with the sea, Wadebridge has always been a bustling place and its establishment as a trading centre began in earnest in the 15th century. The then Rev Lovibond, the vicar of St Petroc's, was looking to convey his flock of sheep across the river safely and so, in 1460s, built the 320 foot long and now 14-arched bridge which can still be seen today. One of the longest bridges in Cornwall today, it did originally have 17 arches and it is said that this bridge, dubbed the **Bridge on Wool**, was constructed on bridge piers that were sunk on to a foundation of woolsacks. The bridge still carries the main road which links the town's two ancient parishes.

The churches of the two parishes that were linked by the bridge can still be seen today: 13th century St Breock's Church stands in a picturesque wooded valley that is known as Nancient (from the Cornish for 'holy well') and, across the river from the main town, stands Egloshayle Church, the church at the centre of Rev Lovibond's ministry and to which he donated the money to build the imposing 80 foot tower.

This major river crossing saw a steady growth in trade through Wadebridge and, with the advent of the railway in the 19th century, the port and town thrived. As a result the town's architecture is chiefly Victorian and, though now a quieter place, this busy shopping centre also draws to it local artists and craftsmen as well as holidaymakers. Each June, just to the west of the town centre, the **Royal Cornwall Agricultural Show** is held.

The town's former railway station is now home to the **John Betjeman Centre** that is dedicated to the life and work of the Poet Laureate. Among the many tributes and intimate artefacts to be seen here there are, in the Memorabilia Room, the late poet's desk, chair and drafts of his books.

Bridge on Wool,

The Platt, Wadebridge, Cornwall PL27 7AQ
Tel: 01208 812750

Dating back to the beginning of the 20th century (although the third storey was not added until the 1920s), the unusually named **Bridge on Wool** is a splendid former hotel that stands right in the heart of Wadebridge. At the time it was built, the pub, like the town, was dependent on horses and, in particular, Romanys would ride their horses into the bar to do their trading - the old stable block can still be seen at the back of the building. Changing its name from the Cornish Arms after World War II to honour the 15th century bridge over the River Camel that, according to local legend, was built on sacks of wool, this quality public house has

been offering superb hospitality to visitors and locals alike for around 100 years.

Today's hosts, Stephen and Carol Harrison have been here since 1996 and they take great pride in the friendly surroundings and high standard of service found here. A pleasant and attractive open plan pub, the Bridge of Wool is well known for always having a good selection of drinks at its bar, including at least two real ales. Bar meals and snacks are also served at lunchtimes and the tasty menu of home-cooked dishes offers traditional pub fayre. A lively, central meeting place during Wadebridge's annual Folk Festival held every August Bank Holiday, throughout the rest of the year Stephen and Carol provide live musical entertainment most Friday and Saturday nights.

The Earl of St Vincent,

Egloshayle, near Wadebridge,
Cornwall PL27 6HT
Tel: 01208 814807

The Earl of St Vincent is certainly one of the most eye-catching inn's in the area as, throughout the summer, the exterior of this old inn is bedecked with an amazing number of colourful, flower filled hanging baskets and window boxes. The sight really has to be seen to be believed and visitors will not be at all surprised that the inn's equally impressive beer garden has won many awards for its fabulous flora displays. Although landlords Anne and Edward Connolly have obviously put a lot of time and effort into their gardening, they have also, since they came here in 1989, put a great deal of work into establishing this inn as one of the best in the area. Well known for its quality ales, there are alsways at least three real ales on tap at the bar, The Earl of St Vincent is also a popular place to come to for a meal. In the wonderful, traditional atmosphere of this old inn, with its fascinating display of over 170 clocks, visitors are treated to a delicious menu of tempting dishes that are all prepared by Anne. Supplemented by a daily specials board, the menu is sure to suit the whole family and, such is the inn's popularity, that booking is essential to avoid disappointment. However, families should note that whilst children are welcome at lunchtimes, in the evenings it is preferred that they be over 12 years of age.

Penwine Farmhouse,

St Mabyn, near Wadebridge,
Cornwall PL30 3DB
Tel: 01280 841783

Situated on the outskirts of the village of St Mabyn, and surrounded by five acres of pastureland, gardens and woodland, **Penwine Farmhouse** is a delightful place to discover. Between 400 and 500 years old this wonderful old building has been lovingly restored using the same materials with which it was built - granite and slate.

Heather and George Hurley, Penwine's owners, have been here since 1994 and they extend a warm welcome to couples and families wishing to take advantage of the splendid bed and breakfast found here. The two comfortable double guest rooms have their own separate entrance and, as they share a bathroom, the second guest room is only let to members of the same party thus ensuring guests have complete privacy and peace. Breakfast is served in the sitting room which is dominated by a large and ancient fireplace complete with a bread oven. However, if the weather is warm enough Heather serves breakfast outside under an attractive loggia. Whilst the glorious gardens make a pleasant place to stroll, Penwine Farmhouse is also close to many interesting walks as well as being ideally placed for many of the area's attractions.

Another reminder that this is an ancient town can be found just to the south of the centre of Wadebridge, at Trevannion Culverhouse. This medieval **Dovecote** is one of only a few such structures in the county that have survived and it was used to provide both fresh eggs and fresh meat for the local manor house.

Although the railway line, which opened in 1899, closed in the 1960s, a stretch of the trackbed has been used to create the superb **Camel Trail**. Either walking or cycling, the trail leads up into the foothills of Bodmin Moor, to the east of Wadebridge, whilst to the west the path follows the River Camel to Padstow through an area that is rich in wildlife and, particularly, in wading birds such as herons.

AROUND WADEBRIDGE

ST KEW
3½ miles NE of Wadebridge off the A39

There are only a couple of buildings

neighbouring the light and airy 15th century church at St Kew, which can be found in a wooded hollow, and they include the large late Georgian rectory and an Elizabethan inn. The village is also home to an **Ogham Stone**, an unusual feature in Cornwall and one that is more commonly associated with southwest Ireland. Given its name because it is inscribed with the Ines of Ogham script, the stone also bears a Latin inscription.

ST ENDELLION
4 miles N of Wadebridge on the B3314

This charming village has a particularly interesting church, built of Lundy Island granite, that houses a major work of the sculptor known as the Master of St Endellion. An anonymous artist in every respect of his life, the Master of St Endellion has, however, been immortalised by his superb tomb that is beautifully carved in black Catacleuse stone. The church itself is dedicated to St Endellienta, a Celtic saint who lived solely, so it is said, on milk. She passed away after her trusty cow was killed in a disputed with a local farmer.

ROOKE FARM COTTAGES,

Rooke Farm, Chapel Amble,
near Wadebridge, Cornwall PL27 6ES
Tel: 01208 880368 Fax: 01208 880600
e-mail Information@Rookefarm.com
website: www.rookefarm.com

Situated in over 230 acres of beautiful Cornish countryside and close to the Camel Estuary, **Rooke Farm Cottages** is an idyllic place for a family holiday. This family run working farm, dates back to the 12th century and, whilst the land still supports sheep, cattle and cereals, the ancient and historic farm buildings have been renovated and converted into superb holiday accommodation. These attractive buildings, all of which are built of mellow stone, vary in size, from The Farmhouse which accommodates seven adults, to cosy cottages for two. Each, however, has been fully furnished to the highest standards whilst the decoration is charming and gives the real feel of sedate country living. The Farmhouse and the cottages all have their own private gardens - which makes them also ideal for children - and the character of each building has also been preserved. The picturesque village of Chapel Amble is within walking distance whilst, close by, are many of north Cornwall's most impressive sights including Port Isaac, Tintagel and the Lost Gardens of Heligan.

THE OLDE HOUSE,

Chapel Amble, near Wadebridge,
Cornwall PL27 6EN
Tel: 01208 813219
Fax: 01208 815689
e-mail: info@theoldehouse.co.uk
website: www.theoldehouse.co.uk

Found at the heart of Penpont Farm, lies **The Olde House**, the home of Andrew and Janice Hawkey and their family. This large working mixed farm has been in Andrew's family for three generations and, in the 1970s, he and Janice began converting a number of stone and slate barns at the farm. The resulting holiday cottages proved a success and now, some 25 years later, the family have a superb holiday facility that not only provides splendid accommodation but also much more besides. There are a variety of cottages here, ranging from those suitable for couples to large family units, but each has been exceptionally well converted and fitted to provide comfortable home from home accommodation. An interesting trail around Penpont Farm takes visitors around the surrounding fields as well as providing an interesting insight into the workings of a busy farm.

Meanwhile, close to the main complex there are numerous amenities for adults and children alike including an indoor heated swimming pool with jacuzzi and sauna, an adventure playground, two tennis courts and a pets' corner. For the under 10's there is an indoor playbarn complete with ballpool and wendy house. This superb establishment is an ideal holiday location and certainly a leader in its field.

THE CROW'S NEST,

4 The Terrace, Port Isaac, Cornwall PL29 3SG
Tel/Fax: 01208 880305 e-mail: mic.mic@virgin.net

Situated on a cliff top overlooking Port Isaac Bay, **The Crow's Nest** is a very aptly named inn and restaurant. Originally two private houses that were built in the late 19th century, they became first a hotel and then an inn, The Shipwright Inn, in 1985. In April 2000, today's owners, Mike and Michelle, bought the premises and, following a complete refurbishment along with a name change, they created a fine inn with hospitality to match. The large picture windows in both the bar and restaurant not only give the rooms a light and airy feel but also allow visitors to enjoy the panoramic views across the bay to Tintagel Head when the weather is too unpleasant to sit on the attractive front terrace.

The stylish and elegant decorations and furnishings complete the relaxed and comfortable atmosphere found here and makes this the place to come to for excellent food and drink. Besides the well stocked bar, Michelle, the chef of the partnership, serves a tempting menu of bar snacks, light meals, main meals and specials board from which to choose - a lot home-made. The emphasis here is on quality and only the freshest local produce is used in the preparation of the mouthwatering dishes. Not surprisingly, the reputation of The Crow's Nest restaurant has spread and it is necessary to book in advance to avoid disappointment. Finally, the inn has four charming en suite guest rooms, some of which have the same seaward views, that provide all anyone could want.

PORT ISAAC
5 miles N of Wadebridge on the B3267

Surrounded, like its neighbour Port Gaverne, by open countryside, Heritage Coast land and an Area of Outstanding Natural Beauty, Port Isaac is a wonderful fishing village that has retained much of its ancient character

Port Isaac

and charm. A busy port since the Middle Ages, fishing is still an important industry here, though the heyday of Port Isaac was in the 19th century when not only fish, but

cargoes of stone, coal, timber and pottery were loaded and unloaded on the quayside.

At one time, huge quantities of pilchard were landed and processed here and, after the arrival of the railway, these were gutted and packed in the village's many fish cellars before being despatched by train to London and beyond. One of these old cellars is now an inshore lifeboat station whilst others have found a wide variety of other uses.

The centre of this conservation village is concentrated around the protected harbour where 18th and 19th century cottages line the narrow alleys and 'opes' that wend their way down to the coast. One lane is particularly narrow and goes by the name of **'Squeeze-ee-belly Alley'**, which provides a warning to visitors of the dangers of indulging in too many Cornish cream teas.

Just inland from the village can be found the double ramparts of **Tregeare Rounds**, a Celtic hill fort that was excavated in 1904. Among the finds uncovered here were pottery fragments thought to be around 2000 years old. Believed to be the Castle Terrible in Thomas Malory's 15th century

ARCHER FARM HOTEL,

Trewetha, near Port Isaac,
Cornwall PL29 3RU Tel: 01208 880522
website: www.archerfarm.com

Set in two acres of wonderful grounds and within walking distance of the north Cornwall coast and the charming village of Port Isaac, **Archer Farm Hotel** is just the place for a relaxing and peaceful holiday. Originally a 15th century farmhouse, the building was extended in early Victorian times and again in the 1970s and now, following a full refurbishment programme in late 1999, it provides excellent accommodation that is both spacious and full of character. Each of the six beautifully decorated and well appointed en suite guest rooms have their own individual style and they all benefit from glorious rural views. Meanwhile, the public rooms are equally well decorated and furnished and whether sitting by the fire in the lounge on a cold winter's evening or enjoying a hearty homecooked breakfast in the dining room, guests can enjoy the friendly and cosy atmosphere which owners, Andy and Lesley, have created.

Observant guests will also notice that there are numerous artefacts relating to lifeboats and the RNLI on display in the hotel and these are part of the collection which Andy has put together during his time as the senior helmsman of the local lifeboat. However, delightful though the interior of Archer Farm Hotel is, the magnificent grounds are well worth strolling around and there is also a patio when guests can enjoy a drink during the evenings.

THE SEASCAPE HOTEL AND RESTAURANT,

Polzeath, Cornwall PL27 6SX
Tel: 01208 863638 Fax: 01208 862940
e-mail: information@seascapehotel.co.uk
website: www.seascapehotel.co.uk

With glorious views over Padstow Bay, **The Seascape Hotel and Restaurant** surely has one of the most splendid positions in north Cornwall. This former farmhouse, which was used as an orphanage for evacuees from east London during World War II, is a now a first class private hotel which has been rejuvenated by owners Paul and Julie Duffield since they arrived here in May 1998. The recent refurbishment has created not only comfortable and stylish accommodation for guests but also a friendly and relaxed environment where Paul and Julie's aim is for guests to "Arrive as strangers and Leave as friends."

Set in picturesque grounds, where the mature and well kept gardens offer quiet alcoves of seclusion and shade, the hotel has 15 en suite guest rooms, many of which have a sea view. Further rooms can be found in the ground floor annex and they have patio doors leading into the garden which makes them ideal for guests wishing to bring their dogs. Although the welcome and the accommodation here is second to none, the hotel's excellent restaurant is an added extra that makes a stay here perfect. Furnished and decorated to the same high standards as the rest of The Seascape, here guests and non residents can enjoy an imaginatively prepared menu which makes the best possible use of fresh local fish, meat and produce. Meanwhile the charming lounge bar is just the place for a pre dinner drink or light bar meal.

epic, Morte D'Arthur, it was here that King Uther Pendragon lay siege to and killed the Earl of Cornwall because he had fallen in love with the earl's beautiful wife, Igerna. After her husband's death, Igerna fled to Tintagel where, with the help of Merlin, Uther seduced Igerna who went on to give birth to the future King Arthur.

PORT GAVERNE
5 miles N of Wadebridge off the B3267

A busy fishing port in the 19th century when, in one season, over 1000 tons of pilchards were landed and processed here in the village's fish cellars or 'pilchard palaces'. Port Gaverne also saw over 100 ships a year docking here to pick up slate from the Delabole quarry. Today, most of the large stone buildings, including some of the old fish cellars, have been converted into holiday accommodation and tourism has taken over as the mainstay of the local economy. One of the safest beaches along the North Cornwall coast, Port Gaverne beach is pebbled and, at low tide, an expanse of sand dotted with rock pools is revealed.

TRELIGHTS
4½ miles N of Wadebridge off the B3314

Close to the village lies the only public garden on the North Cornwall coast - **Long Cross Victorian Gardens**. A real garden lover's delight, there is a fascinating Victorian Maze and a secret garden as well as some superb panoramic views. Granite and water have been used to create imaginative features amongst the 19th century plants and plantings and children will delight in visiting the Gardens' Pets' Corner. Refreshments too can be taken in tea and beer garden.

PORT QUIN
5 miles N of Wadebridge off the B3314

This tiny hamlet, along with its small shingle cove, suffered greatly in the 19th century when the railways took away the slate trade from its once busy quay. The demise of the port was so swift that, at one time, outsiders thought that the entire population of Port Quin had been washed away in a great storm. The village remained deserted for decades but, fortunately, it has now been restored with help of the National Trust and today it has a seasonal community who come here to holiday in the restored cottages that make up this pleasant and peaceful little village.

Situated to the west on Doyden Point, and overlooking Port Quin, stands **Doyden Castle**, a squat 19th century castellated folly which too is now a holiday home.

POLZEATH AND NEW POLZEATH
5 miles NW of Wadebridge off the B3314

Surfers and holidaymakers flock to these two small resorts as the broad west-facing beach is not only ideal for surfing but the fine sands, caves and tidal rock pools make it a fascinating place for children. Well known to and much loved by Sir John Betjeman, to the north of the villages, is a beautiful coastal path that takes in the cliffs and farmland of **Pentire Point** and **Rumps Point**. Much of the coastline here is owned by the National Trust and, on the delightful Rumps Point promontory, stands **Rumps Cliff Castle**, an Iron Age fortification where the remains of its four defensive ramparts - only two of

Polzeath Beach

which were in use at any one time - can still be seen. One of three hill forts that once existed on the headland, this area is also known for its wild tamarisk, an elegant flowering shrub that is more commonly found around the shores of the Mediterranean.

THE MOWHAY GALLERY,
Trebetherick, near Wadebridge, Cornwall PL27 6SE
Tel: 01208 863634

Close to Sir John Betjeman's final resting place at St Endoc church, where there is also a splendid golf course, the **Mowhay Gallery** is another place that is well worth visiting. A fabulous stone and wooden built longhouse which dates from around 1600, this was a derelict barn when Peter and Sandy took it over. They set to work renovating the barn and adding a sympathetically designed extension and, today, they have a wonderful place which pulls together many separate interests.

The first floor of the barn now contains two superb studio apartments, ideal for couples on self-catering holidays. Charmingly decorated and furnished - the kitchens are also fully equipped - they are the perfect place for a holiday away from it all. Meanwhile, on the ground floor is the gallery and coffee shop. The interior of this beautiful barn is the perfect backdrop for the Cornish watercolours, pottery, photographs, jewellery, clothing and other locally made handicrafts that are on sale here.

Here too there is the coffee shop where customers can enjoy a lovely menu of homecooked light meals and snacks that are served either in the barn or on the lawns outside. Seafood is a speciality here but many find that they are also tempted by the excellent cream teas, Cornish ice cream and the homemade patisserie. Also here is Just Kites, an interesting and colourful collection of kites from around the world. Fred is available to advise and sell you a kite to suit your requirements.

SOFT ROCK CAFÉ,

Ferrypoint, Rock, near Wadebridge, Cornwall PL27 6LD Tel: 01208 863841

As its address suggests, the **Soft Rock Café** lies close to the place where the ferry from Padstow moors in this attractive village. Overlooking the beach and Padstow Bay, this delightful place is just the place for a leisurely light lunch or snack at any time of the day. Owner, Sue Male, first came here in 1997 and, following a full refurbishment programme, she has created a flourishing and popular café that is renowned not just for its food but also for its ambience. The large French windows open out on to a paved patio area so that, in the height of summer, customers have the choice of sitting in the coolth of the café or in the sunshine of the patio.

Open everyday throughout the season, from early morning until late afternoon, the menu served here begins with breakfasts and Sue's excellent feast is just the way to start the day. The superb homecooked menu, which is supplemented by a daily specials' board, contains many favourites but the house specialities here are the freshly filled baguettes and the hot toasted paninis. However, it is for Sue's traditional Cornish cream teas that most people find themselves making their way back here time and time again where the delicious scones and fresh clotted cream go down a treat as the gentle background music adds to the style and charm of this establishment.

BODARE COUNTRY HOUSE HOTEL AND RESTAURANT,

Daymer Bay, near Rock, Cornwall PL27 6SA
Tel: 01208 863210 Fax: 01208 863220 website: www.bodare.co.uk

Set in the heart of Sir John Betjeman's favourites area of Cornwall, and just yards from the 12th fairway of the famous St Enodoc Golf Course, the **Bodare Country House Hotel and Restaurant** is a magnificent place from which to explore north Cornwall. Built in the 1920s as a private house and becoming a hotel in the 1930s, the Bodare retains a traditional style and ambience where first class food, accommodation and service are the priorities of manager Norman Evans. The sumptuously decorated and furnished public rooms have log fires to add extra warmth on colder nights whilst, in the summer, guests can make excellent

use of the hotel's mature and extensive grounds. The hotel's restaurant has an enviable reputation and the interesting and imaginative menus change regularly. The emphasis here is very much on fresh local produce and, naturally, fish features heavily whilst the restaurant also bakes all its own bread as well as serving homemade jams and preserves for breakfast and afternoon tea. As might be expected with a hotel of this standard, all the 18 en suite guest rooms are equally stylish and comfortable and all have a sea view. A delightful place for a holiday, golfers will be particularly pleased to here that there are numerous courses in the area and, on some, discount green fees are offered to residents.

In the 1930s, Pentire Head was saved from commercial development thanks to local fund raisers who bought the land and donated it to the National Trust. This lovely stretch of coastline is completely traffic free and offers some excellent walking country with views over the spectacular Camel Estuary.

TREBETHERICK
5 miles NW of Wadebridge off the B3314

The simple yet delightful **Church of St Enodoc**, a Norman building with a squat 13th century stone spire, overlooks Padstow Bay and lies in the shadow of Brea Hill. On a number of occasions throughout its history this church has been all but submerged by windblown sand and, at these times, the congregation would enter the building via an opening in the roof. The sand was finally cleared away in the 1860s, when the church was restored, and the bell in the tower, which came from an Italian ship that was wrecked nearby, was added in 1875.

The beautiful churchyard contains many graves of shipwrecked mariners who came to grief on the local sandbank known as Doom

Bar or at other treacherous places along this stretch of coast. But what draws many people to this quiet place is the grave of Sir John Betjeman who is buried here along with his parents. The fondly remembered Poet Laureate spent many of his childhood holidays in the villages and coves around the Camel Estuary and his affection for the local people and the surrounding countryside was the inspiration for many of his works.

The church is reached across **St Enodoc's Golf Course** which is regarded as one of the most scenic links courses in the country while the beach at Trebetherick is well known for its fine bathing and excellent surfing conditions.

ROCK
4 miles NW of Wadebridge off the B3314

This former fishing village lies in a small estuary inlet and, though today, fishing has all but ceased from here Rock has retained its strong nautical links. With a sailing club and sailing and waterskiing schools, this is an ideal place for those interested in watersports and, during the summer, this is a bustling and popular place. The sandy

QUARRYMAN INN,

Edmonton, near Wadebridge,
Cornwall PL27 7JA
Tel: 01208 816444 Fax: 01208 815674

Found in the heart of Edmonton, and close to the Camel Estuary, the **Quarryman Inn** is a lovely, mellow old building which has, in its time, been both a schoolhouse and a butcher's shop. The slate quarry cottages behind the inn were built many years ago and this is where, long before the building became an inn, ale was brewed. Now a marvellous free house, the Quarryman has only been a pub since 1976, but it does have an enviable reputation as an excellent place to visit. Terry and Wendy, the landlords here since August 1992, have certainly made their mark here and the friendly and welcoming

atmosphere makes it well worth while taking the trouble to find this inn. From the bar there are always four real ales on tap, two of which are local, as well as all the usual lagers, ciders, stouts and spirits. Bar food too is available through out the week whilst, at weekends, the Quarryman's stylish restaurant is also open. The menus are all prepared by the inn's imaginative chef and the dining here, either formally or in the bar, is a pleasure. Entertainment here does not end with the superb food and drink as each Tuesday evening is folk night. Finally, for anyone feeling energetic, opposite the restaurant there is the inn's health club, complete with swimming pool, gym and squash courts, meanwhile, for those who just wish to relax there is a spa, sauna and Jacuzzi.

beach, just north of the cove, is the departure point for the passenger ferry to Padstow which runs a regular service throughout the summer. Anyone wishing to make the journey out of season has to summon the ferry from Padstow by waving the flag that is left at the ferry point for this very purpose.

ST BREOCK
1 miles W of Wadebridge off the A39

To the southwest of this hamlet, with its beautifully placed medieval church found in a steep-sided wooded valley, lies **St Breock Downs**. In the heart of this exposed land stands the ancient **St Breock Downs Monolith**, a striking Bronze Age longstone that is also known as the Men Gurta (the Stone of Waiting). Other prehistoric remains, such as the Nine Maidens stone row, can also be found on the downs.

PADSTOW

For many centuries, Padstow's sheltered

Padstow Village and Harbour

position on the western side of the Camel estuary has made it a welcome haven for vessels seeking respite from the perils of the sea. The only safe harbour along this stretch of the North Cornwall coast, after the rocks, currents and winds of the river mouth have been negotiated, the town has been settled by many different people over the years including the prehistoric Beaker folk, Romans, Celtic saints and marauding Vikings. However, the silting up of the River Camel in the 19th century created a new hazard for shipping coming in and going out of Padstow

PENJOLY COTTAGE GUEST HOUSE,
Padstow Road, Padstow, Cornwall PL28 8LB
Tel: 01841 533535 Fax: 01841 532313 Mobile: 0410 507782

Situated just a mile or so from the centre of Padstow and set in its own lovely grounds, **Penjoly Cottage Guest House** is a tucked away place that is well worth seeking out. Built in the 1930s as a private house, this attractive and deceptively spacious cottage has been owned and personally run by David Crofts since 1998. As well as adding a splendid conservatory to the house, David has also decorated and furnished Penjoly Cottage with style and flair and each room is specifically designed to provide a peaceful and tranquil environment for guests. As well as the three excellent en suite guest rooms, where guests will find little extras that show thought and imagination on David's part, there is a private sitting room in which

they may relax.

Meanwhile, there is also the elegant dining room, a charming place where a splendid breakfast awaits everyone each morning. Though dinner is available here there are a wealth of local restaurants and inns near by ranging from Rick Stein's famous Seafood restaurant to local country pubs and modest, informal bistros. A hidden place offering superb hospitality as well as peace and quiet, Penjoly Cottage is just the place for a relaxing break and, to maintain this, children are not allowed.

harbour and the evocatively named Doom Bar, which restricts entry into the estuary mouth, effectively put an end to this ancient settlement continuing as a major port.

Originally named Petroc-stow, after the Welsh missionary St Petroc landed here in the 6th century. The son of a Welsh chieftain, St Petroc, like St Francis of Assisi had a special relationship with animals and, legend has it, that he drew the splinter from the eye of a dragon, saved a deer from a hunt and, most spectacularly, rescued a seamonster trapped in a lake. Before moving on to Bodmin Moor to continue his missionary work, St Petroc founded a Celtic minster here and the parish **Church of St Petroc Major** still bears his name. Today's building dates from the 13th and 14th centuries and, as well as the octagonal font of Catacleuse stone carved by the Master of St Endellion, there is a striking Elizabethan pulpit and some rather amusing bench ends. Beginning at the door of the church is the **Saints' Way**, a middle distance footpath that follows the route that was taken by travellers and pilgrims crossing Cornwall on their way from Brittany to Ireland.

The monastery that St Petroc founded here was destroyed, along with most of the town, during a Viking raid in the 10th century. Later, in the Middle Ages, King Athelstan granted the town the Right of Sanctuary, enabling criminals to seek refuge from the law here, that was only repealed by Henry VIII at the time of the Dissolution.

Today, Padstow's harbour and nearby shopping streets throng with visitors throughout the summer who come here to see the narrow alleyways and tightly packed slate hung buildings of the old quarter, which has managed to retain much of its medieval character. The influence of the sea is never far away in Padstow and, more recently, it has become linked with seafood and the famous chef and fish restaurateur Rick Stein.

Any exploration of Padstow should begin at the town's focal point, its **Harbour**, which now is home to a fishing fleet and which resists the rise and fall of the tide by means of a sluice gate. Here, too, can be found many of Padstow's older buildings including, on the South Quay, **Raleigh Cottage** where Sir Walter Raleigh lived when he was Warden of Cornwall, and the minute **Harbour**

'Obby 'Oss, Padstow

Cottage. Raleigh's **Court House**, where he collected the taxes, stands close by beside the river. On North Quay is the 15th century **Abbey House** that is now a private residence but was, once, a nunnery. The harbour is also the home of the **Shipwreck Museum** which displays artefacts recovered from ships who floundered on the north Cornish coast.

As well as the annual Fish and Ships Festival Padstow also continues to celebrate May Day in a traditional way that has its origins back in pagan times. Beginning at midnight on the eve of May Day and lasting throughout May 1, the townsfolk sing in the new morning and then follow the **'Obby 'Oss** - a man in a black frame-hung cape and wearing a grotesque mask - around the narrow streets of Padstow until midnight on May 1 when the 'Obby 'Oss dies.

Found on the northern outskirts of Padstow is **Prideaux Place**, a magnificent Elizabethan mansion that, for over 400 years, has been home of the ancient Cornish Prideaux-Brune family. Built on the site of St

RING O' BELLS,

St Issey, near Wadebridge, Cornwall PL27 7QA
Tel: 01841 540251 e-mail: ringersstissey@freeserve.co.uk

Situated right in the heart of St Issey, the **Ring O' Bells** is a charming local inn which certainly dates back to the late 17th century though many believe it to be older. Hard to miss during the summer when the whole of the front of the inn is bedecked with colourful, flower filled hanging baskets and patio tubs, visitors will find that this inn is equally delightful inside. The original ceiling beams, low ceilings and mass of interesting memorabilia on the walls all add to the character of this old building, where, over the years landlords John and Anne Crossley have built up a large and faithful following.

Very much a local pub, the Ring O' Bells has been awarded both the national and the southwest Community Pub of the Year for 1999 prize, the friendly welcome and inviting atmosphere found here is much appreciated by regular customers and visitors alike. As well as the well stocked bar, from which there is always a good range of real ales, this inn is highly regarded for its food. Served in either the cosy and intimate restaurant (for which booking is essential during the weekends) or in the bar the menu of tasty homecooked dishes is extensive. From house specialities such as Steak and Stilton, Gamekeeper's Casserole and Harvest Time Chicken to freshly cut sandwiches, ploughman's lunches and freshly baked Cornish pasties there is certainly something for everyone here.

Finally, hospitality at the Ring O' Bells does not end here as the inn has three comfortable en suite guest rooms.

HAWKSLAND MILL,

Hawksland, near St Issey, Wadebridge, Cornwall PL27 7RG
Tel: 01208 815404 Fax: 01208 816831
e-mail: hjc@hawkslandmill.idps.co.uk website: www.hawkslandmill.co.uk

Tucked away in the hamlet of Hawksland, yet close to Padstow, Wadebridge and the north Cornwall coast, **Hawksland Mill** is a charming group of cleverly converted holiday cottages. Parts of the original mill buildings date back to the mid 19th century, and this attractive and well situated property was purchased, in 1992, by Jane and Richard. Both have used their expertise and flair - Jane's for interior design and Richard's for building - to create these beautiful cottages, which all surround the central lawned courtyard. Pretty from the outside, each of the four cottages has its own private garden or patio and all have splendid views either over the rolling farmland to the south or the coast to the west.

Inside, the cottages are equally attractive and each has been decorated and furnished in a pleasing country style. However, whilst the style is traditional, the modern conveniences of the 21st century have not been forgotten, and guests will find that the kitchens are fully equipped and there are televisions and videos in the lounges. A real home from home with the glorious Cornish countryside on the doorstep, Hawksland Mill is an idyllic setting for a peaceful and relaxing holiday.

Petroc's monastery, this E-shaped house was completed in 1592 although it does display various other architectural styles from later periods. Visitors to the house can see a wealth of family and royal portraits, fine furniture, exquisite porcelain and also a splendid 16th century plaster ceiling in the Great Chamber which was rediscovered by present owner when he was a boy playing in the house. Throughout the house there are reminders of the history of this area of Cornwall, and of events in Britain, and the American Army stationed here during World War II have also left their mark. A wonderful and interesting house, Prideaux Place is surrounding by fantastic gardens and parklands, including one of the oldest deer parks in England, which were laid out in Capability Brown-style in the 18th century.

AROUND PADSTOW

TREDINNICK
3 miles S of Padstow off the A339

To the south of this small stone-built village lies **Shire Family Adventure Park** - one of the county's best kept family parks. Along with the shire horses and new born foals on show here, which include a World Champion, there are numerous other farmyard friends as well as a wealth of other activities to keep the whole family happy for hours. There are woodland trails through the Enchanted Forest to Greengate Meadow, where there is the chance to sight moles, badgers and other shy woodland creatures, whilst the adventure playground, with aerial bridges and slides, provides another source of entertainment. Inside, the fun does not stop as there is a complete indoor play area and, for those needing refreshment, the Camelot Café.

ST ISSEY
2 miles S of Padstow on the A339

This small village is named after the Irish saint, St Issey, who was descended from one of the High Kings. Living around the 5th century, she was christened Daidre but took the name Itha when she decided to dedicate herself to the church.

Whilst visiting Padstow in October 1842, the great novelist, Charles Dickens, inspired by his time in the ancient port, wrote his famous story, *A Christmas Carol*, in which he mentions both Tinnens Cottages and a lighthouse - the one at Trevose Head. His good friend, Dr Miles Marley, whose son, Dr Henry Frederick Marley, practised in Padstow for 51 years, provided the surname for Scrooge's partner, Jacob. In this heartwarming seasonal story, Dickens actually reworks an idea that first began as an interlude in Pickwick Papers and it is plain that the Gabriel Grub character was a prototype for the grasping and miserly Ebenezer Scrooge. Meanwhile, Dr Henry Marley died in 1908, at the age of 76, at his home in Mellingey, St Issey and his funeral took place at the local parish church.

In 1869, the medieval tower of this old church collapsed and, surprisingly, its destruction was captured by an early photographer - the resulting photograph of the tower's demise also shows a top-hatted policeman looking on helplessly. Not only did the tower have to be rebuilt but the Catacleuse stone altar piece by Master of St Endellion had to be meticulously rebuilt piece by piece.

LITTLE PETHERICK
2 miles S of Padstow on the A339

Situated on a branch of the Camel estuary, the tower of the originally medieval church can just be seen amongst the trees. The footpath which follows Little Petherick Creek to its confluence with the River Camel also leads to a splendid viewpoint at which there can also be seen an **Obelisk** that was built in 1887 to celebrate Queen Victoria's Golden Jubilee.

BEDRUTHAN STEPS
5½ miles SW of Padstow off the B3276

By far the best view of this beach, with its curious rock formations, can be found from the grassy clifftops. A steep flight of steps, cut into the cliff, leads the way down to the rock strewn beach which, at low tide, also incorporates a long sweep of sand. The giant slate rocks scattered here have been eroded by the waves and their uniform shape has help to account for them being, according to

OLD MACDONALD'S FARM,

Porthcothan Bay, near Padstow, Cornwall PL28 8LW
Tel: 01841 540829

Found just back from the north Cornwall coast, **Old MacDonald's Farm** is a family attraction primarily aimed at young children but which has plenty to interest all ages on its glorious meadow site. A well established place which has been drawing people for several years between March and October, today's owners, John and Karen Nederpel, took over in 1998 and they have certainly increased the range of amusements here to make this a super day out for all. Three acres of the farm are take up by the many varied attractions here and they include such delights as pony and small train rides, trampolines and crazy golf whilst a further three acres are given over to the numerous animals to be found here. Children of all ages enjoy meeting young animals and here there are plenty including lambs to be bottle fed, goats, rabbits, and piglets. Although the birds of prey here are certainly not cuddly they are beautiful to watch during the displays and make great photographs.

Adults too are catered for here and as well as the locally made craftware in the gift shop and the free scrumpy tasting sessions The Duck Inn Café serves a wide variety of light meals and snacks and is open to everyone - not just farm visitors. An ideal place for a delicious afternoon cream tea, the café's breakfasts are a real feast as is the Old MacDonald special - steak cooked in scrumpy. Finally, the remainder of this entertaining and enjoyable place is taken up with a camping and caravan site which is open all year round. This spacious and open site is an ideal place for a brief or longer stay and along with the electric kook ups there is also a shower and toilet block

TREYARNON BAY HOTEL,

Treyarnon Bay, near St Merryn,
Padstow, Cornwall PL28 8JN
Tel: 01841 520235
Fax: 01841 520239

With spectacular views out over Treyarnon Bay, the **Treyarnon Bay Hotel** is an ideal place from which to enjoy the north Cornwall coast and discover the delights of near by Padstow and Newquay. Dating back, in parts to the 1920s, this well placed hotel is owned and personally run by Malkolm and Jennifer Kenley, along with the help of their sons, Matthew and Benjamin, and daughter Loraine. The family have been here since April 2000, after having lived in America for 18 years but they do have connections with the West Country as Malkolm and Jennifer were in business in Devon before travelling abroad. Open from Easter to the end of October, this friendly and welcoming hotel is especially suited to families as several of the guest rooms are family rooms and the quiet situation is ideal for children.

As well as ensuring that guests are comfortable and their every need catered for, the Treyarnon Bay Hotel offers an excellent level of hospitality. The restaurant here, which is also open to non-residents, serves a tempting and delicious menu at both lunchtime and in the evening. Specialities in this light and airy restaurant include steaks and curries but, with many homemade options from which to choose guests and visitors will find it a hard decision. For less formal eating, the lunchtime tasty bar snacks are available either served in the bar itself or, in good weather, outside overlooking the bay. Add to this the well stocked bar and the regular live music entertainment and the Treyarnon Bay Hotel is a pleasant place that makes a good holiday base.

Coastline at Bedruthan Steps

local legend, thought of as the stepping stones used by the Cornish giant Bedruthan.

One of the most interesting and dramatic sights to be found along this stretch of the North Cornish coast, some of the larger of these massive flat-topped slabs have been given names of their own. **Samaritan Island** is named after a ship wrecked on the beach in 1846 - with the locals 'rescuing' the cargo of luxurious silks and satins for themselves. Another rock, whose curious formation has been likened to the profile of Queen Elizabeth I, is referred to as **Queen Bess Rock**.

However, any resemblance there ever was to the Virgin Queen has long since been wiped away by the wind and the waves.

PORTHCOTHAN
4½ miles SW of Padstow on the B3276

This tiny village overlooks a deep, square cove, with a sandy beach, that is protected by two headlands, one at each side of the cove. Today, much of the land around the cove is owned by the National Trust but, in days gone by, this was the haunt of smugglers, who were able to land their contraband here safely and in secret.

The footpath over the southern headland leads to **Porth Mear**, another secluded cove beyond which, on a low plateau, is a prehistoric earthwork of banks and ditches.

TREYARNON
3½ miles W of Padstow off the B3276

This small hamlet lies at the southern end of **Constantine Bay** and has one of a succession of fine sandy beaches that can be found on either side of Trevose Head. Though

WELL PARC INN,
Trevone Bay, Padstow, Cornwall PL28 8QN
Tel: 01841 520318
e-mail: sally@wellparc.demon.co.uk website: wellparc

With a wonderful view overlooking Trevone Bay from both its large picture windows and the attractive lawned beer garden, the **Well Parc Inn** is a lovely pub to come to whatever the time of year. Originally an extensive private house built in 1904, this did not become an inn until the 1970s and, since 1980, it has been owned and personally run by Ray and Sally Mills. Today, they are joined by their daughters, Jodie and Lee, and they have all worked hard to create the friendly and welcoming atmosphere that is found here. As well as serving an extensive range of drinks from the bar, including several real ales, the Well Parc Inn has

an excellent reputation for the high standard of food on offer. Prepared by both Ray and Sally, the traditional pub style menu is supplemented by a range of home-cooked daily specials dishes and children too will find that many of their favourites are also featured.

Superb food and drink, however, are not all that the Mills family provide for their customers as, during both the summer and the winter there is a full programme of entertainment throughout the week which includes line dancing, whist drives, barbecues and quizzes. Finally, those visiting the area should also note that the Well Parc Inn has 10 well appointed guest rooms and, in the summer, there is a swimming pool available for residents.

conditions here are ideal for surfing, the strong currents around the beach make swimming hazardous.

The sand dunes backing the beaches along Constantine Bay are covered with marram grass and tamarisk shrubs and, through here, runs the **South West Coast Path** on this way northwards to Trevose Head.

TREVOSE HEAD
4 miles NW of Padstow off the B3276

This remote headland, which lies halfway between Hartland Point and West Penwith, is reached via a toll road but it is a trip well worth making as, from the headland, there are wonderful views down the coast that take in bay after bay.

At the tip of the headland stands **Trevose Lighthouse**, which was built in 1847 and has a beam that reaches 27 miles out to sea. Built on the sheer granite cliffs, the light of the house stands some 204 feet above sea level and from here, at night, lights from four other lighthouses can be seen. Still very much a working lighthouse today, a tour can be taken of the building.

After Padstow had lost three lifeboats on the sand bars of the Camel estuary, the lifeboat station was moved to **Mother Ivey's Bay**, on the eastern side of the headland, in the 1960s. Also on the eastern side of Trevose Headland lies **Harlyn Bay** where the site of an Iron Age cemetery was excavated. The remains that were unearthed here can be seen in the Royal Cornwall Museum, Truro.

ST MERRYN
2 miles W of Padstow on the B3276

Found in the garden of a private house in this small village is a modern day Celtic monument that is as equally impressive as the many prehistoric sites found in Cornwall. The **Angles Runway**, three large granite standing stones with a huge, flat capstone, is a direct copy of a Neolithic chamber tomb and there are other copies of famous Cornish stone circles and rocking stones to be seen here.

TREVONE
1½ miles NW of Padstow off the B3276

Sheltered by Trevose Head and Rumps Point, the seemingly gently and quiet sandy cove at Trevone is guarded by vicious offshore rocks. A quiet place that can be reached by way of the coastal path from Padstow, the rock pools that are formed on the beach at low tide, particularly one that is around six feet deep, provide the safest bathing.

4 Mid Cornwall North

With some of the most spectacular coastal scenery certainly in Cornwall if not in the rest of England, the rugged coastline in and around Newquay is well worth exploring. Synonymous with surfing, as well as being a popular seaside holiday resort with all the traditional trappings, Newquay does also retain some of its past, particularly around the harbour. An old fishing village that was very dependent on pilchards, on Towan Headland still stands the Huer's Hut from which the shoals of fish were spotted and their whereabouts passed on to the fishermen.

Further down the coast lies St Agnes, a place that is littered with the reminders of Cornwall's mining tradition and, standing on a clifftop, are the stark yet atmospheric remains of Wheal Coates. Other remains to be seen include, near St Newlyn East, East Wheal Rose Cornwall's richest lead producing mine and also the scene of the industry's greatest disaster. The Poldark novels of Winston Graham, who wrote from his base in Perranporth, brought the beauty, romance and harsh realities of life of this mining area of Cornwall to thousands.

However, the history of this northern coastal area of Cornwall dates back well beyond mining and, as well as the Iron Age remains of Castle-an-Dinas, near St Columb Major, on Penhale Sands, a site associated with St Piran who journeyed here from Ireland on

Newquay and the Town Beaches

a millstone in the 6th century, there stands a splendid Celtic cross and plaque marking the place of St Piran's Oratory.

St Columb Major, though denied the honour of playing host to Cornwall's cathedral in the late 19th century, does still carry on the tradition of hurling the silver ball each year. A cross between hurling and football, this boisterous game, which involves two large teams, has its roots in the ancient kingship contests.

Tucked away in a maze of narrow, leafy lanes, close to Kestle Mill, lies Trerice, a magnificent Elizabethan manor house that is considered a particularly fine architectural gem. The home of the influential Cornish Arundell family, this charming house displays many of its fine, original features, whilst, in one of the outbuildings, is the rather unusual Mower Museum.

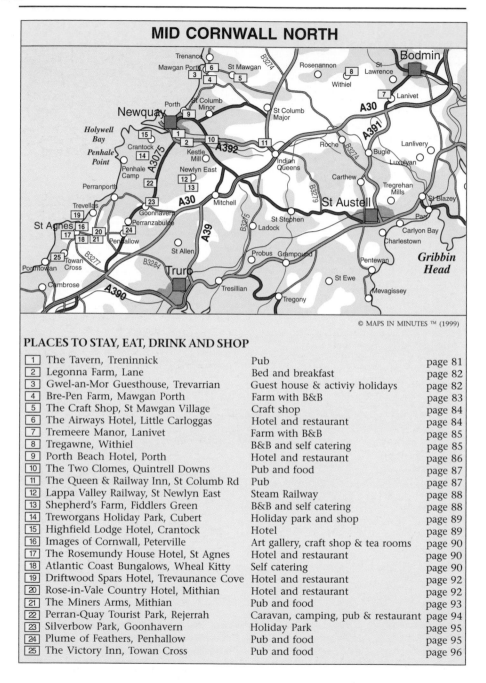

MID CORNWALL NORTH

© MAPS IN MINUTES ™ (1999)

PLACES TO STAY, EAT, DRINK AND SHOP

NEWQUAY

Despite first appearances this is an ancient settlement and there is evidence of an Iron Age coastal fort among the cliffs and caves of **Porth Island** - a detached outcrop which is connected to the mainland by an elegant suspended footbridge. The old part of Newquay is centred around the **Harbour**, which was, for centuries, the heart of this once small fishing community. An important pilchard fishing village right up until the industry's decline at the beginning of the 20th century, the town, with the coming of the railway, also became a major port for both the china clay and the mineral extraction industries. However, with its beautiful rocky coastline and acres of golden sands, Newquay has also developed into a popular seaside resort and one that is famous, throughout the world, for its surfing.

The town takes its name from the 'New Kaye' that was built in the mid 15th century by the villagers who wanted to protect this inlet. As with many other villages along the coast, the main catch of Newquay's fishermen were pilchards and, on Towan Headland, the **Huer's Hut** can still be seen. Here, the Huer would scan the sea looking for shoals of red pilchards and, once spotted, he would alert the fishing crews by calling "hevva" through a long loud-hailer. He would then guide the boats towards the shoal with semaphore-style signals using a pair of bats known as 'bushes'.

Huers House, Newquay

Though there is some Regency architecture to be found in Newquay, the rise of the town's fortunes, in the late 19th century, saw a rapid expansion and many of the large Victorian hotels and small residential houses still remain. One building though has remained from the town's more distant past, the **Trenance Heritage Cottages**, Newquay's oldest dwellings, which are now home to the work of local craftsmen and artists. But it is the sea and beach which draws many here and, along with the more traditional English seaside pursuits, there are also a wide variety of attractions in and around the town that will entertain the whole family.

Situated in Towan Bay, the **Sea Life Aquarium** is home to a wide variety of creatures that live beneath the waves. From the shallowest rock pool to the mysterious depths of the world's oceans, visitors here can see amazing fish and other

THE TAVERN,

Treninnick, near Newquay, Cornwall
Tel: 01637 873564

Surrounded by glorious countryside yet just a short walk from the heart of bustling Newquay, **The Tavern** is a splendid country inn that is well worth seeking out. Dating back to the 18th century, it is only since 1965 that this wonderful old building has been an inn and, for many years, it was a farmhouse. To the front is a beautiful cottage garden and patio area - an ideal place to soak up the sun - and the mass of colourful flowers in the borders, window boxes and hanging

baskets puts most other gardens to shame. Inside, the inn is equally charming and here the olde worlde character of the building has been blended perfectly with the new by owner John Milan. Managed by another local man, Steve Simmons, this inn has is a very popular place with locals, both young and old, and visitors to the area are also given a warm and friendly welcome. Just the place to come to for those who enjoy a good pint of beer - there are always three real ales on tap - this traditional country inn is also has live music each Friday evening and there is a well attended quiz each Sunday evening.

creatures in their natural habitat and, by walking through an underwater tunnel, come face to face with the sharks. Meanwhile, **Newquay Zoo**, where conservation, education and entertainment go hand in hand, offers visitors the chance to see animals from not just the sea but from the land and the air as well. With zebra, antelope and lions from the African plains to the nocturnal world of the Rodrigues bats, there is plenty here to see and do for all the family.

Anyone looking to discover the characters and events that have shaped the history of this part of Cornwall will find that **Tunnels Through Time** holds many attractions. Through realistic life-size figures dressed in authentic costumes and set in carefully constructed tableaux, the days of smugglers and highwaymen, plague victims and miners, King Arthur and Merlin are brought excitingly to life. If the weather here takes a

turn for the worst or the thought of the tropics is too tempting, then a visit to **Water World** is just the thing. A safe environment for all the family, there are waterfalls and fountains, a tropical fun pool and hippo flume, as well as a large swimming pool, for everyone to enjoy and, afterwards, the café is just the place to have a meal or snack.

Towan Beach is one of a succession of fine beaches overlooked by the town and it is also ideal for children as it has a tidal paddling pool. In recent years, Newquay has acquired a reputation as one of the finest surfing centres in Britain and, throughout the year, thousands of surfers arrive here to catch the waves of **Fistral Beach** or to watch the increasing number of national and international competitions held along this part of the North Cornwall coast. Along with the cafés and giftshops, the streets of Newquay are lined with a refreshing variety of shops offering everything for the surfer,

LEGONNA FARM,

Lane, near Newquay, Cornwall TR8 4NJ
Tel: 01637 872272

Hidden away in glorious countryside yet just a couple of miles from the busy beaches of Newquay, **Legonna Farm** is a peaceful and relaxing place to stay. This 140 acre farm lies in a pleasant valley and the farmhouse dates back to 1740 though there are considerable Victorian additions. Still family owned and run, Nora Coombe invites guests to stay at her large and comfortable farmhouse in charming and spacious rooms that will suit both couples and those with children. Throughout the farmhouse is beautifully furnished and decorated and, as well as serving a splendid hearty breakfast each morning, cream teas are served out on the garden lawn in summer and Nora also provides a home-cooked evening meal on request. However, there is much more on offer here as the farm has a large outdoor swimming pool, hard tennis court and snooker table for guests, children can take pony rides, for adults there is a residential bar and coarse fishing in the lake. Nora's daughter, Vanessa, is also happy to teach anyone line dancing.

GWEL-AN-MOR GUESTHOUSE,

Trevarrian, Mawgan Porth, near Newquay, Cornwall TR8 4AQ
Tel: 01637 860437 Fax: 01637 860437 e-mail: tee.gee@zetnet.co.uk
website: www.activityholidayscornwall.co.uk

Gwel-An-Mor Guesthouse is a comfortable and attractive place to stay which offers peaceful and relaxing holidays with a difference. Terry and Gerry Markham, the resident owners, not only provide excellent accommodation for families, including dogs, but they are also experts in organising speciality activity holidays. Fish Cornwall is ideal for anyone interested in boat, shore or freshwater fishing whilst those keen on golf can take advantage of the numerous local courses. Cyclists are also catered for as are those interested in walking, pony trekking and other outdoor activities. Packages can be tailor made and all are based at Gwel-An-Mor Guesthouse.

both to buy and to hire. Another colourful summer attraction involves Newquay's fleet of traditional pilot gigs (30 foot rowing boats) which race each other over a six mile course set out in the bay.

AROUND NEWQUAY

MAWGAN PORTH
4 miles NE of Newquay on the B3276

On the coast at Mawgan Porth, which is little more than a group of beach shops overlooking the delightful horseshoe-shaped sandy bay, the remains of a Saxon settlement can be made out. Various 9th to 11th century dwellings that formed part of this fishing and herding community can be seen near the beach as well as the foundations of a larger courtyard house and a cemetery.

The coastline between here and Padstow, to the north, is rugged and some of the most impressive to be found in Cornwall.

Sunset at Mawgan Porth

ST MAWGAN
4½ miles NE of Newquay off the B3276

This village, found inland from Mawgan Porth and in the beautiful, deep and wooded Vale of Mawgan, provides a real oasis of calm. The restored 13th century church has one of the finest collections of monumental brasses in the country and most are of the Arundell family whose 13th century former manor house, **Lanherne**, was taken over by the closed Carmelite order of nuns in 1794.

BRE-PEN FARM,

Mawgan Porth, near Newquay, Cornwall TR8 4AL
Tel: 01637 860420

Bre-Pen Farm is a National Trust owned mixed working farm that has fantastic views, from both the farmhouse and garden, over Mawgan Porth and Watergate Bay beaches. Surrounded by the farmland and close to the National Trust coastal path, anyone coming to take advantage of the farmhouse's superb bed and breakfast accommodation will marvel at the location.

An ideal place for a relaxing break, Rod and Jill Brake provide a warm welcome to all their guests as well as a choice of comfortable guest room, delicious breakfasts and, if arranged, home-cooked evening meals. Jill's outstanding garden is just the place to sunbathe or have a barbecue whilst those who choose to bring their own horse (for which there is ample stabling) can take advantage of the farm's specially designed cross country course which winds around the farmland. Dogs too are welcome here and children, in particular, will enjoy the Landrover driven farm tours.

Outside, in the churchyard, stands an early 15th century beautifully carved lantern cross whilst here too can be seen an extraordinary timber memorial in the shape of the stern of a boat, that is dedicated to 10 unfortunate souls who froze to death in their lifeboat after being shipwrecked off the coast in 1846.

The village inn, **The Falcon**, is reputed to have been named during the Reformation when it was the practice to release a bird into the air to signal that a secret Catholic mass was about to take place.

ROCHE
10½ miles E of Newquay on the B3274

This old mining village, whose name is

pronounced Roach, has a restored church with a medieval tower and a pillared Norman font. However, what does bring people to this unassuming place lies not in Roche but can be found to the southwest on the granite outcrop of **Roche Rock**. A feat of medieval engineering, the 14th century two storey **Hermitage** perched here has, remarkably, stood the test of time and various legends have grown up around this refuge. It is thought that this cell and chapel were the final retreat of a leper, who survived with the help of his daughter, who brought food and water up the hill each day to sustain her father.

Roche Rock is also associated with the legendary Cornish scoundrel, Jan Tregeagle, who attempted to seek sanctuary in the

THE CRAFT SHOP,

St Mawgan Village, Cornwall TR8 4ER
Tel: 01637 860678

Found on the banks of the River Mawgan, in one of Cornwall's prettiest villages, **The Craft Shop** is a small and charming shop surrounded by a mature cottage garden. Though tucked away, this once carpenter's workshop is well worth a visit as Valerie Codd, the owner since 1980, has on display and for sale an interesting and unusual collection. Open throughout the season, an overwhelming proportion of the items on display are made by local craftsmen and usually come from small cottage industries - generally husband and wife teams. With hand-painted glass, Cornish tin and pewter, prints, watercolours, jewellery, pottery, clothes and much, much more there is not only something to appeal to everyone but also to suit everyone's pocket. A well known and knowledgeable lady, Valerie welcomes back many regular customers each year as well as those discovering The Craft Shop for the first time.

THE AIRWAYS HOTEL,

Little Carloggas, near St Mawgan, Cornwall TR8 4EQ
Tel: 01637 860595 Fax: 01637 860800
e-mail: chrisweaver@compuserve.com
website: www.chrisweaver@compuserve.com

Found close to RAF St Mawgan and Newquay/Cornwall airport, and within easy reach of many of the interesting places along the north Cornwall coast, **The Airways Hotel** is a small and comfortable place to stay. Formerly a farm cottage which was extended in the early 1970s, this family run hotel is owned by Chris and Linda Weaver. The six en-suite guest rooms are both well pleasant and spacious and ideal for a peaceful night's sleep. The bar here is well stocked and Chris ensures that there is always real Cornish ale on tap as well as featuring brews from micro breweries. The Airways Hotel also has an excellent reputation for the high standard of its cuisine and, at the weekends, it is essential to book a table to avoid disappointment. Home-cooked by Chris, the menu and accompanying daily specials board provide plenty of choice of tempting dishes. A quiet and peaceful place to stay, The Airways Hotel has much to offer guests.

TREMEERE MANOR,

Lanivet, near Bodmin, Cornwall PL30 5BG
Tel: 01208 831513 Fax: 01208 832417
e-mail: oliver.tremeere.manor@farming.co.uk

Found just outside the village of Lanivet, and on the edge of Hensbarrow Downs, **Tremeere Manor** is a large working farm that occupies a magnificent position. Chiefly a diary farm, which lies surrounded by lush green pasture, owners David and Margaret Oliver have been here from 1985 and, since 1992, they have also been offering delightful bed and breakfast accommodation from their splendid farm house. The building is very special indeed and, although it dates back in parts to the 13th century, most of this lovely building was constructed in the 17th century. A large house, which dominates the farm, David and

Margaret have three charming guest rooms (each with private or en suite bathrooms) that are not only spacious but also comfortable and homely. There are glorious views in every direction and, whilst enjoying the delights of the surrounding area, guests here are also treated to superb hospitality which is sure to make everyone feel special. Although Margaret does not offer a meal in the evening there are numerous excellent places to eat close by. Children are also welcome at Tremeere Manor and, as well as being made a fuss of, they can also make use of the farm house's large lawned garden that surrounds this lovely old house.

TREGAWNE,

Withiel, Wadebridge, Cornwall PL30 5NR
Tel: 01208 831552 Fax: 01208 832122

Found in the quiet and peaceful countryside of the Ruthern Valley, an area of outstanding natural beauty, **Tregawne** is a marvellous early 18th century farmhouse. Lovingly restored and furnished in an elegant and stylish manner the house is the perfect place to relax and enjoy these glorious surroundings. The brainchild of Peta, Lady Linlithgow and her ex-restaurateur partner, David Jackson, Peta's years of entertaining in style as The Marchioness of Linlithgow have given her valuable experience which is now passed on to guests at Tregawne.

Each of the ground floor public rooms, and the three superb en suite guest bedrooms, are not only spacious and comfortable but they also have fabulous views over the farmhouse's extensive grounds. Here, at the bottom of the meadow can be found the river Ruthern and there is also an outdoor heated swimming pool that is ideal for

dipping into on a lazy summer's afternoon. Accommodation here is on a bed and breakfast basis although the house can be let as a whole. Dinner is available on request. Meanwhile, having restored the farmhouse, Peta and David have also converted the historic mill and barn complex to provide further superb self-catering accommodation in three delightful, self-contained cottages.

David is a member of St Enodoc and Trevose Golf Clubs and is delighted to take guests to play. The exciting Eden project is 15 minutes away and surfing, sea fishing, waterskiing and sailing at Rock and Polzeath are within a 20 minute drive, as is Rick Steins Seafood restaurant!

chapel while being pursued across the moors by a pack of headless hounds. Sadly, his torso became trapped in the chapel window thus exposing his lower body to the frenzied attack of his pursuers.

ST COLUMB MAJOR
6 miles E of Newquay on the A39

Now thankfully bypassed by the main road, this small town was once considered as the site of Cornwall's cathedral but St Columb Major finally lost out to Truro. However, the town's claims for this prestigious prize were not unfounded as the 15th century parish **Church of St Columba** is unusually large and is also home to some of the finest 16th and 17th century monumental brasses in the county - those dedicated to the influential Arundell family. It was several centuries earlier that Sir John Arundell, having supported Edward III in his wars against the Scots, was rewarded by the granting of a Royal Charter, in 1333, which gave St Columb Major market town status.

During the 19th century, this now quiet town enjoyed a period of great prosperity and, so sure were the town's officials of having Cornwall's cathedral sited here, that in 1850, a bishops' palace was built. Now called the **Old Rectory** it retains much of its grandeur though it does not play host to its originally intended guests today. Another interesting building here is **The Red Lion Inn** which is renowned for its former landlord,

James Polkinghorne, a famous Cornish wrestler who is depicted in action on a plaque on one of the inn's external walls.

St Columb Major has also managed to continue the tradition of playing, 'hurling the silver ball', a once common past time throughout the county that is thought to have derived from the ancient kingship contests. Each Shrove Tuesday, and again eleven days later, two teams of several hundred people - the countrymen and the townsmen, endeavour to carry a silver-painted ball made of apple wood through goals set two miles apart. A cross between hurling and football, the game is played here with great passion and enthusiasm, so much so in fact that the windows of houses and shops in the area have to be boarded up for the occasion.

A couple of miles southeast of St Columb Major, on **Castle Downs**, lie the remains of a massive Iron Age hill fort. Called **Castle-an-Dinas**, this was the major fort of the Dumnonia tribe who were in the area in around the 2nd century BC and, from here, they ruled the whole of Devon and Cornwall. The three earthwork ramparts enclose an area of over six acres and those climbing to the gorse-covered remains, some 700 feet above sea level, will be rewarded with panoramic views over the leafy Vale of Mawgan to the northwest and the unearthly landscape created by the china clay industry to the south.

PORTH BEACH HOTEL,

Beach Road, Porth, near Newquay, Cornwall TR7 3NE
Tel: 01637 872447 Fax: 01637 872469 e-mail: enquire@porthbeach-hotel.co.uk
website: www.porthbeach-hotel.co.uk

What makes the **Porth Beach Hotel** so special is its location just yards from award winning Porth beach which has won a coveted Blue Flag for cleanliness and is an ideal spot for beachcombers with its vast expanse of sand and numerous rock pools. A quiet and peaceful place, the hotel is only a short walk along the coast from the bustle of Newquay and it is also the perfect place from which to explore the delights of inland Cornwall.

Owned and personally run by Carl and Jane Goss with the help of their son James, this comfortable family hotel has a relaxed and friendly atmosphere that is appreciated by all who stay here. The 23 en suite guest rooms vary in size and some have stunning sea and coastal views whilst all are decorated and furnished to the same high standard. Dining in the restaurant here, with its splendid views, is an experience worth savouring as is the menu which provides the very best in home-cooked fresh local produce. Less formally, both of the hotel's two bars also serve a tasty range of bar snacks and meals that can be eaten here for taken down on to the beach.

ST COLUMB MINOR
2 miles E of Newquay off the A3059

Lying just to the east of the outskirts of Newquay, this small village, with its impressive 15th century church and pinnacled 115 foot tower, has retained its independence.

PORTH
1 mile E of Newquay on the A3059

Originally a separate village, with its own shipbuilding yards and pilchard cellars, Porth has now been engulfed by its larger neighbour Newquay. However, the fine wide sandy beach here still brings visitors and **Trevelgue Head** becomes an island at high tide.

KESTLE MILL
2½ miles SE of Newquay on the A3058

Found hidden in the lanes two miles west of Kestle Mill is the exceptionally attractive small Elizabethan manor house, **Trerice**, which is now owned by the National Trust. A real architectural gem, this pretty silver-grey stone E-shaped house was built in 1571,

on the site of its medieval predecessor, for the influential Arundell family. As well as the hint of Dutch styling to the gables and the beautiful window in the great hall which contains over 550 small panes of 16th century glass, this beautiful house is noted for its huge ornate fireplaces, elaborate plasterwork and fine English furniture. The grounds in which the house stands are equally charming and, as well as the unusual summer flowering garden, there is an orchard planted with old and, in many cases, forgotten fruit trees. A **Mower Museum**, tracing the history of the lawnmower, tea rooms, shop and plant sales can also be found in the house's various outbuildings.

Meanwhile, to the southeast of Kestle Mill is another place well worth visiting that is rather different from Trerice - **Dairyland Farm World**. This is a real, working dairy farm and, amongst the other attractions here, visitors can see the 140 cows being milked to music. The pets' corner that is home to various friendly animals, is perfect for children while all the family will delight in seeing the baby animals and taking a ride around the farm.

THE TWO CLOMES,
East Road, Quintrell Downs, Cornwall TR8 4PD
Tel: 01637 871163

Dating back to the 18th century, **The Two Clomes** takes its unusual name from the pairs of old ovens that were found in the inn's old inglenook fireplace. An attractive and quaint place, with a pretty beer garden, this lovely pub has the splendid olde worlde feel of a real English country inn. The well stocked bar always has Doom Bar real ales on tap and the inn has an excellent reputation for its food. The

extensive menu contains many traditional pub favourites, as well as more exotic options, and, along with the relaxed and pleasant atmosphere here, makes this a popular and well liked inn.

THE QUEEN AND RAILWAY INN,
St Columb Road, Cornwall TR9 6QR
Tel: 01726 860343

Dating back to the late 19th century, **The Queen and Railway Inn** takes its unusual name after the transfer of licence to these premises from nearby Indian Queens with 'Railway' being added as this too was being laid close by. A welcoming and inviting pub, Nigel and Christine Barnes have been the landlords here for sometime and they are renowned for serving an excellent range of drinks including real ales where they concentrate on offering brews from small, local breweries.

INDIAN QUEENS
6 miles SE of Newquay off the A30

Close to an area dominated by china clay quarries, this chiefly Victorian village is home to **Screech Owl Sanctuary** which lies just to the northeast. A rehabilitation, conservation and education centre, the sanctuary has the largest collection of owls in the southwest of England and, as well as offering visitors the chance to see hand tame owls at close quarters, the centre runs a number of courses on owl welfare.

ST NEWLYN EAST
3 miles S of Newquay off the A3075

A flourishing mining village in the 19th century, the imposing old engine house and chimney stack of **East Wheal Rose** mine can still be seen to the east and can be reached by taking a short journey on the Lappa Valley Steam Railway. Cornwall's richest lead producing mine, East Wheal Rose was the scene, in July 1846, of the Cornwall's worst mining disaster when 39 miners were drowned in a flash flood caused by an unexpected cloudburst. The village's cockpit

LAPPA VALLEY STEAM RAILWAY,
St Newlyn East, near Newquay, Cornwall TR8 5HZ
Tel: 01872 510317 website: www.lappa-railway.co.uk

Running on one of the oldest railway track beds in Cornwall, **Lappa Valley Steam Railway** offers a very different day out for all the family. Boarding the 15 inch guage railway at Benny Halt, visitors alight at East Wheal Rose where there are numerous attractions, such as canoeing, crazy golf, a maze, a coffee shop and much more. From here there is also another line, to Newlyn Halt, which runs through woodland. Glorious nature trails have also been set out through the woodland which is home to a wealth of plant, bird and animal life.

SHEPHERD'S FARM,
Fiddlers Green, St Newlyn East, near Newquay,
Cornwall TR8 5NW
Tel: 01872 540340
Fax: 01872 540340

Situated just a short drive from some of the county's best beaches and tucked away in the glorious Cornish countryside, **Shepherd's Farm** is just the place for a family holiday.

The secluded and picturesque farmhouse, at the centre of this working dairy farm, is over 200 years old and owner, Heather Harvey, has been offering bed and breakfast accommodation here since the early 1960s. A delightful

and friendly lady, Heather ensures that all the family - both children and pets are welcome - have a relaxed and carefree stay at her splendid house. All the four rooms are en suite and guests are free to come and go as they please. There is also a swing in the large and mature farmhouse garden and the farm's ponies are available to guests.

For those wanting more privacy, Heather also has self-catering accommodation in variety of separate dwellings. Ranging from Ashtree House, with four large bedrooms, to two bedroomed Ashtree Cottage, each has been tastefully decorated and furnished as provides a charming setting for a family holiday. Whether staying at the farmhouse or in one of Heather's excellent cottages, a stay here is sure to be a relaxing and refreshing experience.

(where cockfighting had been held for centuries) was restored as a memorial to the dead and, although the mine reopened a year after the accident, it closed for good in 1885.

The village itself is grouped around the handsome church that is dedicated to St Newlina - the fig growing from the walls of the building are said to be her staff.

HOLYWELL
3½ miles SW of Newquay off the A3075

This pretty hamlet, with its attractive beach and towering sand dunes, was, obviously, named after a holy well but its location is unknown although it may have been inside one of the caves on the bay that can be

visited at low tide. **Holywell Bay** is sheltered, at either end, by two headlands, Kelsey Head and Penhale Point and provides superb swimming and surfing which have helped to make this a popular summer seaside resort. An additional attraction here, apart from the dolphins that can sometimes be seen out in the bay, is the **Holywell Bay Fun Park** that offers a whole range of activities for young and old. Ideal for families, there is pitch and putt golf, various rides and a maze among the amusements.

CRANTOCK
2 miles SW of Newquay off the A392

This pretty little village lies across the Gannel estuary from Newquay and was, in

Treworgans Holiday Park,

Cubert, near Newquay, Cornwall TR8 5HH
Tel: 01637 830200

Set in glorious Cornish countryside and yet just a short distance from some of the county's finest beaches, Treworgans Holiday Park is the ideal place for a family holiday. This small and pleasant park has been owned by the Penna family since 1990 and, today, it is personally run by Dawn and Tony, with the help

of their two sons, Ryan and Luke. Very much a family site, the 18 superb holiday homes are set in over two acres of well maintained parkland with paths, lawns and numerous colourful flowerbeds. A safe children's play area ensures that youngsters have every opportunity to amuse themselves whilst adults can enjoy the comforts of the well equipped and stylish holiday homes or sit outside and relax in this peaceful haven. Other site facilities include a shop and laundry room and care is taken to maintain the tranquil surroundings of the park.

Highfield Lodge Hotel,

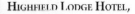

Halwyn Road, Crantock, near Newquay,
Cornwall TR8 5TR
Tel: 01637 830744
e-mail: highfieldlodge@tinyworld.co.uk

Ideally situated for touring the whole of Cornwall and just a few minutes walk from the north coast Highfield Lodge Hotel provides all the ingredients for a successful Cornish holiday. In the peaceful surroundings of this large 1930s family house and gardens, owners Jean and Bob Boston welcome guests to the hotel that they have been running since 1997. Stylishly furnished and decorated throughout, the freshly cooked breakfasts are served in a light and airy dining room whilst, in the evenings, guests will find that the cosy residents' bar is just the place to relax. Each of the nine guest rooms, most of which are en-suite, are equally well appointed and perfect for a refreshing night's sleep. Highfield Lodge is a friendly and comfortable hotel that provides a home from home atmosphere.

IMAGES OF CORNWALL - SAFFRON GALLERY,

Peterville, St Agnes, Cornwall TR5 0QU
Tel: 01872 553674

Just a short stroll from the centre of St Agnes lies Images of Cornwall - Saffron Gallery, a must for anyone interested in the traditional crafts of Cornwall and fine art. First opened by John and Diane Stephens in 1986, this interesting gallery is a charming place to spend a couple of hours browsing and also enjoying some light refreshment in the gallery's first floor coffee shop - the cream teas served here are very popular. Also on the first floor lies the Saffron Gallery, where, throughout the year, there is a programme of exhibitions that feature the paintings of well known and less well known Cornish artists. Meanwhile, the ground floor of this attractive building is home to Images of Cornwall. The wide ranging items on display here illustrate the depth of interest and enthusiasm for craftwork of all kinds in the county. This is the perfect place to find a lasting reminder of a holiday in Cornwall or for those looking for an unusual and imaginative gift.

THE ROSEMUNDY HOUSE HOTEL,

St Agnes, Cornwall TR5 0UF
Tel: 01872 552101 Fax: 01872 554000
e-mail: martin@rosemundy.co.uk website: www.rosemundy.co.uk

Found in sheltered and secluded private grounds, yet only a few minutes walk from the centre of St Agnes, **The Rosemundy House Hotel** is the perfect place for a relaxing and peaceful holiday. The splendid house, which was built around 1780, has a varied history which today's owners, Marion and Derek Faulkner are happy to share with guests. The family bought the property in 1999 and they plan to extend the hotel, but in a style very much in keeping with the original Queen Anne building. Not only is the hotel charming and full of character but also has a very highly regarded reputation. The extensive gardens and grounds provide tranquil walks whilst there is also an outdoor heated swimming pool and other pastimes and amenities on hand. Whilst son Martin is looking after guests' needs at this luxurious hotel, Marion and Derek's other son, Kevin, is the chef. Served in the olde worlde atmosphere of the Tom Noggi restaurant, Kevin's impressive dishes show the range and depth of traditional English cuisine and dinner here is the perfect way to end the day.

ATLANTIC COAST HOLIDAY BUNGALOWS,

Wheal Kitty, St Agnes, Cornwall TR5 0RL Tel: 01872 552485 Fax: 01872 552485
e-mail: atlantic.holidays@virgin.net website: www.atlantic-holidays.co.uk

Hidden in the picturesque village of St Agnes and surrounded by memories of Cornwall's once thriving tin mining industry, **Atlantic Coast Bungalows** makes an ideal location for a relaxing holiday amidst dramatic scenery, ideal for touring the whole of Cornwall. This small group of eight well equipped bungalows are set in spacious grounds that have been carefully laid out with lawns, patios, picnic tables, well appointed laundry, small children's play area and ample parking for guests.

Owners, Lynne and Richard Selby have been running Atlantic Coast Holidays since 1995 and, as well as providing their guests with a superb holiday with the personal touch, they have occupancy all year round and take great care to ensure that each of the bungalows becomes a real home from home, even the beds will be made on your arrival. Fitted with all the latest modern conveniences and appliances, the cosy, clean bungalows are completely self-contained and have heating throughout, perfect accommodation for all ages. Pets and non-smokers are also catered for. Short breaks available in low season.

the 12th century, a famous seat of learning. All that remains from that time is the village church which contains a particularly beautiful rood screen. Although the beach at Crantock looks inviting, with the high dunes backing a large expanse of sand, the currents around the mouth of the River Gannel, which runs into the sea at the northern end of the beach, makes swimming dangerous. At low tide, two bridges become exposed which cross the river but, at all other times during the summer, a small rowing boat ferries passengers over the river. Not surprisingly, a few centuries ago, Crantock attracted smugglers and the village's old thatched inn was a well known hideaway.

ST AGNES

This charming village, which lies at the head of a steep valley, has, since the early 20th century been a popular seaside resort but its sleepy and peaceful appearance today is very far removed from the days when this was a mining village. Once known as the source of the finest tin in Cornwall, this old community still retains reminders of those days and, especially around the narrow-spired parish church, there can be found old miners cottages and mine owners houses. In particular, at the bottom of the village, there is a steeply terraced row of 18th century miners cottages known as 'Stippy-Stappy'.

Surrounding the village are the remains of many mine workings including the picturesque group of clifftop buildings that were once part of one of the county's best known mines - **Wheal Coates**. Now in the hands of the National Trust, the mine was in operation for 30 years between 1860 and 1890 and the derelict **Engine House** is an exceptionally atmospheric local landmark. Many other abandoned pump houses and mine shafts still litter the area (walkers should always keep to the footpaths) and from the remains of **Wheal Kitty**, which closed in 1930, there are view across the landscape to other disused workings. The harsh realities of the lives of the miners and their families is remembered in the story of Dorcas, whose ghost still haunts the village and surrounding area. This poor,

Wheal Coates Tin Mine

unfortunate woman committed suicide in Polbreen Mine, then the richest source of tin in Cornwall, and her ghost would prowl the galleries calling the men from their work and wasting their time. However, one miner, following Dorcas in response to her call, was saved from death when a rock fall landed on the very spot on which he had been standing. The **St Agnes Parish Museum**, which is run by volunteers, aims to promote the heritage of the village and the series of displays here not only cover the mining and seafaring history of St Agnes but also the natural history of the surrounding area.

Whilst today's visitors are reminded of St Agnes' past it is for the beaches and beautiful countryside that they descend upon the village throughout the summer. Renowned as the birthplace of the Georgian society painter, John Opie, this is also a place that was introduced to thousands through the Poldark novels of Winston Graham - in which St Agnes became St Ann. Overlooked by the buildings of Wheal Coates, **Chapel Porth** is a sandy shingle-backed beach where both swimmers and surfers should be aware of the strong currents and undertows. A cave found on the beach is linked with the giant Bolster, who fell in love with Agnes, a local young maiden. As proof of his devotion to her, Agnes asked the giant to fill a small hole on the beach with his blood - a task he willingly undertook as the hole

seemed tiny. However, unknown to Bolster beneath the hole was a large cave and, as his blood drained away, he became so weak that he fell into the sea and died.

A footpath from the beach leads northwards, along the coast, to **St Agnes Head** and **St Agnes Beacon**. A local landmark now in the hands of the National

THE DRIFTWOOD SPARS HOTEL,

Trevaunance Cove, St Agnes, Cornwall TR5 0RT
Tel: 01872 552428/553323 Fax: 01872 553701

Found along the rugged Cornwall coastline, in the sandy Trevaunance Cove, **The Driftwood Spars Hotel** is a splendid hotel and inn that dates back to 1660. Taking its name from the enormous ships' spars used in their construction, this welcoming establishment offers guests several bars, an atmospheric restaurant and comfortable accommodation in a choice of individually styled en suite rooms. A wonderful place to relax, owners Jill and Gordon Treleaven ensure that everyone here receives the very best in Cornish hospitality. A variety of ample meals is available, and during the season there is an upstairs carvery. Delicious Sunday Lunches and Big Breakfasts are popular all year round. Meanwhile, in the bar, guests and visitors can make their choice from a wide variety of drinks that include not only a vast selection of malt whiskies but also Cuckoo Ale which is brewed in the hotels own micro brewery. Just up the road there is also a craftworkshop, owned by Jill and Gordon, that is sure to have the perfect memento of a visit to Trevaunance Cove.

ROSE-IN-VALE COUNTRY HOUSE HOTEL,

Mithian, near St Agnes, Cornwall TR5 0QD
Tel: 01872 552202 Fax: 01872 552700
e-mail: reception@rose-in-vale-hotel.co.uk website: www.rose-in-vale-hotel.co.uk

Hidden away in a wooded valley and surrounded by extensive gardens and grounds, **Rose-in-Vale Country House Hotel** is a wonderful, attractive 18th century house that offers its guests a very special experience. Originally built in 1760 as the winter residence of a mine captain who owned all the tin mines in the Perranporth area, this delightful Georgian house has been expertly transformed into a hotel without losing any of the style and elegance of the beautifully proportioned rooms. Furnished and decorated to create a relaxing and comfortable environment all the hotel's luxurious en suite guest rooms, as well as the public rooms, provide the ideal atmosphere in which to completely unwind. After spending

the day exploring the local area or enjoying the superb gardens at Rose-in-Vale, guests are treated to a sumptuous dinner in the Opie's Room, the splendid dining room. Both the table d'hôte and à la carte menus offer diners a mouth-watering choice of interesting and imaginative dishes that make excellent use of fresh local produce including fish and seafood from Newlyn. The addition of an equally excellent wine list makes dining here, as well as staying at the Rose-in-Vale, a very memorable experience.

Trust, it is from the beacon that St Agnes derives its Cornish name, Bryanick, meaning pointed or prominent hill. At 629 feet above sea level the beacon is well worth climbing as, from the summit, both coasts of Cornwall and, at night, some 12 lighthouses can be seen. It was from this summit that, in the 16th century, a fire was lit to warn of the coming of the Spanish Armada though, more recently, in 1977, another fire was lit as part of the Queen's Silver Jubilee celebrations.

The beach to the north of the village is now popular with surfers and fishermen although, up until 1915, **Trevaunance Cove** was the main harbour for the mines in and around St Agnes. Outgoing cargoes were delivered to the harbour by means of a chute whilst incoming goods were hoisted up the hillside using a horse. In 1915 a great storm all but obliterated the harbour and only a few granite blocks can be seen today.

AROUND ST AGNES

TREVELLAS
2 miles NE of St Agnes on the B3285

Close to the village and now located in a shaded and leafy valley lies **Blue Hills Tin Streams**, a fascinating place where guided tours show visitors the fascinating process of tin production. In the 19th century this pretty combe was a dusty place that

resounded to noise of tin mining and it became known locally as Jericho Valley.

PERRANPORTH
3 miles NE of St Agnes on the B3285

From a one time pilchard fishing and mining village that had also played host to smuggling gangs in the past, the arrival of the railway, at the beginning of the 20th century, ensured that Perranporth would survive, this time as a pleasant and popular holiday resort. The three mile long stretch

Perranporth Beach

of golden sand lies at the heart of Perranporth's success and it is a place that draws both surfers and bathers though because of the strong currents care has to be taken.

Though there is little left to see around Perranporth of its mining past, this small town's Celtic heritage is still remembered, on

THE MINERS ARMS,

Mithian, near St Agnes, Cornwall TR5 0QF
Tel: 01872 552375

One of the older buildings in this pretty village, **The Miners Arms** dates back to 1577 and, over the years, it has been a chapel and an office for the local mine owners from which they dispensed the workers wages. Throughout, many of the building's original features remain, giving it a true olde worlde feel, and, in particular one of the upstairs rooms which was used as a court has a barrel ceiling whilst two others have lovely decorative

ceilings. However, interesting surroundings are not the only features of The Miners Arms which makes it so popular as experienced landlords, Andrew and Michele Bown also provide superb hospitality. As well as serving a splendid range of drinks, including real ales and a selection of fine wines, this inn has a delicious menu of imaginative home-cooked food. Served throughout the inn, and outside on the patio area during the summer, Andrew puts together a lovely range of traditional and modern dishes that features plenty of fresh, local seafood and meats from a local butcher.

an annual basis, during the **Lowender Peran Festival**, which brings all the Celtic nations together through music and dance. Meanwhile, found about a mile from the town, high up in the sand dunes overlooking Penhale Sands, lies **St Piran's Oratory**. Built on the site of St Piran's grave, the remains of this 6th or 7th century building lay covered under the shifting sands until, in 1835, they were revealed. Reburied today, a simple plaque marks the site of the burial place of the saint who is said to have travelled from Ireland to Cornwall on a millstone. The saint's landing place is marked by a tall granite cross, **St Piran's Cross**, which is one of only a very few three-holed Celtic crosses in the county.

For most people, however, Perranporth will forever be linked with Winston Graham, the author of the Poldark novels. Born in Manchester, Graham settled in Perranporth in the 1930s and, whilst staying here, wrote the first volumes in the series which were published between 1945 and 1953. Local beauty spots, towns, villages and various old mine workings all appear either as

themselves or in disguise in the books and, in some cases, his characters take their names from local villages.

PENHALE CAMP
6 miles NE of St Agnes off the A3075

According to local legend, the old town of **Langarroc**, a supposedly beautiful place with seven fine churches, lies buried beneath the dunes of Penhale Sands. The town gained its wealth from mining and it also proved to be the cause of the town's undoing as, during a great storm that lasted three days, Langarroc and its inhabitants were engulfed - some said as retribution for their ungodly ways. On stormy nights it is said that ghostly cries for help can still be heard above the sound of the wind and the waves.

ROSE
4½ miles NE of St Agnes off the B3285

Close to this tiny village lies **St Piran's Round**, an Iron Age enclosure that was used for miracle plays in the Middle Ages. Possibly the oldest theatre site in Europe, it is still used on occasions today.

PERRAN-QUAY TOURING PARK,

Hendra Croft, Rejerrah, near Newquay,
Cornwall TR8 5QP
Tel: 01872 572561
e-mail: rose@perran-quay.co.uk
website: www.perran-quay.co.uk

Set in over seven acres of scenic countryside and just a short drive from the coast, Perran-Quay Touring Park provides everything that the holiday maker could wish for whilst exploring the county. Run by Ralph, Gloria, Ray and Rose this attractive and peaceful site has ample room for caravanners and campers who can take advantage of the level

and large pitches, many with electric hook-ups, modern shower block and site shop.

There is a safe, purpose built children's play area and a special dog walking area so that all the family can enjoy a holiday here. Unusually, Perran-Quay Touring Park also has a friendly and inviting bar, the ideal place to relax with a drink after a day out sightseeing. Food too is available at the bar but, in the evenings, the site's friendly restaurant opens so that staff and tourers can enjoy the evenings. The chef prepares a tasty and tempting menu and the house speciality, Aberdeen Angus steaks, ensures that no one will go hungry whilst staying here.

PERRANZABULOE
3½ miles NE of St Agnes on the A3075

This village's curious name means 'St Piran in the sand' as it was here, in the 6th century, that the missionary saint, St Piran, is reputed to have arrived after journeying from Ireland.

ST ALLEN
6½ miles E of St Agnes off the A30

Like many parts of Britain that have a Celtic tradition, Cornwall has its own 'little people' - the piskies. One legend surrounding these mischievous people tells of a boy, living in St Allen who was out picking wild woodland flowers near his home. When he failed to return home for supper, his mother and other villagers began a frantic search. After three days, the boy was found, sleeping peacefully in exactly the same spot where he was last seen and he had no idea what had happened to him in the intervening days. However, what he could remember was that whilst he had been picking the flowers he had heard a bird singing so beautifully that he had followed the sound of the bird deep into the woods. As day turned into night and the stars came out, the boy had realised that the stars were, in fact, piskies and they had led him to a fantastic cave with crystal pillars studded with jewels where he had been fed on the purest honey. When he awoke from this incredible adventure he found himself back in the woodland close to his home.

SILVERBOW PARK,

Goonhavern, near Truro, Cornwall TR4 9NX
Tel: 01872 572347 Fax: 01872 572347

Found on the outskirts of Goonhavern village and close to Perranporth beach, **Silverbow Park** is a wonderful holiday location that caters for all the family. An award winning park - it has the title Best Park in Britain and also the David Bellamy Environmental Gold Medal - owners, Mr and Mrs Taylor have created a peaceful and relaxing site, with splendid amenities, that also blends in with the local environment. Surrounded by fields, the park has a variety of luxury holiday homes available as well as numerous pitches for touring caravans and all are found in the beautifully landscaped and well maintained grounds. As well as enjoying the peace and quiet of the park, there is also plenty to do here. The heated outdoor swimming pool is set within a formal walled garden and therefore is not only a sheltered spot for lounging around but also a real sun trap. There are two all weather tennis courts and short mat bowls here too, and a safe, purpose built adventure play area for the children. All in all this superb park provides the ideal holiday location - dog included but no teenagers.

PLUME OF FEATHERS,

Penhallow, Truro, Cornwall TR4 9LT
Tel: 01872 571389

Over 250 years old and originally three cottages, the **Plume of Feathers** is a lovely traditional English country inn with a true olde worlde atmosphere. However, this has not always been the case and, until June 2000 when Patrick and Sue purchased the inn, it was in a very dilapidated state. Enthusiasm and hard work

has, fortunately, restored this charming pub and now, with feature fireplaces, a mass of memorabilia and exposed beams, it is just the place to enjoy warm and friendly hospitality. The couple too have come across the inn's ghost who, thankfully, is only mischievous not malicious. There are always several real ales on tap at the bar and the Cornish ale is labelled with bilingual signs (English and Cornish). Excellent home-cooked traditional pub food is also served here and, wherever possible, fresh local produce is used. This is a delightful pub where the whole family will feel at home.

THE VICTORY INN,

Towan Cross, Mount Hawke, near Truro, Cornwall TR4 8BZ
Tel: 01209 890359

Believed to date back to the late 16th century and now the only
remaining inn of the many that were in this area during the
heyday of the copper and tin mining industry, The Victory Inn
is a place well worth discovering. Owned and personally run
by Derek and Di House, a very experienced local couple, this
free house has plenty to offer all its visitors - both locals and
those new to the area. As well as the excellent range of real ales and other drinks, The Victory Inn is well
known for Di's superb culinary skills and the meals served here are a real treat. An attractive and
comfortable place with a real olde worlde feel, there is also a lovely rear conservatory which overlooks the
well tendered beer garden.

PENHALLOW

3 miles E of St Agnes on the A3075

Just south of the village lies the **Cider Farm**, a
commercial farm that is also open to visitors.
There are tours of the fruit orchards from
which over 40 varieties of delicious fruit
products are made, including jams, country
wines, honey, mead and, of course, cider and
traditional farmhouse scrumpy. Whatever
the season there is always something to see
here of the cider making process, from
harvesting and pressing to bottling and
labelling, and after the tour, there is the
opportunity to sample the product. Here,
too, is the **Cider Museum** where the
fascinating history of cider making is
charted, through displays of old equipment
and artefacts, that include a horse-drawn mill
and a cooper's workshop.

TOWAN CROSS

2 miles S of St Agnes off the B3277

The countryside around this village was one
of the richest tin and copper mining areas in
the country and the minerals were extracted
here until the 1920s. To satisfy the thirst of
the miners, there were once many inns here
and in the surrounding area and the village's
name comes from the horizontal stone cross
that lay outside Towan Cross's 16th century
inn, on which coffins were rested while the
bearers called in for refreshment in the days
of walking funerals.

5 Mid Cornwall South

The discovery of china clay in the countryside around St Austell in 1748 saw a dramatic change to the mining town and also the surrounding landscape. Mines opened, villages grew, St Austell prospered and the ports along the coast expanded. Still one of the world's largest producers of the surprisingly versatile china clay, St Austell has fortunately managed to keep its market town appearance and it is still an interesting place to visit. However, the countryside around St Austell has suffered from the industry and the great conical spoil heaps, the industries waste product, have lead to the area being dubbed the Cornish Alps. Landscaping of the heaps is changing the horizon again and,

Mevagissey Harbour

in particular, there is the ambitious Eden Project, built on the site of an old pit, which aims to explain and provide understanding of the "vital relationship between plants, people and resources."

To the southwest lies Truro, another town built on the proceeds of the mineral extraction industry, that became, in the 1870s, a city when the decision to grant Cornwall its own bishop was made. The magnificent Truro cathedral, with its splendid triple spire front, was completed in 1910 and it is said to have some of the finest Victorian stained glass in the country. At the entrance to Carrick Roads, at the top of which Truro lies, is Falmouth, a key deep-water anchorage that is also the world's third largest natural harbour. A busy port, Falmouth and the other ports in the shelter of Carrick Roads have been protected for centuries by Henry VIII's two fine fortresses, Pendennis and St Mawes Castles.

Surrounding these three major Cornish towns are numerous pretty villages and coastal ports that are certainly well worth exploring. The countryside of the beautiful Roseland Peninsula offers visitors the chance to investigate the area's wealth of flora and fauna whilst, those interested in gardens, will find that there is plenty of choice. The famous Lost Gardens of Heligan have been restored to their original 19th century splendour whilst other gardens in south Cornwall all show the benefits of the Gulf Stream which create this mild and pleasant climate.

Falmouth Beach

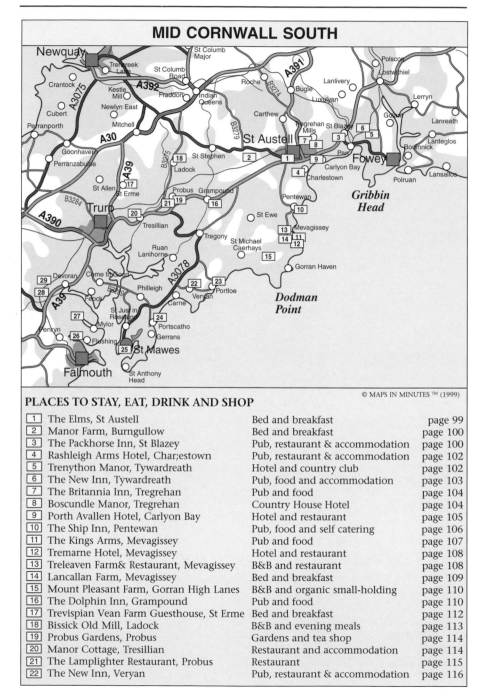

MID CORNWALL SOUTH

© MAPS IN MINUTES ™ (1999)

PLACES TO STAY, EAT, DRINK AND SHOP

1	The Elms, St Austell	Bed and breakfast	page 99
2	Manor Farm, Burngullow	Bed and breakfast	page 100
3	The Packhorse Inn, St Blazey	Pub, restaurant & accommodation	page 100
4	Rashleigh Arms Hotel, Char;estown	Pub, restaurant & accommodation	page 102
5	Trenython Manor, Tywardreath	Hotel and country club	page 102
6	The New Inn, Tywardreath	Pub, food and accommodation	page 103
7	The Britannia Inn, Tregrehan	Pub and food	page 104
8	Boscundle Manor, Tregrehan	Country House Hotel	page 104
9	Porth Avallen Hotel, Carlyon Bay	Hotel and restaurant	page 105
10	The Ship Inn, Pentewan	Pub, food and self catering	page 106
11	The Kings Arms, Mevagissey	Pub and food	page 107
12	Tremarne Hotel, Mevagissey	Hotel and restaurant	page 108
13	Treleaven Farm& Restaurant, Mevagissey	B&B and restaurant	page 108
14	Lancallan Farm, Mevagissey	Bed and breakfast	page 109
15	Mount Pleasant Farm, Gorran High Lanes	B&B and organic small-holding	page 110
16	The Dolphin Inn, Grampound	Pub and food	page 110
17	Trevispian Vean Farm Guesthouse, St Erme	Bed and breakfast	page 112
18	Bissick Old Mill, Ladock	B&B and evening meals	page 113
19	Probus Gardens, Probus	Gardens and tea shop	page 114
20	Manor Cottage, Tresillian	Restaurant and accommodation	page 114
21	The Lamplighter Restaurant, Probus	Restaurant	page 115
22	The New Inn, Veryan	Pub, restaurant & accommodation	page 116

ST AUSTELL

This old market town that had, for many centuries, been at the centre of the local tin and copper quarrying and mining industries was transformed, in the second half of the 18th century, when William Cookworthy discovered large deposits of kaolin, or china clay, here in 1748. A chemist from Plymouth, Cookworthy saw the importance of the find as china clay was, and still is, a constituent of many products other than just porcelain, including paper, textiles and pharmaceuticals. Over the years, the waste material from the clay pits to the north and west of the town has been piled into great conical spoil heaps which dominate the landscape around St Austell and these bare, bleached uplands have caused this area to be dubbed the *Cornish Alps*. More recently, steps have been taken to soften the countryside and the heaps and disused pits have been landscaped with acid-loving plants, such as rhododendrons, and they now have gently undulating footpaths and nature trails.

Although the china clay industry has dominated St Austell since it was first discovered, the town is also the home of another important local business - the St Austell Brewery. Founded by Walter Hicks, a farmer from the parish of Luxulyan, in 1851,

the brewery began as a malting house before, having moved into premises in the Market Square, Hicks built a steam brewery in 1867. Boosted by the town's expansion on the

St Austell Railway Station

proceeds of the china clay industry the brewery continued to flourish and, still a family run business today, it continues to go from strength to strength. The history of the company and an insight into the brewing process can be found at the informative **St Austell Brewery Visitor Centre**, from where visitors are also taken on a guided tour of the brewery.

The narrow streets of old St Austell create an atmosphere more befitting a market town than a busy mining and industrial

THE ELMS,

14 Penwinnick Road, St Austell, Cornwall PL25 5DW
Tel: 01726 77283
e-mail: sally@theelm.co.uk website: www.theelm.co.uk

Found in a quiet and leafy residential area on the outskirts of St Austell, **The Elms** is an attractive and spacious family house that is surrounded by a large and mature garden. Since April 1999, owner, Sally Wilkins, has been offering superb bed and breakfast accommodation here in four comfortable en suite guest rooms that are as well furnished and decorated as the rest of her delightful property. A real home from home, this highly regarded establishment is well known not only for its splendid hospitality but also for the magnificent breakfasts served each morning. In addition dining restaurant facilities will be available from 2001.

MANOR FARM,

Burngullow, near St Austell, Cornwall PL26 7TQ
Tel: 01726 72242 Fax: 01726 72242
e-mail: suzannemanuell@tinyworld.co.uk

Tucked away down a quiet country lane but easily found and close to St Austell, **Manor Farm** is the perfect location for a farmhouse holiday. At the heart of this 450 acre working dairy farm stands the impressive, grade II listed farmhouse which dates back to the mid 18th century. The home of Suzanne and William Manuell, William is the third generation of his family to farm here, the couple have, since 1983, been offering superb bed and breakfast accommodation and over the years the popularity of this exceptional establishment has spread.

The en suite guest rooms have been decorated and furnished to provide the very best in comfort whilst the views from the windows all add to the peace and tranquillity of this charming house. Downstairs there is a cosy guests' lounge, with a log fire should the weather turn cooler, and guests can also sit out in the lovely and well maintained garden. A hearty Aga-cooked breakfast is served each morning and, though there are no evening meals served here, there are plenty of local pubs and restaurants close by.

THE PACKHORSE INN,

Fore Street, St Blazey, near Par,
Cornwall PL24 2NH
Tel: 01726 813970

The Packhorse Inn dates back to the early 19th century and was, many years ago, used as the local Tax Office. An attractive stone building, which is softened in summer by the addition of a mass of hanging baskets and window boxes, the interior of this old place is both inviting and full of character.

With very much the atmosphere of a traditional English country inn, landlords Phil and Gill Baines, who have only been here since spring 2000, welcome both locals and visitors alike. There is a well stocked bar from which customers can enjoy a full range of drinks, including at least three real ales, and food too is served here, either in bar or in the separate comfortable dining room. Most of the dishes are home-cooked by Gill and the well chosen menu is sure to satisfy all the family and the traditional Sunday roast lunches are also proving to be popular so it is best to book in advance. During the summer, customers can make excellent use of the inn's pretty beer garden and, on Friday and Saturday evenings, Phil and Gill lay on a variety of live music and other entertainments for their loyal customers. Finally, The Packhorse Inn has three comfortable and well appointed guest rooms.

community. The main thoroughfares all radiate from the parish church of the Holy Trinity, an imposing building with a tall 15th century tower that has, inside, a curious Norman font that is carved with an assortment of grotesque human heads and mythical creatures. Elsewhere in the town there are some other notable older buildings including the 17th century Market House, a Quaker Meeting House built in 1829, and the White Hart, an old posting inn.

Meanwhile, just to the east of the town centre, lies, among rhododendrons and beech trees, **Menacuddle Well**. Another of Cornwall's many holy wells, this particular source of curative water is housed in a small granite shrine.

AROUND ST AUSTELL

CARTHEW
2½ miles N of St Austell on the B3274

Situated in the heart of the Cornish Alps, this tiny village, which lies in a small valley, is surrounded by the spoils of the china clay industry. Just to the south lies Wheal Martyn, an old clay works that is now home to the **Wheal Martyn China Clay Heritage Centre**. At this open-air museum, the 200 year story of the industry is explored and, through a wide variety of displays including a stimulating audio-visual show, visitors can take a journey back through time. Home to Cornwall's largest working water wheel, an early source of power for the works, the centre also has various steam engines on display, such as the Great Fal Valley Oil Engine which is now in working order. The land around this once busy mine has been replanted and it now has a unique range of habitats. The nature trail through the surrounding countryside offers visitors the opportunity to discover many different birds, small mammals, plants and insects.

BUGLE
4 miles N of St Austell on the A391

This relatively modern village was built in the 19th century to house miners and their families, who were brought into the area to work at the numerous china clay pits. In common with other mining communities throughout the country, Cornwall mining villages also have a musical tradition and, in Cornwall, it was common for villages to have their own brass band. Each year, the musicians came together to show off their skills and compete and, as the music festival was held here, Bugle has a particularly apt name.

LUXULYAN
4 miles NE of St Austell off the A390

Found lying between the moorland above and the steep, wooded Luxulyan Valley below, this old village of granite cottages has a very scenic location. Across this boulder strewn valley stands the remarkable **Treffry Viaduct**, which was built between 1839 and 1842 as part of the railway line between Par and Newquay. Over 100 feet high and 200 yards long, the viaduct was important in the establishment of the newly-created port of Par. Mineral ores, quarried stone and fresh water were all transported along the line to the port.

CHARLESTOWN
1 mile SE of St Austell off the A390

Originally the small fishing village of West Polmear, in the 1790s Charles Rashleigh (after whom Charlestown is named), a local mine owner, built a harbour here to support the growing china clay industry and also for the importing of coal. Other ports with better facilities, such as Fowey and Plymouth, led to the decline of trade through Charlestown's harbour in the 19th century and, today, this harbour and village remains a Georgian time capsule. As well as providing a permanent berth for square-rigged boats it is a popular

Shipwreck Centre, Charlestown

RASHLEIGH ARMS HOTEL,

Charlestown, near St Austell, Cornwall PL25 3NJ
Tel: 01726 73635 Fax: 01726 73635

A popular place with both locals and tourists, **Rashleigh Arms Hotel** is a welcoming and inviting inn that is well known for offering friendly hospitality. Dating back to the 19th century, this traditional family inn not only has charm and character but also a superb atmosphere that is appreciated by all its customers. Managed by Patricia Bailey, a lady with many years experience in the licensing trade, this free house serves an extensive range of drinks from the bar including at least 10 real ales!

The food here has put the Rashleigh Arms Hotel on the map and as well as the lunchtime carvery

that is served every day of the week, there is an comprehensive restaurant menu, a tasty list of bar snacks and a daily specials board. The house speciality is freshly caught local fish and succulent steaks and, with all this choice, there is sure to be a delicious dish to tempt even the most jaded palate. Patricia also lays on live musical entertainment for customers on Thursday and Saturday evenings and there is a delightful beer garden to the rear that is a real bonus during the summer. Finally, comfortable bed and breakfast is available here in a choice of five en suite guest rooms.

TRENYTHON MANOR HOTEL AND COUNTRY CLUB,

Tywardreath, near Par, Cornwall PL24 2TS
Tel: 01726 814797 Fax: 01726 817030
e-mail: info@trenython.co.uk

Built in 1872 by Italian patriot Garibaldi as a thank you to Colonel Peard, **Trenython Manor Hotel and Country Club** is a superb English country house set within a peaceful 25 acre estate. Over the years, the house has seen several interesting owners, including the third bishop of Truro Bishop Gott and, for some years, it was also a convalescent home for the Great Western Railway. Now beautifully restored and renovated this splendid house, in the grand Italian style, is a luxury hotel and country club which offers its customers the perfect environment for relaxation.

The accommodation here comprises beautifully designed and well appointed self-contained lodges individually located in the hotel's grounds. Meanwhile, at the main house there is a complete indoor leisure complex with heated swimming pool, sauna and gymnasium and, outside, a tennis court and mini golf course. However, whilst the accommodation and facilities here are superb, it is Trenython Manor's restaurant that excels. The lavish dining room is panelled in oak which dates back to the 16th century and, among the other artefacts on display, is Lord Nelson's sea chest and General Wolfe's headboard. However, the surroundings will not distract guests from the wonderful menu that presents a mouth-watering choice of imaginative dishes prepared from only the finest ingredients. This is a top class establishment that offers the perfect setting for a relaxing and luxurious holiday.

destination with holidaymakers and was also used as the location for both *Poldark* and *The Onedin Line* television series.

Close to the docks, and housed in an historic clay building, is the **Charlestown Shipwreck, Rescue and Heritage Centre**, which offers an insight into the town's history, local shipwrecks and the various devises that have been developed over the years for rescuing and recovering those in peril at sea. As well as the typical scenes from village life in Charlestown, visitors can see a large collection of artefacts that have been recovered from shipwrecks, one of the largest underwater equipment collections that includes John Lethbridge's famous wooden barrel of 1740, and try the life raft and breeches buoy that form part of the Life Savers display. An interesting, informative and fun centre that covers many aspects of Cornish life.

PAR
3 miles E of St Austell on the A3082

The harbour was built here in the 1840s as part of the expansion of the china clay

industry and, today, the terminals, erected in the 1960s, still handle the clay. The tall and slender chimneys of the clay processing plants can be seen from **Par Sands**, where at low tide the flat beach can extend over half a mile out to sea. Contrastingly, to the east of the beach lies a low rocky cliff where, at low tide, **Little Hell Cove** can be reached.

Close by can be found **The Butterfly House**, at Wyevale Garden Centre, where hundreds of vividly coloured butterflies fly freely, feed and breed in near natural surroundings. There are over 20 species of butterflies in the house living amongst a wonderful range of tropical plants and, as well as taking photographs, there is plenty of information here on these beautiful creatures and their habits.

TREGREHAN MILLS
2 miles E of St Austell off the A391

Lying just southeast of the village is Tregrehan Gardens, where visitors can not only see many mature trees from places such as North America and Japan, but also rhododendrons and a range of Carlyon

THE NEW INN,

Fore Street, Tywardreath, near Par, Cornwall PL24 2QP
Tel: 01726 813901

Close to St Austell Bay, the ancient village of Fowey and only 2½ miles from the Eden Project, **The New Inn** can be found in the centre of this rural village. Dating back to the early 18th century, this impressive Cornish stone building, which is bedecked by colourful, flower filled baskets and tubs, is just the place to call in to for a drink, bar food or bed and breakfast accommodation. Well known for the excellent selection of real ales, well kept beers and lagers, and wide range of spirits, the inn also serves food of a simple

nature such as ploughmans lunches, home-made curry, toasted sandwiches or ham, egg and chips etc - using as far as possible local produce.

The inn has three comfortable guest rooms on the first floor, all with hot and cold water, colour TV and tea-making facilities, which are let on a bed and breakfast basis. Evening meals can be provided by arrangement.

An ideal place for all the family, with a huge, attractive rear beer garden that is just the place to sit on a warm summer's day, The New Inn is certainly worth seeking out.

Hybrid Camellias. The house and estate has been the home of the Carlyon family from 1565.

ST BLAZEY
3½ miles E of St Austell on the A390

To the west of the village, in the heart of the china clay area, lies a disused pit that has become the centre of the ambitious **Eden Project**. The aim of this on-going project is to "promote the understanding and responsible management of the vital relationship between plants, people and resources." At the bottom of a giant crater are the largest conservatories in the world where, in the space of a day, visitors can walk from steamy rainforests to the warmth of the Mediterranean.

THE BRITANNIA INN,

Tregrehan, near Par, Cornwall PL24 2SL
Tel: 01726 812889

Easily found as it lies on the main Lostwithiel to St Austell road, **The Britannia Inn** is a large and welcoming country pub that is a pleasant and inviting place to stop and relax. A former coaching inn, the oldest parts of this building date back to the 16th century, this quality freehouse has been offering customers excellent hospitality for many years and, since 1982, at the hands of owners, Frank Rogers and business partner Philip Lafferty. Now joined by Frank's son Richard, this family run inn is as popular as it has ever been and, certainly at weekends, customers come from far and wide to enjoy the well kept ales and delicious food served here.

The well stocked bar offers a choice of at least six real ales and, as well as the usual beers, lagers and ciders, there is also a selection of wine by the glass. Food too is a feature of The Britannia Inn and the extensive menu is sure to tempt even the most jaded palate. The house speciality curries and lasagne are well worth trying and both children and vegetarians will find that they have a specially prepared list of tasty options. Spacious and comfortable inside, the extensive rear beer garden is the ideal place to enjoy this inn's superb fayre when the weather allows.

BOSCUNDLE MANOR COUNTRY HOUSE HOTEL,

Tregrehan, near St Austell, Cornwall PL25 3RL
Tel: 01726 813557 Fax: 01726 814997
e-mail: stay@boscundlemanor.co.uk
website: www.boscundlemanor.co.uk

More a luxurious private house, **Boscundle Manor Country House Hotel** is a very special place that is found in its own secluded woodland grounds. This wonderful 18th century manor house was purchased by Mary and Andrew Flint in 1978 and, since then, they have continuously improved both the house and gardens so that, today, guests here can enjoy a peaceful and relaxing holiday in splendid surroundings. Each of the manor house's charming rooms is furnished with fine antiques and paintings and, throughout, the comfort of guests is paramount. Dinner is in the elegant dining room with bone china and silver, and the menus offer fresh local food beautifully cooked. The wine list here is also considered to be one of the best in the county. Whilst Boscundle Manor offers exceptional hospitality, the hotel's grounds and outbuildings provide guests with all manner of amusements that include both an indoor and outdoor swimming pool, golf, croquet and a fully equipped gymnasium and games room.

Throughout, the long and sometimes fragile relationship between man and plants is explored with a view to informing and educating visitors as well as looking ahead towards the future. A whole range of other displays and attractions at the visitor centre mean that, not only is a visit here an enjoyable and informative assault on the senses but all the family are thoroughly entertained. As this unique project has yet to be completed, visitors to the Eden Project are, at present, confined to the visitor centre. Before taking a trip here it is worth contacting the project, by telephone (01726 811911) or through their website (www.edenproject.com).

CARLYON BAY
2 miles SE of St Austell off the A390

This modern seaside resort lies almost at the centre of the long and sweeping **St Austell Bay**. Sheltered by Gribben Head and Dodman Point, this bay is home to numerous beaches, including, at Carlyon Bay, Crinnis and neighbouring Polgaver, Cornwall's only accredited naturist beach.

PENTEWAN
3 miles S of St Austell off the B3273

The east-facing shoreline, to the south of St Austell, shelters some pretty villages, including Pentewan, which is pronounced Pen-tuan. Famous for its stone, which has been used in the construction of many of Cornwall's churches and larger houses, that has been quarried from nearby for centuries, Pentewan also became a china clay port. Unfortunately, the silting up of the harbour led to the village's decline as a port although, today, it is another popular holiday destination with the harbour now playing host to sailing boats and pleasure craft.

Inland from the village lie the famous **Lost Gardens of Heligan**, one of the country's most interesting gardens. Found at the heart of one of the most mysterious estates in England, the seat of the Tremayne family, this world famous garden was originally laid out in 1780 but it lay undisturbed, or 'lost', for 70 years before being rediscovered in 1990. Following one of the largest garden restoration projects, the gardens, after spending years under brambles and ivy, have

PORTH AVALLEN HOTEL,

Sea Road, Carlyon Bay, near St Austell,
Cornwall PL25 3SG
Tel: 01726 812802 Fax: 01726 817097
e-mail: nmarkris@aol.com
website: www.web-direct.co.uk/porthavallen

Originally built as a family house in 1920 on the cliffs overlooking Carlyon Bay, **Porth Avallen Hotel** is now a superb establishment that offers its guests all the luxury of a top class hotel in the relaxed atmosphere of a family home. Owned and personally run by Martin and Kris Shone, with the help of their daughter Helen, this is the perfect place to stay for those looking for a country house hotel by the sea. Care and attention to the smallest detail - fresh flower arrangements can be found throughout - add the finishing touches to this lovely establishment where, throughout, all the rooms have been beautifully decorated and furnished to create a comfortable as well as elegant environment in which to relax.

Dinner in the stylish and sophisticated restaurant makes the perfect end to any day here and the superb menus prepared by resident chef, Julie Ramphry, are an interesting and imaginative blend of modern European cuisine and exotic flavours and through the very best is made of the freshest locally sourced produce. With a superb à la carte menu and a tempting luncheon table d'hôte menu it is easy to see why this restaurant is one of most popular and most highly regarded in the area. After a peaceful night's sleep in one of the hotel's well appointed en suite rooms, guests will find that there is plenty to enjoy here without travelling far as, not only do most of the public rooms have glorious views out over the bay, but there is also a sun lounge and, right from the hotel's doorstep, a footpath leads down to the safe sandy beach.

The Ship Inn,

West End, Pentewan, near St Austell, Cornwall PL26 6BX
Tel: 01726 842855

Hidden away just off the beaten track, **The Ship Inn** is a picturesque pub that is well worth seeking out. Dating back to the early 18th century, this charming old inn not only offers visitors excellent food and drink but also an interesting and atmospheric interior where many of the building's original features remain. Everyone, visitor or local, is assured of a warm welcome at The Ship Inn from experienced managers, Tony and Pam Francis and their helpful staff. As well as good choice of drinks served from the bar there are also

several real ales from which to choose and they include the intriguingly named Daylight Robbery.

Pam takes charge of the kitchens at the inn and, at both lunchtime and in the evening, she serves a delicious menu of tasty home-cooked dishes that are sure to please all the family. Finally, adjacent to this lovely traditional English country inn, which has so much to offer customers, is a holiday flat which is an ideal place for up to six visitors to enjoy the beauty of this area and the delights of this inn.

been restored to their original beauty and Heligan is a real living museum of 19th century horticulture. There are walled gardens, a formal Italian garden, hothouses and a subtropical jungle garden to be found here, as well as many others, that all benefit from the mild Cornish climate. A delightful place that will interest not only keen gardeners, a visit to Heligan is a treat not to be missed.

Lost Gardens of Heligan

From the village, a charming walking and cycling trail leads up the beautiful **Pentewan Valley** which follows the course of the White River. Taking in both woodland and wetland, there is plenty to see and the trail is relatively flat so aiding both walkers and cyclists.

MEVAGISSEY
5 miles S of St Austell on the B3273

Once aptly known as Porthilly, Mevagissey was renamed in the early 14th century after the Welsh and Irish saints: St Meva and St Issey. The largest fishing village in St Austell Bay, Mevagissey was once an important centre of the pilchard industry and, in the 19th century, catches of over 12,000 tons a year were landed here. The catching and processing of the fish employed nearly everyone in the village and, as well as smoking, salting and packing the fish, there were boatbuilders, net makers, rope

Harbour Wall, Mevagissey

makers, coopers and fish merchants here. Some pilchards were exported to southern Europe or supplied to the Royal Navy - the sailors used to refer to the fish as 'Mevagissey Ducks'. The need to process the catch within easy reach of the harbour created a labyrinth of buildings separated by steeply sloping alleyways, some of which were so narrow that the baskets of fish sometimes had to be carried on poles between people walking one behind the other.

Mevagissey's **Inner Harbour**, as it appears today, dates from the 1770s when an Act of Parliament allowed the construction of the 'new' pier and jetties although the original pier dated back as far as 1430. Many of the buildings around this area of the town date from the late 18th century when stone cottages and warehouses were built in place of the town's original cob cottages. The **Outer Harbour** was built so that the size of the port could be increased to cater for the needs of the growing fishing fleets. However, before it was finally completed the harbour was destroyed in the Great Storm of 1891 and it was not finally finished until 1897.

As well as still being an interesting place from which to watch the boats, the harbour here is also home to **Mevagissey Folk Museum**. Housed in a museum piece itself, the building dates from 1745, the museum

THE KINGS ARMS,

17 Fore Street, Mevagissey, Cornwall PL26 6UQ
Tel: 01726 843869

Found just a short distance from Mevagissey's harbour and down one of this historic village's many interesting and picturesque narrow streets stands the impressive **Kings Arms**. Dating back over 250 years, this eyecatching public house has been run by landlords Bob and Gerry Wilson since early 2000 and, although the couple are relatively new to inn keeping they have certainly made their mark.

Now a charming and bustling local inn, perhaps some of the couple's success comes from Bob's years as a Mevagissey fisherman and knowing just what the regular customers are looking for. A cosy and inviting inn, the bar here stocks an excellent range of ales, including several real ales, and there is always a good choice of lagers and cider as well.

Bob sees to the food here too and, available at lunchtimes only, there are, given Bob's previous work, always some delicious seafood and fish dishes on the menu. Fresh, locally caught crab is the house speciality and certainly well worth trying. Sunday lunches too are special as Bob puts on a roast lunch for his customers who can

help themselves without being charged. Add to this the weekly live musical entertainment, and in particular Bob's appearances on Sundays with his friend Mick, and this inn really does have a lot to offer its happy and loyal customers.

has a broad collection of artefacts that cover not only the pilchard industry but also old agriculture machinery, a collection of 19th and 20th century photographs depicting village life and the story behind Pears soap. In 1789, Andrew Pears, a young Cornish barber, went to London where he began to groom the rich and influential. His customers' complaints about the harshness of the available soap led Andrew to experiment and develop a softer soap that was more gentle on the skin - the still popular Pears soap.

Another attraction found around the harbour is the **World of Model Railway Exhibition** which houses a fascinating display of over 2000 models and over 40 trains and the detailed scenery through which the trains run is exceptional as are the many moving accessories. A well stocked model shop caters for everyone, from the enthusiast to the complete beginner, and those interested in Thomas the Tank Engine will also not be disappointed. Meanwhile, the old lifeboat station that was built, in 1897, on the quay side to allow for quick and easy launching has now become **The Aquarium**. The lifeboat station closed in the 1930s after this original building had sustained regular and repeated storm damage.

Today, all but a handful of inshore fishing craft have gone and, in common with most of

TREMARNE HOTEL,

Polkirt, Mevagissey, Cornwall PL26 6UY
Tel: 01726 842213 Fax: 01726 843420
e-mail: tremarne@talk21.com
website: www.tremarne-hotel.co.uk

Just 10 minutes walk away from the centre of Mevagissey, **Tremarne Hotel** has a splendid elevated situation with views over Chapel Point from its south facing gardens. A comfortable and relaxed family hotel, owned and personally run by Helen and David Dudley-Smith, this friendly and welcoming establishment dates back to the 1930s when it was built as a gentleman's residence. Guests here have the choice of relaxing in either of the hotel's two charming lounges or lazing around the open air heated swimming pool before enjoying a predinner drink in the cosy lounge bar. Dinner here too comes highly recommended and the hotel's restaurant, which is also open to non residents, is well known for its excellent cuisine. With only 14 superb en suite guest rooms, this establishment remains small and intimate and David and Helen are always looking to improve this already exceptional hotel further. The hotel is graded AA ** and ETC** and is open all year including Christmas.

TRELEAVEN FARMHOUSE AND RESTAURANT,

Mevagissey, Cornwall PL26 6RZ
Tel: 01726 842413 Fax: 01726 842413
e-mail: annehennah@bun.com
website: www.treleaven.co.uk

Standing at the crest of a valley overlooking Mevagissey, **Treleaven Farmhouse and Restaurant** is a wonderful modernised establishment that offers guests comfortable bed and breakfast accommodation, a distinguished restaurant and an ideal base from which to explore the area's many places of interest - it lies on the fringes of the Lost Gardens of Heligan and just 8 miles from the Eden Project. Owners, Anne and Colin Hennah have lived here since 1960 and for much of that time they have been offering excellent family accommodation. As well as the six well appointed en suite rooms, guests can enjoy a delicious breakfast, play the 18 hole putting green and relax in the solar heated outdoor swimming pool. The guest lounge overlooks the farmhouse's garden as does the restaurant which, over the years, has gained an enviable reputation locally for its traditional home-cooked cuisine. Fish and grills feature strongly here but the list of house specialities certainly adds another dimension to the excellent cuisine found here. This is a charming place to stay and eat.

Mevagissey

Cornwall's coastal communities, the local economy relies greatly on tourism. Thankfully though the annual influx of visitors, which has given rise to a proliferation of cafés and gift shops, has not diminished the port's essential character. However, in the 1750s, when John Wesley first came to Mevagissey to preach at the Market Square, he was greeted to a barrage of rotten eggs and old fish and had to be rescued from the crowd and taken to safety. In return for their hospitality, Wesley gave his hosts, James and Mary Lelean, his silver shoe buckles. Visitors to Mevagissey today need not fear such a welcome.

GORRAN HAVEN
7 miles S of St Austell off the B3273

Once a community with a history to rival that of Mevagissey, Gorran Haven is now a small and unspoilt village with a sheltered sandy beach that connects, at low tide, with the longer **Great Perhaver Beach** to the north. To the southeast, the land rises into the impressive headland of **Dobman Point**,

LANCALLAN FARM,

Mevagissey, near St Austell, Cornwall PL26 6EW
Tel: 01726 842284 Fax: 01726 842284

Found just a short drive from Mevagissey and surrounded by 700 acres working diary, arable and beef farmland, **Lancallan Farm** is the ideal place for a holiday base in the heart of this attractive rural area of Cornwall. At the centre of the farm is the large 17th century farmhouse which has, since 1985, been the home of Dawn and Michael Rundle. Traditionally decorated and furnished throughout in a comfortable and pleasing style, Dawn and Michael offer friendly farmhouse bed and breakfast accommodation in a choice of four spacious guest rooms.

Well appointed and ideal for families - pet dogs are welcome at no extra charge - this welcoming house is the perfect place to relax and feel at home and there are glorious views from the windows either over the surrounding farmland or the house's attractive cottage garden. Guests are greeted each morning with a splendid breakfast served in the spacious dining room and, though there are no evening meals served here, there are numerous pubs and restaurants close by. There is also a cosy lounge here where guests can make the most of this peaceful location and relax with a good book or enjoy an interesting conversation.

MOUNT PLEASANT FARM,

Gorran High Lanes, near St Austell,
Cornwall PL26 6LR
Tel: 01726 843918
e-mail: jlucas@mpfarm.fsnet.co.uk

Just three miles away from the famous Lost Gardens of Heligan lies **Mount Pleasant Farm**, a large property situated in a quiet and peaceful location and surrounded by glorious Cornish rural countryside. Rebuilt in the 1970s, the farmhouse still retains part of the original 18th century cottage. The spectacular south Cornish coastline is only one mile away from the small holding.

Owned by Jill and Nick, they offer guests the opportunity to enjoy superb bed and breakfast accommodation in their attractive and comfortable home. There are spacious guest rooms all lie on the first floor and, downstairs, a separate guest lounge, complete with log fire on cooler evenings, and the elegant dining room. Apart from the friendly and welcoming environment at Mount Pleasant Farm, what makes this a special place to stay are the organic traditional vegetarian and vegan breakfasts which they serve. The couple also cater for other special diets with prior notice. Although no longer a farm, Jill and Nick keep chickens and bees and grow their own organic vegetables on the small holding so the superb quality of the dishes served here can be assured.

THE DOLPHIN INN,

Fore Street, Grampound, near Truro, Cornwall TR2 4RR
Tel: 01726 882435

Situated on the main road through this historic old village, **The Dolphin Inn** is an attractive old coaching inn that is well worth taking the time to visit. Although landlords, Nigel and Kirsty Wakeham, have only been here since early 2000 they have many years experience of the trade between them and Nigel was, at one time, the head chef at The Crown Inn in St Ewe. A warm and inviting inn with a traditional olde worlde atmosphere, the bar at The Dolphin Inn is very well stocked - the range of beer,

ciders and lagers is extensive and there are always several real ales on tap too.

However, what does draw people here is the traditional menu of pub food that is served at both lunchtimes and in the evenings. All freshly prepared and cooked to order, as expected with Nigel on the premises, the inn's reputation for high quality food is increasing week by week. Although both the food and drink found at The Dolphin Inn are superb what makes the inn special is the pleasant surroundings and the friendly atmosphere which greets everyone.

Gorran Haven

which marks the southern point of St Austell Bay and is owned by the National Trust. Sometimes known locally as Deadman Point, this headland, which stands over 370 feet above sea level, was the site of a substantial Iron Age coastal fort.

GRAMPOUND
5½ miles SW of St Austell on the A390

Though it is hard to imagine today, Grampound was once a busy port and market town at the lowest bridging point of the River Fal. As well as having a number of interesting buildings, such as the Guildhall, Clock Tower and Toll House, at its centre there is a tall cross in the market square. Grampound, too, was once a parliamentary borough, returning an member of Parliament at each election. However, corruption in this constituency was so rife that, in 1821, the town was disenfranchised following a special act of Parliament.

ST STEPHEN
4½ miles NW of St Austell on the A3058

This village, on the edge of the clay quarrying area, is also home to **Automobilia**. Established in 1980, this is just the place to step back in time and reveal in motoring nostalgia. There are over 50 vehicles on display here which chart the history of motoring from its infancy in the 1900s through to the post World War II sports cars of the 1950s and 1960s. Anyone looking for a particular item for a vehicle restoration project should take time to look through the Autojumble whilst others may like to take in the audio-visual presentation and enjoy some refreshment at Automobilia's grill room.

TRURO

This elegant small town has grown to become the administrative and ecclesiastical centre of Cornwall. Its site, at the head of a branch of the River Fal, besides which there are now pleasant walks, has been occupied for

Cathedral Lane, Truro

TREVISPIAN VEAN FARM GUEST HOUSE,

St Erme, near Truro, Cornwall TR4 9AT
Tel: 01872 279514 Fax: 01872 263730 website: www.guesthousestruro.com

Found tucked away in the village of St Erme and surrounded by 300 acres of farmland, **Trevispian Vean Farm Guest House** offers holidaymakers the chance to experience real Cornish hospitality in a friendly and comfortable family environment. The large and spacious farm house is around 300 years old and, for as long as owner Ernie Dymond can remember, there has never had a summer here without guests. Ernie was born on the farm and, today, he and his wife, along with son Nick and daughter-in-law Jaqui, carry on the Dymond family tradition.

A relaxed guest house in a wonderful location, there are six splendid en suite rooms here and everything has been done to ensure that guests awake refreshed and, after one of Bridget's splendid breakfasts, everyone will be ready for a day exploring the local countryside. There is too plenty to occupy the whole family at the farm: the scenic location, the horses, donkeys and pigs on the farm, the farm's games room, the children's play area and coarse fishing.

Bridget also prepares dinner on three evenings a week for guests and this is a chance to experience more fabulous home-cooking that should not be missed. With a choice of dishes, including vegetarian options, this is a great opportunity to relax and chat with the hosts and fellow guests.

Afterwards, before retiring for another restful night's sleep, the farmhouse has several comfortable lounges and, in winter, roaring log fires are lit to add an extra warming glow. All in all, Trevispian Vean Farm Guest House is a true home from home which draws many visitors back who wish to experience the farm's unique appeal.

Truro Cathedral

with local granite and serpentine stone, this graceful three-spired building incorporates the early 16th century south aisle of St Mary's Church, which originally occupied the site, and the Victorian stained glass in the cathedral is some of the finest in England.

The **Royal Cornwall Museum**, itself housed in one of the city's fine Georgian buildings, explores the history of the county from the Stone Age right up to the present day whilst, Truro's **Art Gallery**, is home to the works of Constable and Lowry as well as paintings by the Newlyn School of Artists.

Much of the town's architecture dates back to those prosperous times and, in particular, there are the handsome Assembly Rooms and Theatre and Lemon Street, one of the finest complete Georgian streets in the country.

The arrival of the railway in 1859 confirmed Truro's status as a regional capital and, in 1877, it became a city in its own right when the diocese of Exeter was divided into two and Cornwall was granted its own bishop. Three years later, the foundation stone of **Truro Cathedral**, the first Anglican cathedral to be built in Britain since Wren's St Paul's, was laid by the future Edward VII. The next 30 years saw the construction of this splendid Early English style building, that was designed by architect John Loughborough Pearson, and it was finally completed in 1910. Finished

Although the city has the trappings of modern day life, there is an excellent shopping centre but one ancient tradition continues to survive here. At Christmas time, Wassailers circulate through Truro drinking from a decorated wassail bowl and collecting money for charity. The original custom was designed to ward off evil spirits and the word, 'wassail' comes from the Old English and means 'to be of good cheer'.

Along with the elegantly planned streets there are attractive formal public parks, such as **Victoria Gardens** and **Boscawen Park**, and there is also **Bosvigo** - a small garden surrounding a private house that is beautifully planted, with summer herbaceous plants, to give the impression of moving from one 'room' to another.

BISSICK OLD MILL,

Ladock, near Truro, Cornwall TR2 4PG
Tel: 01726 882557 Fax: 01726 884057

Dating back to the 17th century **Bissick Old Mill** only ceased working in the 1960s and, today, this splendid ancient stone building is the home of Mikhail and Sonia Vichniakov. Both professional musicians, Mikhail and Sonia came in October 1998 and since then they have carefully refurbished this marvellous old property to provide superb accommodation with the friendly and traditional

atmosphere of bed and breakfast but with many features of a small country hotel. The guest rooms in the old mill building are spacious and extremely comfortable, they even include a minibar, and there is also an annexe which can provide self-catering accommodation. The breakfasts here are a real feast and include both English and continental style dishes and, in the same attractive surroundings, guests can enjoy a superb home-cooked dinner each evening. Changing daily, the dinner menu offers traditional French cuisine whilst also making use of fresh local produce. There is also an equally comfortable sitting room and Bissick Old Mill holds a residential licence and a good selection of fine wines.

PROBUS GARDENS,

Probus, near Truro, Cornwall TR2 4HQ
Tel: 01726 882597 Fax: 01726 883868
e-mail: enquiries@probusgardens.org.uk
website: www.probusgardens.org.uk

Set up in 1971 as a major demonstration garden, **Probus Gardens** is, today, run by a dedicated group of volunteers, aided by the ever-growing Friends of Probus Gardens, with Gary Lavis as the Head Gardener and Brenda Thatcher as the Under Gardener. Called 'The Really Useful Garden', Probus is a unique place which, over its five and a half acres, is a series of small gardens that bring together the exotic and the ordinary.

A typical Cornish garden site, shelter for more delicate plants has been created by using over 35 different hedges and here can be seen a wide range of plants from herbs, fruits and vegetables

to trees and shrubs. There is a national collection of Salvias, a dye plant garden collection, a collection of culinary and medicinal herbs and a low-allergen garden for asthma sufferers. As well as the wide variety of plants here, Probus Gardens also run a series of events throughout the year, which include visits to other gardens and exhibitions, and a whole range of courses that cover every aspect of horticulture. Back at Probus, visitors can not only wander around enjoying the many displays but also take well-earned refreshment at the Log Cabin Coffee Shop where there is a splendid menu of delicious home-made treats served all day.

MANOR COTTAGE RESTAURANT WITH ROOMS,

Tresillian, near Truro, Cornwall TR2 4BN
Tel: 01872 520212 e-mail: man.cott@cwcom.net
website: www.manorcottage.com

Dating back over 200 years, **Manor Cottage Restaurant** with Rooms is a delightful old place in a charming and secluded setting but it is also within easy reach of both the north and south coasts of Cornwall, Truro and St Austell.

The cottage has been owned and personally run by Carlton and Gillian since 1993 and, in this time, they have established an excellent reputation for the high standard of cuisine served in their restaurant. Dining takes place in the stylish and informal surroundings of the cottage's light and airy conservatory. Carlton is the chef here and the fixed price, three course menu provides diners with a tantalising choice from the list of imaginative and tempting dishes. The emphasis here is very much on using the best possible local produce and, along with the attention to the smallest detail, it is easy to see why this intimate restaurant is so popular. Only open on Thursday, Friday and Saturday evenings, those who are staying in one of the Manor Cottage's five comfortable and homely guest rooms should certainly not miss out on such a treat.

AROUND TRURO

PROBUS
4½ miles NE of Truro off the A390

This large village is famous for having the tallest parish church tower in the county: built of granite in the 16th century and richly decorated, it stands 124 feet high.

Just to the west of the village lies a place that will be of great interest gardeners - **Trewithen House and Gardens**. An early Georgian house whose name literally means 'house of the trees', Trewithen stands in glorious woods and parkland. Laid out in the early 20th century by George Johnstone, the gardens are planted with many rare species of flowering shrubs, including magnolias and rhododendron species. The nursery and café at Trewithen complete the facilities at this world renowned garden.

ST CLEMENT
1½ miles SE of Truro off the A390

The 14th century church in this quiet hamlet has long been a favourite with painters and photographers, perhaps, because it has an unusual lych gate, with an upper room that, some say, was once used as the village school. Evidence of previous inhabitants of the area can be found on a stone near the church porch that is dedicated to Isniocus Vitalis, a 3rd century Roman, but which also bears inscriptions in the ancient Ogham alphabet of the Celts.

TREGONY
6 miles SE of Truro on the B3287

Often referred to as the 'Gateway to the Roseland Peninsula', this village was, in the 14th century, a busy river port long before Truro and Falmouth had developed. Built on the wealth of the local woollen trade the surrounding mills produced a rough serge known as Tregony Cloth. The silting up of the river left Tregony's quayside unusable though parts of it can still be made out today.

The **Roseland Peninsula** is the name given to the indented tongue of land which forms the eastern margin of the Fal estuary which is always known by its Cornish name - **Carrick Roads**.

ST MICHAEL CAERHAYS
8 miles SE of Truro off the B3287

Close to the village lies **Caerhays Castle and Gardens**, one of only a few remaining examples of a castle built by John Nash that is surrounded by informal woodland gardens.

Caerhays Castle and Gardens

Created by J C Williams in the early 20th century and planted with trees and shrubs that were brought back from expeditions to China, the gardens are famous for their camellias, magnolias and rhododendrons.

THE LAMPLIGHTER RESTAURANT,

Fore Street, Probus, near Truro, Cornwall TR2 4JL
Tel: 01726 882453

The Lamplighter Restaurant is a charming and atmospheric establishment that has an enviable reputation throughout this area for the high standard of its cuisine as well as its ambience. Owned and personally run by Tony and Maria Davis, the intimate interior of this splendid 18th century building is just the place to enjoy the interesting and imaginative dishes that make up the evening à la carte menu and the less formal but equally impressive bistro menu. A marvellous experience that is not to be missed booking here is essential at all times. Tony and Maria also offer comfortable bed and breakfast accommodation above the restaurant.

RUAN LANIHORNE
4 miles SE of Truro off the A3078

Situated on the old main coaching route from London to Penzance, this now quiet village is a bird lovers' paradise as the creek is a haven for waders and waterfowl.

VERYAN
6 miles SE of Truro off the A3078

This charming village, set in a wooded hollow, is famous for its five **Roundhouses** which lie at the entrances to Veryan. Built in the early 19th century for the daughters of the local vicar, Jeremiah Trist, the whitewashed cottages each have a conical thatched roof with a wood cross at the apex. It was believed that their circular shape would guard the village from evil as the Devil would be unable to hide in any corners.

Roundhouses, Veryan

PORTLOE
7½ miles SE of Truro off the A3078

The stone cottages of this small and unspoilt fishing village surround Portloe's tiny harbour which is overshadowed by the steep cliffs

THE NEW INN,

Veryan, near Truro, Cornwall TR2 5QA
Tel: 01872 501362 Fax: 01872 501078
e-mail: jack@veryan44.freeserve.co.uk
website: www.veryan44.freeserve.co.uk

Formerly a pair of 16th century cottages, **The New Inn** is an attractive and quaint old inn run by landlords, Jack and Penny Gayton, that offers customers the very best in English country hospitality. Inviting and welcoming, the cosy interior is full of olde worlde charm and character whilst, outside, there is a secluded and well maintained beer garden. There is always a good selection of beers, ales, lagers, ciders and spirits from the well stocked bar, including local real ale, and The New Inn too has an excellent reputation for the high standard of the food. Prepared by Penny, the menu includes local favourites as well as a range of imaginative dishes and booking here, throughout the summer, is essential. As the inn has three comfortable and attractive guest rooms, with an enormous breakfast served each morning, those visiting the area can take full advantage of the friendly and welcoming hospitality offered by the charming and interesting hosts.

TREGAIN,

Portloe, near Truro, Cornwall TR2 5QU
Tel: 01872 501252

Found in a picturesque and quaint 300 year old building **Tregain** is a well known and highly regarded tea rooms and licensed restaurant that has received several awards including Best Restaurant in Cornwall, 2000. Owned and personally run by Clare Holdsworth, the daytime menu is a wonderful list of sweet and savoury dishes that includes such mouthwatering specialities as home-made crab soup, meringues and treacle pudding. The ever changing evening à la carte menu is equally delicious and offers a wealth of sumptuous dishes that make the very best of locally caught fish and seafood and locally produced meat and cheese. Not only is this an elegant and superb place to eat but Clare also offers bed and breakfast accommodation.

along this stretch of coast. In stormy weather, it is impossible for boats to fight their way against the wind and waves through the narrow gap into the safety of the harbour.

CARNE
6½ miles SE of Truro off the A3078

Overlooking Gerrans Bay, and on land owned by the National Trust, stands **Carne Beacon**. One of the largest Bronze Age barrows in the country, this ancient burial mound is thought to be the grave of King Geraint, who, in the 5th century, is said to have rowed across the bay in a golden boat with silver oars. Reputed to have been buried in full regalia, recent excavations have failed to confirm this story.

PORTSCATHO
7 miles SE of Truro off the A3078

This pleasant and unspoilt fishing village, with its sandy beach on Gerrans Bay, is well worth a visit and may appear familiar to anyone who watched the television drama, *The Camomile Lawn*, as it was used as the filming location.

ST ANTHONY HEAD
9 miles S of Truro off the A3078

This little hamlet lies towards the bottom of the Roseland Peninsula and, from **St Anthony Head**, there are splendid views across Carrick Roads to Falmouth. At the foot of this squat headland stands **St Anthony Lighthouse**, which was built in 1834 and replaced a coal beacon that, for centuries, had warned sailors off the infamous Manacles rocks.

This headland, which guards the entrance into Carrick Roads, has had a strategic importance for many years and, on the cliff top behind the lighthouse, are the remains of **St Anthony Battery**. In military use right up until the 1950s, this was a significant World War II observation post and the old officers' quarters, which are now in the hands of the National Trust as is the headland, have been converted into holiday cottages.

ST MAWES
7½ miles S of Truro on the A3078

A popular and exclusive sailing centre in the shelter of Carrick Roads, St Mawes is a

TREWINCE MANOR,

Portscatho, near Truro,
Cornwall TR2 5ET
Tel: 01872 580289
Fax: 01872 580694
e-mail: bookings@trewince.co.uk

Tucked away in a splendid and unique location, between the river and the sea, **Trewince Manor** is a superb place for a peaceful and relaxing holiday.

The grade II listed Georgian manor house was built in 1750 for a sea captain and, today, it forms the centre piece of Peter and Liz Heywood's marvellous and secluded holiday retreat. The first floor of this charming house has been tastefully converted into apartments whilst, adjacent to the house, there is an attractive 18th century cottage that provides guests with the latest in modern convenience.

Elsewhere on the large estate, Peter and Liz have a range of excellent luxury lodges, each of which has a sea view. Guests can also enjoy the wonderful sea views from the manor's attractive sitting room, have a drink in the friendly and cosy bar and dine on delicious fresh local produce in the elegant dining room. Children and dogs are welcome here and there is provision for touring caravans and campers.

St Mawes Harbour

St Mawes Castle

charming small town with a safe anchorage and good beaches. From here ferries take passengers across the river to Falmouth and, during the summer, a boat also takes passengers down the river to the remote and unspoilt area of Roseland around St Anthony. The town is dominated by its artillery fort, **St Mawes Castle**, that was built in the 1540s as part of Henry VIII's coastal defences. Guarding the entrance into Carrick Roads, the castle stands opposite Pendennis Castle with which it shared the duty of protecting Falmouth and the river. A fine example of

THE ST MAWES HOTEL,

The Sea Front, St Mawes, Cornwall TR2 5DW
Tel: 01326 270266 Fax: 01326 270170
e-mail: stmaweshotel@compuserve.com
website: stmaweshotel.co.uk

Found right in the heart of St Mawes and overlooking the quay, The **St Mawes Hotel** is an outstanding place that is well worth taking the time to discover. Dating back to the 16th century, the hotel has been in the Burrows family since 1972 and today it is personally run by Emma. The hotel's bar is a popular meeting place for locals, as well as visitors who come here to quench their thirst from the well stocked bar.

Here, too, a tasty menu of bar snacks and meals - anything from a light scallop salad to a Ribeye steak - is served at both lunchtimes and in the evening. For more formal dining, the hotel's restaurant is a comfortable and intimate choice and, in these pleasant surroundings not only is there an extensive list of dishes but also an excellent daily table d'hôte. The house speciality is local fish and seafood and both feature heavily on the menus and, for children, there is also plenty of choice from their own special list. Finally, the eight en suite guest rooms here are as exceptional as the rest of the hotel and are sure to provide visitors with the perfect restful night's sleep. All in all The St Mawes Hotel is a charming establishment that is a pleasure to find.

Tudor military architecture, the castle's cloverleaf, or trefoil, design ensured that, whatever the direction of any attack, the castle could defend itself. However, a shot was never fired from its canons in anger and, today, the castle has been restored and visitors can look round the Tudor interior which is in remarkably good condition. St Mawes Castle is in the custodianship of English Heritage.

ST JUST IN ROSELAND
6 miles S of Truro on the B3289

This enchanting hamlet has an exquisite 13th century church which lies in one of the most superb settings in the country. Concealed in a steep wooded tidal creek of the Percuil River, the church, which has been described as one of the most beautiful in England, is

St Just in Roseland

surrounded by gardens that contain many subtropical trees and shrubs, including African fire bush and Chilean myrtle. Unfortunately, the interior of the church does

not live up to expectations as it underwent a clumsy Victorian restoration.

TOLVERNE
4 miles S of Truro off the B3289

During World War II, this quiet village was taken over by the American army and was used as an embarkation point for Allied troops during the D-Day landings. On the shingle beach the remains of the concrete honeycomb mattresses that covered it in the 1940s can still be seen. Whilst in the area, General Eisenhower stayed at **Smugglers Cottage** and, today, this simple dwelling is home to a large collection of memorabilia from that period.

FEOCK
4 miles S of Truro off the B3289

The charming collection of whitewashed thatched cottages that make up this tiny hamlet, along with its glorious position, have led to Feock being considered one of the most attractive little village's in the county. A pleasant creekside walk to the west of the village follows the course of an old tramway which dates from the time when this area was not as peaceful and tranquil as it is today but was a bustling port serving inland Cornwall. To the south of Feock, a country lane leads to the tip of **Restronguet Point** and, at the mouth of Restronguet Creek, stands the Pandora Inn. A typical whitewashed and thatched 17th century inn, it was named after the ship which was sent out to capture the mutineers from the *Bounty*.

TRELISSICK
3½ miles S of Truro off the B3289

Situated on a promontory that is bound by the River Fal and two creeks, lies the estate of **Trelissick**, a private 18th century house that is surrounded by beautiful gardens and parkland from which there are marvellous views over Carrick Roads. Several miles of paths lead around the estate, which takes in rolling parkland and dense woodland, and visitors will see an abundance of subtropical trees and shrubs that live happily alongside native plants. The estate's Cornish apple orchard is another interesting feature here and it was created to preserve many traditional apple

Trelissick Gardens

species. Various of the house's outbuildings have been converted to take visitors and, in the stables, there is a display of saddlery while another building is home to an arts and crafts gallery.

Close to the estate is the landing point of the **King Harry Ferry** which takes passengers across the narrow, yet deep, stretch of water to

the Roseland Peninsula. The reason for the ferry's curious name has been lost in the mists of time and the nearby old Ferry Boat Inn would suggest that this now chain ferry has been operating in one way or another for several centuries.

MYLOR
5½ miles SW of Truro off the A39

The two attractive villages of **Mylor Churchtown** and **Mylor Bridge**, on the south side of Mylor Creek, have blended into one another and, today, are popular yachting centres with a club and many watersports activities. Mylor Churchtown, at the mouth of the creek, is the larger of the two and was once a dockyard and landing place for the packet ships which carried mail throughout the world. In the churchyard of the ancient St Mylor Church can be seen the graves of many sea captains as well as, close to the south porch, a round headed **Celtic Cross** which, at

CREEKSIDE HOLIDAY HOUSES,

Restronguet, near Falmouth,
Cornwall TR11 5ST
Tel: 01326 372722 Fax: 01326 372722

Overlooking the sheltered waters of Restronguet Creek in a tucked away corner of the Fal Estuary, **Creekside Holiday Houses** are the ideal place for a real get-away-from-it-all holiday. The three houses, which are all owned and privately let by Peter Watson, are perfect for those who enjoy sailing and boating as, not only are the conditions here some of the best

in the country, but holidaymakers here have the use of the private beach, quay and extensive water frontage. They are also well situated for visiting National Trust gardens. Dogs are welcome.

Although the three houses vary in size the are all beautifully appointed and decorated and furnished to a very high standard. The largest, Marlow, sleeps six adults comfortably and, as well as being a delightful spacious house it is also surrounded by its own sheltered and mature garden. The Quarter

Deck is a self-contained and completely separate wing of Peter's own house and, as well as being well furnished and decorated, it also has wonderful views out over the water from both its windows and garden. The third house, Rhinos Barn, is a charming barn conversion that has, again, its own garden. Many of the building's original features remain which go to make this a place of character. Three delightful holiday houses in an outstanding location, Creekside Holiday Houses are also close to the equally exceptional Pandora Inn which is noted for its bar snacks and restaurant.

over 10 feet, is one of the tallest in Cornwall. Dating from the 10th century, it was rediscovered in Victorian times after having been used for centuries to prop up the south wall of the church.

FLUSHING
7 miles S of Truro off the A39

This small village, which is another popular yachting centre, was built by settlers from Vlissingen in Holland, in the 17th century and it still retains a Dutch appearance. A prosperous port in the 17th and 18th centuries, Flushing's narrow streets are home to some fine Queen Anne houses, many of which were built to house sea captains and naval officers.

FALMOUTH
8 miles S of Truro on the A39

In Britain's Western Approaches and guarding the entrance into Carrick Roads, Falmouth is a spectacular deep-water anchorage that is the world's third largest natural harbour. Although a settlement has existed here for hundreds of years, it was not until the 17th

century that the port was properly developed. However, in the 16th century, Henry VIII sought to guard this strategically important harbour from attack. Standing on a 200 foot promontory overlooking the entrance to Carrick Roads, Henry's **Pendennis Castle** is one of Cornwall's great fortresses and, along with St Mawes Castle on the opposite side of the river mouth, it has protected Britain's shores from attack ever since its construction. Its low circular keep has extremely thick walls and it stands within a 16-sided enclosure - the outer curtain wall was added in response to the threat of a second Spanish Armada in Elizabethan times. One of the last Royalist strongholds to fall during the Civil War, and then only after a grim five month siege, Pendennis Castle remained in use up until the end of World War II. Now under the ownership of English Heritage, the castle is a fascinating place to visit as, through a variety of displays and exhibitions, the 450 year old history of the fortress is explained.

In the 17th century, the arrival of the Packet Ships at Falmouth, which sailed between Britain, Europe and the Americas carrying mail and goods, saw the

THE LEMON ARMS,

Lemon Hill, Mylor Bridge, near Falmouth, Cornwall TR11 5NA
Tel: 01326 373666

Still very much a local pub, **The Lemon Arms** has been providing the people of Mylor Bridge and the surrounding area with generous hospitality since the mid 19th century. There has, however, been an inn on this site since at least 1765 and, as well as being a local meeting place, the inn has also been used to hold the Manor Court, where, on quarter days, rents were paid and other business transacted.

Today, the inn is still run by a local couple, Allan, who comes from Falmouth, and his wife Leane who has lived in the village all her life. Inviting and full of character inside, this charming old inn is a popular place where both locals and visitors alike can expect a warm welcome.

As well as having a well stocked bar which includes several real ales, The Lemon Arms also has a fast growing reputation for the high standard of the food served here. Leane is the cook of the partnership and, along with the regular menu, she also prepares a mouth-watering list of daily specials. Steaks and fresh fish dishes are the house speciality and the traditional roast lunches on Sundays are particularly impressive - booking for this is essential. A delightful inn for all the family, The Lemon Arms is a friendly place where everyone will feel welcome.

Pendennis Castle

ships coming into Falmouth also brought exotic plants from such places as China, Australia and the Americas. Many of the subtropical trees and shrubs ended up in private gardens but the town's four central public gardens, **Fox Rosehill**, **Queen Mary**, **Kimberley Park** and **Gyllyngdune** are also packed with such plants as magnolias and palms which all benefit from the mild south Cornwall climate.

development of the port. During its heyday, in the early 19th century, Falmouth was the base for almost 40 such sailing ships which carried cargo to every corner of the globe, but, a few decades later, the introduction of steam-powered vessels heralded the end of Falmouth and, by the 1850s, the packet service had moved to Southampton. Despite this the town has maintained its maritime links and today it plays a dual role as a commercial port and holiday centre. The docks continue to be used by merchant shipping but the town's traditional activities are being overshadowed by its increasing popularity as a yachting and tourist centre.

Falmouth's nautical and notorious past is revealed at the **Cornwall Maritime Museum** where a wealth of displays explain the rise in prosperity of the town due to the arrival of the packet ships. Pirates and smugglers too were attracted to Falmouth and, on **Custom House Quay**, stands an early 19th century brick-built incinerator known as the **Queen's Pipe**. It was here that contraband tobacco seized by Falmouth's customs men was burnt.

As well as carrying commercial cargoes around the world, the

Visitors here can also find fine sandy beaches, from which there is good, safe swimming, while, for those looking for a wilder time there is the **Ships and Castles Leisure Pool** complete with its rapid river run and wave machine. For those keen to explore

River Fal, Falmouth

the upper reaches of Carrick Roads by boat, a number of pleasure trips depart from Prince of Wales pier, as does the passenger ferry to St Mawes and several others destinations along the coast. A short distance from the pier is the tree-lined square known as the 'Moor' where the town hall and Falmouth's **Art Gallery** can be found.

PENRYN
7 miles SW of Truro on the B3292

Mentioned in the Domesday Book, this ancient town, at the head of the Penryn River, was, before Falmouth's rise to prominence in Tudor times, the controlling port at the mouth of Carrick Roads. During medieval times it was also the home of Glasney College, an important collegiate church which survived until the Dissolution of the Monasteries in 1539. At one time, granite quarried close by was shipped from here all over the world and

it has been used in both the Thames embankment and Singapore harbour. The availability of the stone has also left its mark on Penryn as there are many fine Tudor, Jacobean and Georgian houses to be seen here and, now restored, they can be found in the town's conservation area.

Another reminder of the town's maritime past is the sad story that forms the basis of the play, *The Penryn Tragedy*. After years at sea, a young sailor from Penryn returned home to his parents' inn and, as a joke, he disguised himself but not before first telling his sister of his plan. His parents, overcome with temptation on meeting this rich stranger, murdered the young man for his money. Next morning, the sister came in search of her brother and the full horror of their crime caused her parents to commit suicide.

SPINDRIFT COTTAGE,

Green Lane, Perranarworthal, Cornwall TR3 7PE
Tel: 01872 863129 Mobile: 07773 470384 e-mail: rgrant9998@aol.com

The village of Perranarworthal lies halfway between Truro and Falmouth. Hidden from the main road through the village and surrounded by its own half acre, wooded garden **Spindrift Cottage** is a spacious mid 19th century stone house. The home of Ros Grant since 1998, she offers superb B&B accommodation in her comfortable and relaxed house that is sure to appeal to everyone looking to escape the pressures of every day life. Most of the guest rooms are en suite and there is also a bunk house available in the garden. Children and dogs are very welcome here too. Ros is keen to conserve the environment and this extends beyond recycling to providing a wonderful breakfast menu that features fair trade produce, free range eggs and the extensive use of organic ingredients.

THE ROYAL OAK,

Perranwell Station, near Truro, Cornwall TR3 7PX
Tel: 01872 863175

Dating back to the mid 19th century and found on the main road through this picturesque village, **The Royal Oak** is a warm and welcoming inn that is owned and personally run by Richard and Lydia Rudland. A true traditional English country inn, the interior of The Royal Oak is full of character and charm and, along with the stone walls, heavy ceiling beams and open fire, there is also a mass of interesting memorabilia on display. Cosy and comfortable this is just the place to relax and enjoy a drink from the well stocked bar where the choice includes at least three real ales. Food too is served at The Royal Oak and with the couple's experience of running a steak and seafood restaurant in Puerto Rico for 15 years ensures that not only is the food here excellent but not the usual pub grub. Caribbean and American style cuisine features heavily here and, along with the many daily specials, a meal at The Royal Oak is certainly a different experience that is sure to be memorable.

6 Camborne, Redruth and the Lizard Peninsula

This area of Cornwall is often called Poldark country after the series of successful novels, set in the county's tin and copper mining region, became popular following their appearance on television. At the centre of the industry are the twin towns of Camborne and Redruth, which now form Cornwall's largest conurbation, and where most of the mines were found. Although the industry closed down in the early 20th century, unable to compete against the great mineral finds in South Africa, Australia and the Americas, there is plenty to see in the region from those days.

The world famous School of Mines, along with the Geological Museum, are based in Camborne, but for visitors wishing to find out more about the lives of the miners and the industry itself will find that the Poldark Mine Heritage Complex - where there are underground tours - and the Cornish Mines and Engines - with its splendid working beam engines - will be able to answer most questions.

As well as being mining country this is also land that has been settled for centuries and Carn Brea, to the southeast of Camborne, is the site of the earliest known Neolithic settlement in southern Britain. Another curious feature of this landscape is Gwennap Pit, a large natural amphitheatre, probably created by a collapsed mine shaft, that was used on many occasions by John Wesley, the founder of Methodism.

Old Lifeboat Station, The Lizard

Meanwhile, to the south lies the Lizard Peninsula, the southern most point of mainland England. An area of contrasts - there are beautiful secluded wooded inlets around the Helford estuary, areas of bleak moorland and dramatic cliffs - exploration of the peninsula is very worthwhile. Warmed by the Gulf Stream, the Lizard is home to some of the county's most interesting and most exotic gardens, including Trevarno where there is also a Gardening Museum.

CAMBORNE, REDRUTH & THE LIZARD PENINSULA

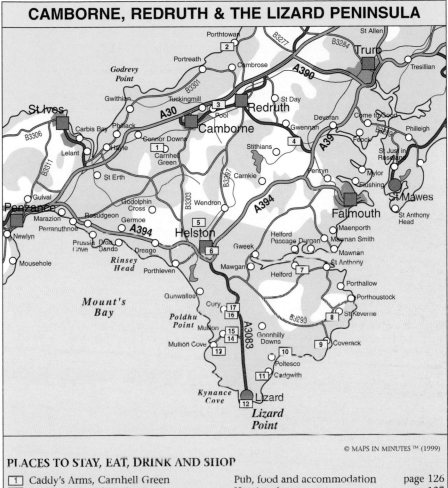

© MAPS IN MINUTES ™ (1999)

PLACES TO STAY, EAT, DRINK AND SHOP

CAMBORNE

Once the capital of Cornwall's main tin and copper mining area, Camborne and neighbouring Redruth have combined to form the largest urban centre of population in the county. In the mid 19th century, the area surrounding Camborne was the most intensely mined in the world and the district is still littered with evidence of this lost era. In the 1850s, Cornwall had well over 300 mines which, together, produced some two thirds of the world's copper and employed around 50,000 workers. However, most had to close in the first few decades of the 20th century when the discovery of extensive mineral deposits in the Americas, South Africa and Australia rendered the local industry no longer economically viable.

Before the mining industry took off in the 18th century, Camborne was a small place and the results of the rapid expansion of the village at the time can still be seen in the numerous terraces of 18th and 19th century miners' houses. Contrasting with these densely populated streets and alleyways, the **Literary Institute**, built in 1829 in granite, has a grand, Tuscan style. A **Town Trail** now guides visitors around this historic former mining town, introducing the many interesting buildings, which could easily be missed amongst the bustle of Camborne's busy town centre.

As the town's, and indeed the area's, livelihood has depended on mining for several hundred years it is not surprising that Camborne is the home of a world famous **School of Mining**. One of the specialists in mining education, Robert Hunt, is remembered here in the school's impressive **Geological Museum** which displays minerals and rocks from all over the world. The School of Mines is now part of the University of Exeter and close by also lies **Camborne's Art Gallery**.

Outside the town's library is a statue to a Richard Trevithick who, as an accomplished amateur wrestler, became known as the Cornish Giant. Trevithick was also an inventor and he was responsible for developing the high pressure steam engine, the screw propeller and an early locomotive which predated Stephenson's Rocket by 12 years. The home of this pioneering Cornish engineer can still be seen close to Camborne, at Penponds, but though a genius, Trevithick died penniless and was buried in an unmarked grave in Dartford, Kent. The town still celebrates the achievements of its great son, each year, with the **Trevithick Day Festival**.

AROUND CAMBORNE

PORTREATH
3½ miles N of Camborne on the B3300

Now a thriving holiday centre, Portreath developed in the 18th century as a port from

CADDY'S ARMS,

Carnhell Green, near Camborne, Cornwall TR14 0NB
Tel: 01209 832116

Found in the centre of the hamlet of Carnhell Green and on part of the Cornish Way - an ancient route that was once used by monks, missionaries and miners - **Caddy's Arms** is a splendid old country inn that is well worth finding. Formerly a coaching stop, this lovely 300 year old building is now owned and personally run by Mark and Jane Hollis who, since they came here in 1998, have gained enviable reputation for the high standard of hospitality served here. Well known throughout Cornwall, this charming inn has a well stocked bar, which includes the local real ale Doom Bar, as well as an excellent wine list. However, what really draws people to this popular inn is the superb menus of delicious food that are served throughout the week. In comfortable and friendly surroundings visitors will have an interesting choice to make from either the tempting lunch time or the more formal evening menu. The emphasis here is on traditional country fayre and it is the use of fresh local ingredients that makes these lovely dishes so mouth-watering. Always a busy place, it is essential to book for the Sunday lunches and, finally, Caddy's Arms also has quality bed and breakfast accommodation.

THE BEACH HOTEL,

West Cliff, Porthtowan, Cornwall TR4 8AE
Tel: 01209 890228 e-mail: colin@hardwick63.freeserve.co.uk
website: www.thebeachhotel.net

Situated so close to the sandy shore that the rhythmic lapping
of the waves on the beach provides the soothing background
music, **The Beach Hotel** has to have one of the best possible
locations in the county. A small, family hotel personally run by
owners Sian and Colin Hardwick, this cosy and imtimate place
is perfect for those wishing to find a relaxing retreat on the coast.
Each of the 12 comfortable guest rooms here is en suite and most
come with a sea view. The rest of the public rooms are equally well furnished and decorated and, again,
they offer a pleasant environment in which to unwind from the stress of everyday life. Pre dinner
cocktails can be taken in either the hotel's quiet bar or out on the terrace overlooking the calm of the
beach and sea beyond. The Beach Hotel's fully licensed family restaurant is well known and highly
regarded locally with wonderful views from its picture windows. Both children and dogs are welcome
here and Colin and Sian are happy to meet guest coming by rail when arranged.

which copper was exported and coal
imported. Prior to the quay being constructed
here by the Bassett family in 1760, copper ore
from the mines around Redruth had to be
loaded on to ships from the beach which was
not only a slow job but also a dangerous one.
Some years later, in 1809, the new **Harbour**
was connected to the mines by the first
railway in Cornwall.

The remains of the inclined plane, on
which the ore laden wagons were lowered
down the steep gradient to the quayside, can
still be seen as can the white conical daymark
that stands on the cliffs above the harbour.
Built in the 19th century, the locally
nicknamed Pepperpot, still guides ships safely
into the harbour. During the 19th century,
this now quiet village was at its busiest with
over 100,000 tons of copper passing through
the port and equally vast quantities of coal
were received here from the coalfields of
South Wales.

A popular destination with surfers and
families, the village also marks the starting
point of the **Mineral Tramway Walks** whilst,
just to the south, lies the **Tehidy Country
Park**.

PORTHTOWAN
5 miles NE of Camborne off the B3300

This small holiday resort has a gently sloping
beach that is sheltered by the cove. An
excellent family beach, the sea also provides
good surfing whilst the seaside cafés and
shops cater for almost every holiday makers'

needs. Evidence of copper mining is never far
away in this part of Cornwall and, in the
village, a 19th century mining engine house
has been converted into a private residence.
Inland, at **Tywarnhale**, more evidence can be
seen in the remains of various copper mine
buildings.

ST DAY
4 miles E of Camborne off the B3298

A **Heritage Trail** around this village takes in
the historic sites which are all that remain
from the time when, in the 19th century, St
Day was known as the richest square mile in
the world due to the number of copper and
tin mines in the area.

GWENNAP
4 miles E of Camborne on the A393

The mysterious **Gwennap Pit**, found just to
the southeast of Redruth, is a round, grass
covered amphitheatre that is thought to have
been created by the collapse of a subterranean
mine shaft. Used as a cock pit, this curious
theatre is sometimes referred to as the
'Methodist Cathedral', as it was here that John
Wesley, the founder of the nonconformist
denomination, preached on many occasions
from 1762 onwards. In 1806, the seating
terraces were cut into the banks and, the
following year, a Whit Monday service was
held which has continued and is now the
annual focus for Methodist pilgrimage from
around the world.

THE PLUME OF FEATHERS,

Fore Street, Pool, near Redruth, Cornwall TR15 3PF
Tel: 01209 713513 e-mail: mtking@talk21.com

Found on the main road between Redruth and Camborne, **The Plume of Feathers** is an attractive stone built inn that dates back to the early 19th century. A former coaching inn, this welcoming pub, which is in the experienced hands of landlords Maggie and Tony King, continues to offer excellent and traditional hospitality to all its customers. This secluded rear beer garden, with its children's playarea, and the patio are ideal for summer's days whilst, inside, this charming place has an authentic olde worlde atmosphere that is highlighted by the feature fireplace, exposed stone walls and gleaming brassware. From the bar there is a wide choice of beers, lagers, cider and stout, as well as two real ales, whilst a tasty menu of bar snacks are also offered. The Plume of Feathers is highly regarded for its separate restaurant where the tempting à la carte menu offers customers a superb selection of dishes that range from traditional steaks and simply cooked locally caught fish to elaborate classical French cuisine and spicy Oriental stir fries. Certainly with something to interest every one, this is an inn for all the family that is well worth finding.

THE STAG HUNT,

20 St Michael's Road, Ponsanooth, near Truro,
Cornwall TR3 7EE
Tel: 01872 863046

Found on the main road through this inland Cornish village, **The Stag Hunt** is an inviting inn where both locals and visitors alike will receive a warm welcome. Originally three 18th century cottages, one of which was used as a morgue in the 19th century, the interior still retains much of the character and charm of the old buildings as well as some of their features, including the stone walls and fireplace. Although owners Mike and Brenda Beckett, along with their daughter Michelle, have only been here since spring 2000, they have lived in Cornwall for over 20 years and they certainly know how to offer superb Cornish hospitality. The range of drinks served from the bar includes several real ales and there is also a delicious menu of tasty dishes served at both lunchtime and in the evenings. Michelle is a qualified chef and the marvellous array of tempting delights she conjures up each day has greatly helped to establish The Stag Hunt as one of the most popular places for food and drink in the area.

The **Museum of Cornish Methodism**, nearby, was opened in the 1980s and provides an interesting and informative series of displays and exhibits on the religion and its founder.

POOL
2 miles NE of Camborne on the A3047

Pool is one of several villages that has been consumed into the Camborne and Redruth conurbation. Very much in the heart of Cornwall's mining area, here can be found **Cornish Mines and Engines**, where the secrets of the county's dramatic landscape can be discovered at the **Cornwall Industrial Discovery Centre**. The two historic Cornish beam engines still stand in their original engine houses and whilst one of them was built by the local firm, Holmans, in 1887, as a winding engine for raising ore up and lowering miners down the shaft, the other was built by Harveys, in 1892, for pumping water up from a depth of 1700 feet. The world of Cornish mining is explained here through the displays and guided tours and there are specially designed activities for children.

Tin Mine Engine House, Redruth

REDRUTH
2 miles E of Camborne on the A393

This market town was once, along with much of the surrounding area, at the centre of the county's mining industry and, as such, was a prosperous town. Some pockets of Victorian, Georgian and earlier buildings still remain and, particularly at Churchtown, there are some attractive old cottages and a Georgian church with a 15th century tower whose lychgate has an unusually long coffin rest that was built to deal with the aftermath of mining disasters.

Redruth was also the home of the Scottish inventor William Murdock who was responsible for such innovations as coal-gas lighting and the vacuum powered tubes that were once a common feature in department stores.

The countryside immediately to the south of Redruth is dominated by dramatic **Carn Brea** - pronounced Bray - which rises to some 738 feet above sea level. The summit of this windswept granite hill is crowned with a 90 foot monument to Francis Basset, a benevolent Georgian land and mine owner who did much to improve the lot of poor labourers. Also to be found on Carn Brea, on the lower eastern summit, is a small castle, a part medieval building, that had once been used as a hunting lodge and has since been restored. However, this land has been occupied for centuries and Carn Brea is the site of the earliest known Neolithic settlement in southern Britain.

Each year, in June, Carn Brea sees the Midsummer Bonfire ceremony, a pagan ritual in which the lighting of a fire on the summit of the beacon is the signal to light further fires that stretch across the county from Land's End to the River Tamar. Each fire is blessed by a clergyman in Cornish and, after burning flowers and herbs, young people leap across the dying embers to ward off evil and bring good luck.

TUCKINGMILL
1½ miles E of Camborne off the A3047

Whilst most places in this area devoted their energies to the mining industry, Tuckingmill was home to a fuse factory (the last fuseworks closed in the 1960s) that went on to become world famous for the production of safety fuses. Invented in 1830 by William Bickford, the fuses were used widely in Hollywood films and, most notably, as dynamite fuses in *Mission Impossible*.

STITHIANS
5½ miles SE of Camborne off the A393

This quiet rural village is home to the second largest agricultural show in Cornwall, which takes place every July. **Stithians Reservoir**, just to the west of the village, is a watersports centre and also home to a bird sanctuary.

THE CROWN INN,

Crowntown, near Helston,
Cornwall TR13 0AD
Tel: 01326 565538

Once part of the Trevano Valley Estate, **The Crown Inn** is a splendid stone pub that was originally built by the Lord of the Manor as a hunting lodge. A welcoming and inviting inn that is owned and personally run by Chris and David Hopkinson, this is an ideal place to stop for a drink and good food in pleasant surroundings. There are always at least five

real ales on tap behind the bar as well as other keg beers, draught ciders and a comprehensive wine list. The couple's daughter, Katie, prepares the dishes here and, along with the regular menu of traditional pub fayre, each Wednesday evening is devoted to curries which prove to be very popular as do the carvery Sunday lunches. Adjacent to the inn is a cottage which David and Chris rent out on either a self-catering or a bed and breakfast basis. An excellent place to visit throughout the year, The Crown Inn is cosy in winter and, during the summer, customers spill out into the attractive rear beer garden.

MAENPORTH
10½ miles SE of Camborne off the A39

The sheltered sandy beach at this village overlooks Falmouth Bay and is not only a pleasant place for families but is also a watersports centre from which diving equipment, sailboards and other accessories can be hired.

MAWNAN SMITH
10½ miles SE of Camborne off the A39

Just to the west of this pretty village, which overlooks the River Helford, lies **Glendurgan**, a marvellous valley garden that is owned by the National Trust. Set in a wooded valley that drops steeply down to the hamlet of Durgan and the shores of the Helford estuary, this subtropical garden was first laid out at the beginning of the 19th century and still includes many exotic trees and shrubs. The famous **Heade Maze**, created in 1833 from laurels, and the **Giant's Stride** - a maypole - are two features that are particularly popular with younger visitors to this beautiful and secluded garden.

MAWNAN
11½ miles SE of Camborne off the A39

Its elevated position, above this hamlet, has led the to the 15th century Church of St Mawnan, and particularly its tower, to have been used as a landmark by sailors for centuries. Built on a spur at the mouth of the River Helford, this tower is an excellent viewing point not only for those wishing to take in this sweeping coastline but it was also used as a lookout post during times of war and potential invasion.

DURGAN
11 miles SE of Camborne off the A39

This tiny hamlet, which today is owned by the National Trust, was, for centuries, a fishing village whose daily catch was transported to Falmouth by donkey. Now a peaceful backwater, with cottages overlooking a sand and shingle beach on the River Helford, Durgan is also home to **Trebah Garden** - often dubbed the garden of dreams. The ravine in which the garden has been created was, in the 11th century, owned by the Bishop of Exeter and, in the 1830s, the land was bought by the Fox family. The then owner, Charles Fox, set out to create a garden of rare and exotic plants and trees that were collected from all over the world. Reaching maturity some 100 years later, Trebah was then regarded as one of the most beautiful gardens in Britain.

Unfortunately, shortly after, in 1939, the estate was sold and, for the next 40 years, Trebah was left to become submerged under weeds, ivy and other creepers. However, following a massive restoration programme in the 1980s, Trebah Garden has been returned to its original impressive state and is open to the public. The 25 acres of the garden fall down to a private beach on Helford River and here visitors can discover glades of subtropical shrubs and trees, 100 year old rhododendrons, waterfalls and ponds of giant Koi carp.

HELFORD PASSAGE
11 miles SE of Camborne off the A39

Situated on the opposite bank of the estuary from Helford, this hamlet is a popular mooring point, with sailing and motor boats for hire, that also has a sand and shingle beach. During the summer a ferry runs from here across the estuary, as one has done since the Middle Ages. Until the early 20th century, whilst a cart was allowed on the ferry the horse, led by a rope, swam alongside the craft.

WENDRON
7 miles S of Camborne on the B3297

Close to this bleak village is one of the many mines that have been worked in this area since the 15th century. Now reopened as the **Poldark Mine Heritage Complex**, it is one of the Cornwall's most interesting attractions. As well as the underground tours which take visitors into the mine's tunnels, there is famous 18th century Poldark village, which brings to life the living conditions of Ross and Demelza Poldark, and numerous machinery exhibits, some of which are in working order. The complex is laid out with award winning gardens and both young and old will find there is plenty here to keep them amused such as fairground rides, a toddlers' play room and a gift shop.

GODREVY POINT
5 miles NW of Camborne off the B3301

Marking the northern edge of St Ives Bay, the low cliffs here lead down to a sandy beach on the eastern side of the headland. Godrevy Point is a well known beauty spot that, along with **Navax Point** where seals that can be sighted off shore, is owned by the National

Island and Lighthouse, Godrevy Point

Trust. A short distance from the point lies **Godrevy Island** on which stands a **Lighthouse** that not only provides a useful landmark from both sea and land but also featured in Virginia Woolf's *To the Lighthouse*.

HELSTON

Dating back to Roman times, when it was developed as a port, Helston is the westernmost of Cornwall's five medieval stannary towns. During the early Middle Ages, tin was brought here for assaying and taxing before being shipped from the once

The Bell Inn,

Meneage Street, Helston, Cornwall TR13 8AA
Tel: 01326 572134

Situated right in the heart of Helston, **The Bell Inn** is a traditional small town inn that is easily spotted by its elegant Georgian façade and welcoming open front door. Owned and personally run by Neal and Carol-Jane Hicks, the couple, who only arrived here in spring 2000, have already begun to make a name for the inn and their superb hospitality. Specialising in offering their customers a superb choice of real ales, beer, lagers and cider, The Bell Inn is certainly the place to come to for a drink. What does make this inn special, apart from the relaxed atmosphere, is that customers bring their own food - whatever they wish. A lovely place to enjoy some quiet refreshment whilst discovering the town, The Bell Inn also has, tucked away at the back, a secluded garden. An ancient well provides the centre piece of this landscaped garden and, with both children and dogs welcome, this has to be one of the most family friendly pubs in the area.

busy quaysides. However, in the 13th century a shingle bar formed across the mouth of the River Cober, preventing access to the sea, and goods were transported to the newly formed harbour at Gweek.

Helston's long and colourful history has left it with a legacy of interesting old buildings: **The Blue Anchor Inn** was a hostel for monks in the 15th century whilst 16th century **Angel House** was the former town house of the Godolphin family. In the 1750s, the Earl of Godolphin rebuilt the parish Church of St Michael and, in the churchyard of this unusual granite structure, lies a memorial to Henry Trengrouse, the Helston man responsible for inventing the rocket propelled safely line which saved so many lives around the British coast. Trengrouse devoted himself to its development after the frigate Anson ran aground on nearby Loe Bar in 1807 and 100 people lost their lives unnecessarily. Elsewhere, there are a surprising number of Georgian, Regency and Victorian buildings which all help to give Helston a quaint and genteel air.

Housed in one of the town's old market halls, close to the classical Victorian **Guildhall**, is Helston's **Folk Museum**. Covering local history, the displays here including trades associated with Helston such as fishing, agriculture and mining, along with exhibits depicting domestic life. As well as honouring Henry Trengrouse, the museum also features another famous Helston born man - Bob Fitzsimmons - who was a famous

prize fighter in the late 19th century.

Still very much a market town today, which serves much of the Lizard Peninsula, Helston has managed to escape from the mass tourism that has affected many other Cornish towns. However, what does draw people here is the famous **Festival of the Furry**, or **Flora Dance**, a colourful festival of music and dance. The origins of the name are unclear but it could have been derived from the Middle English word 'ferrie' which suggests a Christian festival or from the Celtic 'feur' which means holiday or fair. As it is held in early May this would suggest that the festival has connections with ancient pagan spring celebrations. There are various stories and legends surrounding the Furry Dance and one tells how the Devil, flying across Cornwall carrying a large stone to block the gates of Hell, was intercepted by St Michael. During the ensuing encounter, the Devil dropped the boulder and the place where it fell became known as Hell's Stone, or Helston. The people of Helston took to the streets dancing to celebrate St Michael's victory and this is said to be the original Furry Dance which takes place on the nearest Saturday to St Michael's Day (8 May).

Just to the northwest of the town lies **Trevarno Estate and Gardens**, a beautiful and rare estate that has a long history that stretches back to 1296 when Randolphus de Trevarno first gave the land its name. Over the centuries the gardens and grounds have been developed and extended so that, today,

Church Street, Helston

Trevarno has become known as one of the finest gardens in the county that displays a great gardening tradition. From walled gardens and Victorian and Georgian gardens to mature woodlands, there are many different styles to be discovered here along with an extensive collection of rare trees and shrubs. The estate's **Gardening Museum** compliments the grounds and highlights the ingenuity of gardeners down the ages by the range of gardening implements that are exhibited here.

To the east of the town lies another interesting attraction that will keep all the family amused for hours - **Flambards Victorian Village**. With its recreation of a lamp lit Victorian street where over 50 shops and domestic situations have been authentically furnished and equipped, a visit to Flambards it is just like taking a step back in time. However, there is much more to see and do here: the Britain in the Blitz, a recreated bombed street from World War II; the award winning gardens and the country's most southerly rollercoaster.

Close to Flambards is the Royal Navy's land and sea rescue headquarters at **Culdrose**. One of the largest and busiest helicopter bases in Europe, aircraft from here have been responsible for a great many successful search and rescue operations since the base was established in the 1940s. Though not open to the public, there is a special public viewing area from which the comings and goings of the helicopters can be observed.

AROUND HELSTON

GWEEK
3 miles E of Helston off the A394

Situated at the westernmost branch of the River Helford, Gweek was once an important commercial port that grew up after nearby Helston harbour became silted in the 13th century. The same fate befell Gweek many years later and today it is a picturesque village that has replaced it cargo vessels with small pleasure craft. However, the village has maintained links with its maritime past and the rejuvenated harbour now plays host to such delights as craft shops and small boatyards.

Just a short distance from the centre of Gweek, and found along the north side of the creek, is the **National Seal Sanctuary**, the country's leading marine rescue centre. Established over 40 years ago, the centre cares for many sick, injured and orphaned seals as well as being home to a community of seals and sea lions who are unable to fend for themselves. Visitors to the sanctuary can not only witness the joyful antics of the seals at feeding time but also explore the **Woodland Nature Quest** around an ancient coppiced wood.

LIZARD PENINSULA
Area SE of Helston on the A3083

Physically separate from the main part of Cornwall and with a unique landscape the Lizard Peninsula has been designated an Area of Outstanding Natural Beauty. Must of the coastline around this most southerly part of mainland Britain is in the hands of the National Trust and the **South West Coast Path** winds around the peninsula providing

THE SHIPWRIGHT'S ARMS,

Helford, near Helston, Cornwall TR12 6JX
Tel: 01326 231235

Dating back to the early 18th century **The Shipwright's Arms** is one of the best known and certainly one of the most attractive inn's on the Lizard Peninsula. With a tiered garden leading down to the River Helford and a real olde worlde air, it is easy to believe that this charming thatched building was once the haunt of smugglers. Run today by experienced landlords, Charles and Maria Herbert visitors can relax and enjoy the superb hospitality. As well as having a well stocked bar, The Shipwright's Arms is famous locally for the excellent home-cooked food that is on offer. Fish is a speciality and, when available, the crab and lobster should certainly not be overlooked although the inn has many other tasty dishes from which to choose.

beautiful scenery for walkers of all ages and abilities. From the luxurious greenery of the Helford River to the dramatic cliffs around Kynance, Mullion and Lizard Point, there is a variety of landscape that is matched only by the vast range of both rare and common plants and many species of birds that make this their home.

The Lizard is also known for its unique Serpentine rock, a green mineral that became fashionable in Victorian times when ornaments were, and still are, made as souvenirs and objects d'art.

MAWGAN
3½ miles E of Helston off the B3293

This small village lies beside a creek in the Helford estuary that inspired the setting for Daphne du Maurier's novel *The Frenchman's*

Creek. An isolated inlet that is overhung with trees, the creek is more reminiscent of the Amazonian rainforest than Cornwall and many local people down the ages have believed that the area is haunted.

Trelowarren House, in the village, is an impressive part-Tudor country mansion, that has been the home of the Vyvyan family since the 15th century.

HELFORD
6½ miles E of Helston off the B3293

This picture postcard village stands on the secluded tree lined southern bank of the Helford estuary and it must be one of the most attractive settings in the whole of the county. Once the haunt of smugglers, who took advantage of the estuary's many isolated creeks and inlets, the series of deep tidal creeks in the area are rumoured to be the home of Morgawr, the legendary Helford monster. The first recorded sighting of Morgawr was in 1926 and, ever since, there have been numerous other sightings of this "hideous, hump-backed creature with stumpy horns".

Now a popular sailing centre, this charming and relaxed village is also linked, during the summer, to Helford Passage, across the river, by a ferry.

Helford Jetty and Ferry

Helford

ST ANTHONY
8 miles E of Helston off the B3293

This small and remote hamlet, on the northern bank of the Gillan Creek, is little more than a cluster of old cottages and a church. Said to have been founded by shipwrecked Norman sailors grateful that they

St Anthony Head from St Anthony

had reached dry land, the Church of St Anthony does, in some ways, verify this claim as it is built of a stone that is not found in Cornwall but in Normandy.

PORTHKERRIS DIVERS,

St Keverne, near Helston, Cornwall TR12 6QJ
Tel: 01326 280620 Fax: 01326 280620
e-mail: mike@porthkerrisdiver.demon.co.uk
website: www.porthkerrisdiver.demon.co.uk

Found on the sheltered, eastern coast of the Lizard Peninsula, **Porthkerris Divers** is a very different establishment which offers excellent facilities for diving, fishing and other

watersports. A family business, this resort is staffed by experts and the aim here is to introduce as

many people as possible to the delights of both under and above water activities. Courses are run at all levels and can be tailored to anyone's specific needs. Back on dry land, Porthkerris Divers is also home to a flourishing ostrich farm and there is also a superb restaurant at the centre. As well as enjoying the glorious views from the windows, diners at the Conservatory Restaurant are treated to a delicious home-cooked meal.

The Paris Hotel,

Coverack, Cornwall TR12 6SX
Tel: 01326 280258 Fax: 01326 280774

Found in the heart of this charming and unspoilt fishing village and surrounded on three sides by the sea, **The Paris Hotel** provides excellent hospitality to all those coming here. Built in 1907, by the Redruth Brewery Company, the hotel is named after a ship which, in 1899, was grounded on the rocks that guard the approach to Coverack harbour. Finally salvaged and rebuilt in Belfast, she was renamed the *Philadelphia*. In addition to being remembered in the name of this hotel there is a scale model of the ship in the bar area. Not surprisingly the main theme is the sea and shipwrecks, and throughout the hotel the pictures and memorabilia illustrate this to great effect.

With the harbour just across the road, fish and seafood features heavily on the à la carte menu offered in the comfortable restaurant overlooking the sea. For less formal dining there is available a tempting bar menu. Meanwhile, those staying in the well appointed en suite guest rooms will also be able to watch the activity of this still busy harbour.

Seaview Chalet and Caravan Park,

Gwendreath, Kennack Sands, Ruan Minor,
near Helston, Cornwall TR12 7LZ
Tel: 01326 290635 or 01326 290836

With spectacular views over Kennack Bay, **Seaview Chalet and Caravan Park** is a superbly positioned holiday location on England's most southerly point. In the heart of an area of outstanding natural beauty and only 10 minutes walk away, through a wooded valley, to safe sandy beaches, this spacious and well maintained holiday park is ideal for a relaxing family holiday. Owned and personally run, since June 1997, by Keith, Les and Judy Snaith and their close friend Jeffrey Fenton, this friendly park offers holidaymakers a wide range of accommodation as well as excellent facilities such as the heated indoor swimming pool, sauna, solarium, children's adventure play ground and park shop. The accommodation comprises family sized cottages and chalets, modern, spacious caravans and there is also a site for touring caravans and campers. Any one wishing to take a rest from the kitchen will also be glad of the park's popular licensed restaurant, just the place to relax after a day out sightseeing.

A path from the church leads to **Dennis Head**, from which there are views across Falmouth Bay to **St Anthony Head**, and the hamlet has its own small beach of sand and shingle that is also used by sailing boats and sailboarders.

ST KEVERNE
9 miles SE of Helston off the B3293

This pleasant village, which is something of a focal point for this part of the Lizard Peninsula, has a handsome square, an unusual feature in a Cornish village. St Keverne's elevated position, on a high plateau, has led to its church spire long being used as a landmark for ships attempting to negotiate

the treacherous rocks, **The Manacles**, which lie just offshore. In the churchyard are some 400 graves to those who have fallen victim to the dangerous reef and, as well as a stone marking the graves of nearly 200 emigrants who drowned in 1855 on their way to Canada, there is a large granite cross marking the mass grave of the 106 passengers and crew who lost their lives when the *Mohegan* floundered on the rocks in 1898.

Just outside St Keverne, a statue commemorates the 500th anniversary of the **Cornish Rebellion** of 1497 and, back in the church, is a plaque in memory of the executed rebel leaders.

Whilst the sea has dominated the life of St

Coverack Harbour

Keverne for centuries the village also has an agricultural heritage and here the ancient custom of Crying the Neck is continued. Dating back to pagan times, when it was believed that the corn spirit resided in the last wheatsheaf cut, on the last day of harvest, the last wheatsheaf, or neck, is taken to the farmhouse where it is plaited and hung over the fireplace until the spring when it is ploughed back into the ground.

COVERACK
10 miles SE of Helston on the B3294

This old and unspoilt fishing village, where crab, mullet and monkfish are still landed at the small harbour, has a sheltered, sweeping beach of sand and shingle. Once the haunt of smugglers, Coverack was, for many years, home to an RNLI station because of its proximity to The Manacles.

GOONHILLY DOWNS
5½ miles SE of Helston off the B3293

This area of windswept granite and Serpentine heathland is littered with prehistoric remains including some large Neolithic standing stones that are thought to have been erected to aid communication with the heavenly gods. Rather more up-to-date communications can be explored at the **Earth Satellite Station** whose giant dishes can be seen from many miles away. The largest such station in the world, the Earth Station was

opened in the 1960s and, since then, there have been few world events that have not been transmitted or received through here. The guided tour around the station, which takes in all manner of telecommunications including the internet and videophone links, is a fascinating and rewarding experience.

POLTESCO
8½ miles SE of Helston off the A3083

Just a few minutes walk from this pretty National Trust owned village lies the deserted **Carleon Cove** which was, until the early 19th century, a busy pilchard fishing and processing harbour. However, with the rise in interest in Serpentine stone, the processing buildings were converted into a factory to work the stone and the pilchard cellars were extended to house steam engines. The finished articles, from ornaments to shop fronts, were carried to the waiting ships on flat bottomed barges at the start of a journey that could lead half way across the world. All that now remains of the stone works is the ruined warehouse.

Earth Station, Goonhilly Downs

CADGWITH
9 miles SE of Helston off the A3083

Fishermen at Cadgwith Beach

This minuscule and very picturesque fishing village, with its cluster of pastel coloured thatched cottages and two shingle beaches, is, perhaps, everyone's idea of the typical Cornish village. However, in the 19th century this was a busy pilchard fishing centre and the fleet from Cadgwith, in 1904, landed a record 1,798,000 pilchards in just over four days.

Separating the main cove here from Little Cove, is **The Todden**, a grass covered mushroom of land. A walk to Little Cove also leads to the curiously named **Devil's Frying Pan**, a collapsed sea cave that is filled with water at high tide.

THE OLD PILCHARD CELLAR RESTAURANT,

Cadgwith Cove, near Helston, Cornwall TR12 7JU
Tel: 01326 290727

The **Old Pilchard Cellar Restaurant** is a wonderful place that is housed in a listed building that dates back to 1782 and was originally used for the pressing and salting of pilchards. A quaint and extremely atmospheric building, the restaurant is owned and personally run by Michael and Mark, who were both fishermen in the cove for many years, and Mark does still fish with some of his catch ending up on the tables here. Opening all day as a café the character changes in the evening when the cobbled courtyard is transformed by candles and lanterns. Naturally the speciality here is fish and seafood and fresh shellfish, lobster and scallops from the fishermen of Cadgwith feature heavily on the menu. This is a superb fish restaurant that offers charm, character and the smell of the sea as well as fabulous food.

THE WAVE CREST CAFÉ,

Lizard Point, Cornwall TR12 7NU
Tel: 01326 290898

Situated on England's most southerly point and overlooking the old lifeboat station **The Wave Crest Café** is one of the county's best known places. First established in 1927, this famous café was taken over by Elizabeth Hart and her mother Joan in 1964 and they have been personally running it ever since. Open every day during the summer from mid morning, the café serves all manner of beverages, home-made hot and cold meals and snacks ice creams. As well as being a superb place to relax and enjoy the spectacular view, The Wave Crest Café also lies on the well used coastal path and is a wonderful place to stop for refreshment, a rest and charming hospitality when on a long walk.

Lighthouse at the Lizard

LIZARD
10 miles SE of Helston on the A3083

The most southerly village in mainland Britain, Lizard is a place of craft shops, cafés, art galleries and an inn, all clustered around the village green. Following a visit to Cornwall by Queen Victoria in the 19th century, when she ordered many items made from Serpentine stone for her new house on the Isle of Wight, Osborne, this richly coloured green stone has been popular and Lizard is a centre for its polishing and fashioning into ornaments.

To the south of the village lies **Lizard Point**, the tip of the Lizard Peninsula, whose three sides of high cliffs are lashed by the waves whatever the season. There has been a form of lighthouse on Lizard Point since the early 17th century but the present **Lighthouse**, which warns ships away from the treacherous cliffs, was built in 1751 despite protests from the locals fearing that they would lose a regular source of income from looting ships wrecked around the point.

KYNANCE COVE
9 miles S of Helston off the A3083

A famed beauty spot, that is owned by the National Trust, Kynance Cove has a marvellous sandy beach and dramatic offshore rock formations. A favourite

destination with wealthy Victorians, after a visit here by Prince Albert and his children in 1846, one of the giant rocks on the beach became known as **Albert Rock**. Meanwhile, out to sea is **Asparagus Island**, where, at one time, wild asparagus grew. The cove is also the site of the largest outcrop of Serpentine rock, the rock unique to the Lizard, that is dark, mottled and veined with green, red and white. The caves to the west of the cove can be explored around low tide and these include the **Devil's Bellows**, a cave that, at high tide, becomes a dramatic blowhole.

Kynance Cove

MULLION COVE
6 miles S of Helston on the B3296

The pretty, weather worn harbour here is overlooked by a few ancient buildings and huge walls of Serpentine rock. Much of the land surrounding this secluded cove of white

Mullion Cove

largest settlement on the Lizard Peninsula and an ideal base from which to explore this remarkable part of the county. The parish church, dedicated to the French saint, Malo (or Mellane of Rennes), has some interestingly carved bench ends and there is also a 'dog door' in the south door that was used by sheep dogs who were allowed to attend church with their masters. This sturdy 15th century building also has a tower built of granite and Serpentine rock.

sand, as well as the harbour and offshore **Mullion Island**, is owned by the National Trust and the views from here extend westwards, across Mount's Bay, to Penzance and Newlyn.

MULLION
5 miles S of Helston on the B3296

A mile inland lies the village of **Mullion**, the

POLDHU POINT
5 miles S of Helston off the A3083

A memorial on the cliffs above the popular sandy beach of Poldhu Cove, commemorates the work of Guglielmo Marconi, the radio pioneer who transmitted the first wireless message across the Atlantic from here in 1901. Marconi had chosen this lonely spot a year earlier and had gone on to build one of the

MULLION COVE HOTEL,

Mullion, Cornwall TR12 7EP
Tel: 01326 240328 Fax: 01326 240998
e-mail: mullion.cove@btinternet.com
website: www.mullioncove.com

Commanding spectacular views from its cliff top position over Mullion Cove to St Michael's Mount and Penzance, **Mullion Cove Hotel** certainly has one of the best coastal locations in Cornwall. A striking white building, erected at the beginning of the 20th

century by the Cornish Railway, this large and spacious hotel has

much to offer holidaymakers who are seeking a quiet and relaxing place to stay with a discreet and friendly staff.

The splendid outlook can be enjoyed from the tranquillity of the hotel's cosy lounge and the dining room also has the same view. Eating here is certainly a pleasure not to be missed and the menus are a sumptuous blend of local seafood and fish combined with other locally sourced produce that is expertly prepared by a team of talented chefs. Predinner drinks are served in the conservatory bar, a pleasant place to meet other guests and also watch the sun setting over Land's End.

Finally, the hotel's 32 luxury en suite guest rooms provide all that is needed for a restful night's sleep.

largest wireless stations in the world - the pylons and aerials of which survived until the 1930s. The small granite obelisk, the **Marconi Monument**, was unveiled by his daughter after the inventor's death.

GUNWALLOE
4 miles S of Helston off the A3083

A tiny fishing hamlet with a charming cove, in 1785 a ship carrying a consignment of gold coins ran aground in adjoining **Church Cove** and this place is still popular with treasure hunters who comb the sands with metal detectors hoping to unearth more coins from the sunken galleon. The 15th century Church of St Winwaloe, which gives the cove its name, lies protected in the sand dunes behind

the rounded cliffs of Castle Mound and its bell tower has been, unusually, built separately right into the rock.

PORTHLEVEN
2 miles SW of Helston on the B3304

This pleasant fishing town developed in the 19th century when, in 1811, London industrialists built its three section harbour to export tin and import mining machinery. Although this scheme to establish Porthleven as a major tin exporting centre failed, the inner basin can still be sealed off from the worst of the southwesterly gales. A number of the small town's old industrial fixtures have been converted into handsome craft galleries, restaurants and shops and the charming old

---

MULLION GALLERY,

Nansmellyon Road, Mullion, near Helston, Cornwall TR12 7DQ
Tel: 01326 241170 e-mail: mulliongallery@supanet.com website: www.mulliongallery.co.uk

Found just outside the village, on the way to Mullion Cove, **Mullion Gallery** is a wonderful place that is dedicated to the many artists who live and work on the Lizard Peninsula. Established by owners, Agnes and Tony Lewis in 1990, Agnes originally started the gallery for local artists who had nowhere to display their work and, since then, the gallery has gone from strength to strength. As well as work by

well established names on display here the gallery also promotes lesser known but equally highly skilled artists and there is sure to be plenty of interest to anyone who is visiting the area. Whilst the gallery began with the work of painters, other craftspeople have also been inspired by the natural beauty of the Lizard Peninsula and their work can be found here too. From pottery and metal sculpture to engraved glass and woodcarvings, there is a wide range of artefacts here that provide a unique and special memento of a holiday in this area.

THE OLD VICARAGE,

Mullion, near Helston, Cornwall TR12 7DQ
Tel: 01326 240898 Fax: 01326 240879
website: www.accomodata.co.uk/061298.htm
or www.SmoothHound.co.uk/hotels/oldvicar.html
The Old Vicarage is the home of Jacqui Valender and her family. It is a large and spacious house with many original features and is set in delightful gardens near the centre of Mullion. The front of the house was added onto the existing vicarage in 1834 and has an interesting history. Conan Doyle stayed here

and included The Old Vicarage in his Sherlock Holmes novel "*The Devils Foot*". Jacqui's love of decorating and furnishing is apparent throughout the house. The four guest rooms - each having it's own bathroom - are situated at the front of the house and thus enjoy the views towards the sea. The relaxed and warm atmosphere of this family home, where all ages are welcome, makes The Old Vicarage a special place to stay.

harbour is overlooked by an assortment of attractive residential terraces and fishermen's cottages. One street is named after Porthleven's most famous son, Guy Gibson, the inventor of the famous bouncing bombs used in the Dambusters raids during World War II. A popular and pleasant town, Porthleven is gaining a gastronomic reputation as there are many excellent and tempting restaurants and inns to be found here in such a small area.

When the shingle bar formed across the mouth of the River Cober in the 13th century and dammed the river, it created the largest natural freshwater lake in Cornwall. Lying just to the east of Porthleven and once forming part of the Penrose estate (which is now owned by the National Trust) **Loe Pool** is a haven for sea birds as well as waterfowl and is surrounded by the woodlands of the old estate.

A Cornish folk tale links Loe Pool with the Arthurian legend of the Lady of the Lake: like Bodmin Moor's Dozmary Pool, a hand is said to have risen from the depths of the water to catch the dying King Arthur's sword. Another local story connects **Loe Bar** with the legendary rogue, Jan Tregeagle, who was set the task of weaving a rope from its sand as a punishment.

THE FAYREWAY RESTAURANT,

Mullion Golf Club, Cury, near Helston, Cornwall TR12 7BP
Tel: 01326 241231

Housed in Mullion Golf Club's clubhouse but privately run by experienced Anne Hobbs, **The Fayreway Restaurant** is just the place to enjoy lunch before or after a round of golf or a relaxing dinner. Open to members, green fee players and invited guests of the club this excellent restaurant also overlooks this attractive links course and customers can watch as players tee off and hole out. For lunchtime, Anne offers an extensive menu of wholesome dishes that are particularly designed to fortify golfers before or after playing. The all day breakfast and the mixed grills being favourites with many but there is sure to be something to suit everyone. On Sunday's there is a popular carvery lunch that is very well attended. The evening à la carte menu provides a sumptuous choice of dishes that make the very best of locally sourced produce and the mix of traditional English cuisine with tastes from Europe makes the choice an interesting one. However, once a month, Anne really excels when she puts on the very popular and entertaining themed evenings and the choice of menu here provides an excellent opportunity for her to show her creativity and flair in the kitchen.

TREGADDRA FARMHOUSE,

Cury, near Helston, Cornwall TR12 7BB
Tel: 01326 240235 Fax: 01326 240235

Dating back to the early 18th century and set within a well kept garden, **Tregaddra Farmhouse** lies at the centre of a working arable and beef farm. The home of Jon and June Lugg, whose family have lived here since 1864, the couple first began welcoming bed and breakfast guests in 1992 and have not looked back since. Although the farmhouse

has been completely modernised the work has been undertaken sympathetically and the result has left a comfortable home which retains much of its original character. One of the more interesting features is the splendid inglenook fireplace in the lounge which comes alive when the logs are lit on colder nights. As well as the six superb en suite guest rooms, some of which have balconies overlooking the garden, guests can also make use of the outdoor swimming pool, tennis court and relax in the large sun lounge. The wonderful farmhouse breakfast and excellent evening meal served here both use fresh home grown produce when in season and are a treat not to be missed.

7 Penzance and Land's End

This, the most southwesterly area of mainland Britain - a region often referred to as Penwith - juts out into the Atlantic and as a result of the warm waters of the Gulf stream experiences

Tate Gallery, St Ives

a mild climate. The area has been settled for over 4000 years and, dotted around the lonely and under-populated countryside, there are numerous prehistoric relics. The Iron Age village of Carn Euny, the Merry Maidens standing stones and Zennor Quoit are just some of the ancient remains that are well worth visiting. First fishing and then the tin and copper mining industries were the economic mainstay of this region and, whilst many of the little seaports have now become picturesque holiday villages, Newlyn is still one of the busiest fish landing ports in the country. Reminders of the days of mining abound and, near Pendeen, there are the Geevor Tin Mine and Heritage Centre and the Levant Beam Engine which give an excellent insight into what was, until the beginning of the 20th century, a vast industry in southwest Cornwall.

This area has also, since the 1880s, become a place for artists who come here for the clear, natural light as well as the spectacular scenery. St Ives and Newlyn both still have large communities of painters and sculptors and, as a result, there are numerous commercial galleries as well as the superb Tate Gallery and Newlyn Art Gallery displaying their works.

Sunset, Land's End

However, one of the most famous places in Great Britain, Land's End, is most people destination when visiting Penwith. The dramatic series of steep granite cliffs, the most western point in Britain, are a great pull and, as well as enjoying the view out over the Atlantic, the area around Land's End has a series of exhibitions that are connected with the people and surrounding area. Whilst a visit to this point is a must on everyone's itinerary, other places equally worthy of visiting for their beauty alone are the almost perfect fishing village of Mousehole and Marazion, from where the spectacular granite island of St Michael's Mount, sitting out in Mount's Bay can be both seen and visited.

PENZANCE AND LAND'S END

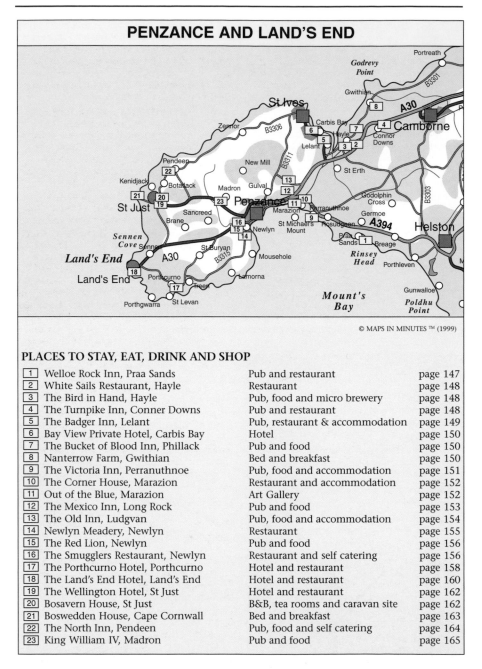

© MAPS IN MINUTES ™ (1999)

PLACES TO STAY, EAT, DRINK AND SHOP

ST IVES

With its five sandy beaches, maze of narrow streets and picturesque harbour and headland, this beautifully situated old fishing town still retains much of its charm despite being deluged with tourists for much of the late spring, summer and early autumn. The original settlement of St Ives took its name from the 6th century missionary, St Ia, who is said to have landed here having sailed from Ireland on an ivy leaf. The 15th century parish church, near the harbour, bears her name, along with those of the two fishermen Apostles St Peter and St Andrew. Nearby on **St Ives Head**, stands another ecclesiastical building, the mariners' Chapel of St Nicholas.

Known locally as **The Island**, St Ives Head is also home to a Huer's Hut, from where a lookout would scan the sea looking for shoals of pilchards. One of the most important pilchard fishing centres in Cornwall, until the industry declined in the early 20th century, St Ives holds a record dating back to 1868 for the greatest number of fish caught in a single

St Ives Beach and Island

seine net. On catch days, the streets of St Ives would reek of the smell of pilchard oil as the fish were pressed before being salted and packed ready to be despatched throughout Europe. A local speciality, heavy or hevva cake, was traditionally made for the seiners on their return from fishing.

As well as providing shelter for the fishing fleet, St Ives' harbour was developed for exporting locally mined ores and minerals and the sturdy main pier was built by John Smeaton, the 18th century marine architect who was responsible for designing the famous Eddystone Lighthouse. The town's two industries led to the labyrinth of narrow streets and alleyways to become divided into two communities: Downalong, where the fishing families lived, and Upalong, a district of mining families. In fact, **St Ives Museum** is housed in a building belonging to an old mine and here can be seen a wide range of artefacts that chronicle the natural, industrial and maritime history of the area. There is also a display here dedicated to the exploits of one of St Ives most colourful people, John Knill. Mayor of the town in 1767 and a customs officer by profession, it was widely rumoured that Knill was an energetic smuggler himself and that the tall monument he built to the south of the town, supposedly as his mausoleum, served to guide ships carrying contraband safely to the shore. Though buried in London, Knill left a bequest to the town so that, every five years, they could hold a ceremony in his honour when a procession, led by a fiddler, two widows and 10 young ladies, dance from the town centre to his monument and then sing the Hundredth Psalm.

As both the fishing and mining industries declined in the late 19th century, St Ives developed as an artists' colony. Since the 1880s, the town has attracted many diverse painters, brought here by the special quality of the light, and they have included such talents as Turner, Whistler, Sickert, McNeill, Munnings and Hepworth. Many of the old pilchard cellars and sail lofts were converted into studios and a 'St Ives School' quickly became established which gained an international reputation.

Art still dominates the town and, as well as the numerous private galleries there is the **Tate Gallery**, on a hillside overlooking the beach of Porthmeor, where the work of 20th

Barbara Hepworth Sculpture Garden

century painters and sculptors is permanently on display. More intimately, there is also the **Barbara Hepworth Sculpture Garden and Museum** at Trewyn Studio, where she lived and worked until her death, in a fire, in 1975. Among the many pieces of her work displayed in the garden, visitors can also see the little summerhouse where Barbara used to rest in the afternoons and her workshop, which has been left untouched since her death.

However, it is not only artists that have been inspired by the beauty of St Ives and the surrounding area. As a child in the late 19th century, Virginia Woolf holidayed in the town, staying at Talland House overlooking St Ives Bay. Said to be the happiest time of her life, she recaptures the mood of those days in her novel, *To the Lighthouse*. Although Rosamunde Pilcher was born close to St Ives in 1924, she moved away long before publishing her two novels *The Day of the Storm* and *The Shell Seekers*, but they both have Cornish settings.

AROUND ST IVES

GODOLPHIN CROSS
8 miles SE of St Ives off the B3302

To the northwest of the village lies **Godolphin House**, an exceptional part Tudor, part Stuart house that still retains its original

Elizabethan stables. The former home of the Earls of Godolphin, a prominent Cornish family who made their fortune through mining, the house is noted for its splendid King's Room, fine Jacobean fireplaces and the unique north front which was completed shortly after the Civil War and incorporates an impressive granite colonnade. Meanwhile, outside, the gardens still retain traces of their original ancient raised walks and the carp ponds. However, it is the family itself that is most interesting: one Godolphin, Sidney the poet, was killed during the Civil War whilst supporting the king; Sidney, the 1st Earl was a Lord High Treasurer; and it was the 2nd Earl who imported the famous Godolphin Arabian, one of the three stallions from which all British thoroughbreds are descended. A painting of this magnificent horse, by John Wootton, hangs in the Dining Room. Used as a location for the *Poldark* television series, Godolphin House has limited opening.

BREAGE
9 miles SE of St Ives off the A394

Pronounced Braig (to rhyme with vague), this village is noted for the superb 15th century wall paintings that were discovered in the parish Church of St Breaca in the 19th century. The building too dates from the same time and this remarkable set of murals, which feature such subjects as St Christopher and Christ blessing the trades, lay beneath a layer of whitewash until the 1890s. Meanwhile, in the north aisle there is a rare Roman milestone from the 3rd century AD that provides evidence that the tin was extracted here on behalf of the Roman Empire.

RINSEY
9 miles SE of St Ives off the A394

Around this hamlet is evidence of tin mining: to the east is **Wheal Prosper**, where the restored 19th century engine house can be seen and, further on, there are the ruins of another copper mine, **Wheal Trewavas.**

PRAA SANDS
8 miles SE of St Ives off the A394

Two headlands and high dunes enclose the mile long crescent of sand that have helped to build Praa Sands reputation as one of the

Praa Sands Beach

finest family beaches in Cornwall. An ideal place for bathing and surfing, the beach here never gets too crowded and the village

provides a variety of accommodation that is suitable for a small family resort.

GERMOE
7½ miles SE of St Ives off the A394

This small rural village is home to the ancient Church of St Germoe, or St Germochus, an Irish king and missionary who was the brother of St Breaca. Dating from the 12th century, the present church contains a remarkable Celtic font that is carved with a mysterious human head. Meanwhile, built into the churchyard wall is **St Germoe's Chair**, a curious covered seat under which, some believe, St Germoe was buried.

ROSUDGEON
7 miles SE of St Ives on the A394

A narrow, winding lane from the village leads to **Prussia Cove**, a clifftop settlement that was

WELLOE ROCK INN,

Praa Sands, near Penzance, Cornwall TR20 9TQ
Tel: 01736 763516

Overlooking the beach at Praa Sands, the **Welloe Rock Inn** has been here since 1975 and it is named after a rock that lies out at sea. The views from the front terrace of the inn are quite outstanding and, just a few steps away, customers will find themselve on this well known beach. John Andrews bought the inn in 1991 and he continues to personally run this popular establishment that sees many people coming here to enjoy the superb hospitality as well as the location. As well as the well stocked bar, where there are always at least two real ales on tap, there is a tempting menu of tasty bar snacks that are sure to please those who have been spending time on the beach. There is also an attractive restaurant, where booking is essential for their traditional Sunday lunches, that offers hungry customers a wide range of delicious dishes. Fish is the house speciality and the selection of dishes here is both interesting and imaginative. Finally, Welloe Rock Inn is gaining a reputation for the high standard of live music that is presented here on Friday evenings and Sunday lunchtime.

WHITE SAILS RESTAURANT,

17-19 Commercial Road, Hayle, Cornwall TR27 4DE
Tel: 01736 753272

Situated on Hayle's main street and with a secluded rear patio overlooking the Hayle estuary, **White Sails Restaurant** is a charming and attractive place for a delicious evening meal out. Owned and personally run by Rob and Debbie Evans, not only does this restaurant have an enviable reputation for the high standard of cuisine served here but it also has a very pleasant atmosphere that is just perfect for a relaxing meal. Beautifully decorated and furnished throughout, customers are treated to a splendid menu that is supplemented daily by the tempting specials board. As well as fish, which features heavily here, the well chosen list of tasty dishes includes such delights as Goats' cheese and red onion tart, Sirloin Vignerons and Pork fillet with Bramley compote. Combining the very best of fresh local produce and prepared in a modern European style, this imaginative and interesting menu is sure to provide customers with a difficult yet enjoyable decision when it comes to choosing a meal. Children are welcome at the White Sails and, during the high season, it is essential to book a table.

THE BIRD IN HAND,

Trelissick Road, Hayle, Cornwall TR27 4HY
Tel: 01736 753974 Fax: 01736 753974

Found adjacent to Hayle's popular attraction, Paradise Park, **The Bird in Hand** is a rather grand building that was originally the old coaching house to the park before being converted into an inn in the 1970s. Both inside and out there are many reminders of this building's past life and, in such interesting surroundings, landlords George and Lesley offer superb hospitality that has gained the inn many regular customers. Well known for serving an excellent range of real ales, there are always six on tap, George has a micro brewery, Wheal Ale Brewery and his two ales, Millers and Speckled Parrot can also be tasted here. Although there is no food served throughout the winter, during the season a traditional menu of pub grub is on offer that is supplemented by the everchanging specials board. During the summer, when the weather allows, barbecues are held in the attractive and very well maintained rear beer garden whilst, throughout the year, there is a popular happy hour. An inn with a difference, The Bird in Hand provides its customers, both old and new, with good hospitality in charming surroundings.

THE TURNPIKE INN,

Turnpike Road, Connor Downs, near Hayle, Cornwall TR27 5DT
Tel: 01736 752377 e-mail: robertsaxby@care4free.net

Once believed to have been called The Why Not, **The Turnpike Inn** is a late 17th and early 18th century property that lies in the centre of Connor Downs. Although landlords, Robert and Monica Saxby have only been here since 1999, they have plenty of experience in the trade and this shows in the excellent hospitality that is offered here to both locals and visitors alike. With a secluded beer garden and patio seating to the front, this is an ideal place to come to during the summer whilst, the interior of this old inn is warm and cosy - perfect on a cold winter's night. There are always at least three real ales served from the bar, as well as a good selection of draught ales, bitters, lagers and stouts. Served in the bar or in the inn's small restaurant, a delicious menu of home-cooked dishes is sure to please everyone and, while fish from nearby Newlyn is the house speciality, there is also a superb roast lunch on Sundays that proves popular. Along with the friendly welcome, good food and charming hospitality, The Turnpike proves to be a lovely country inn for all the family.

named after a notorious 18th century smuggler, John Carter, who modelled himself on Frederick the Great. One story surrounding this unsavoury man tells how he used a cannon mounted on the cliffs to scare off revenue officers. The smugglers' wheel tracks can still be seen in the steep stone slipway leading up from the water's edge.

HAYLE
3 miles SE of St Ives on the B3302

Established in the 18th century as an industrial village where copper was smelted and foundries made industrial machinery, Hayle was also a seaport with a harbour in the shelter of Hayle estuary. It was here, in the early 1800s, that the great Cornish inventor, Richard Trevithick built an early version of the steam locomotive and, not long afterwards, one of the first railways in the world was constructed to carry tin and copper to the town from Redruth and the mines between. At the height of the foundry industry, in the 19th century, steam powered engines built by the famous company, Harveys of Hayle, were being used in the majority of Cornwall's mines and beyond.

Found on the southern outskirts of the town is **Paradise Park**, the country's leading conservation zoo that has won much recognition, both here and around the world, for its work. This sanctuary is home to some of the world's rarest and most beautiful birds, including the Cornish chough that is extinct in the wild, and various other animals such as

otters and squirrels. Set in wonderful gardens and with something new to see on a regular basis this is a superb place for all the family. Meanwhile, the Hayle estuary and sands around the town are an ornithologists delight.

LELANT
2½ miles SE of St Ives on the A3074

A thriving seaport in the Middle Ages, until the silting up of the Hayle estuary caused traffic through here to divert to St Ives, Lelant is now a popular holiday village with a golf course and a scenic rail link to St Ives. Though little remains from the heyday of the port here, the parish church, which overlooks the golf course, dates from the 15th century and it is dedicated to St Uny, a Celtic saint said to be the brother of St Ia.

Overlooking the saltflats of the Hayle estuary, Lelant is another place particularly popular with ornithologists who come here to view a wide variety of wildfowl and waders and, near by, in the grounds of Quay House, is an RSPB hide that is open to everyone.

CARBIS BAY
1 mile SE of St Ives off the A3074

The sheltered beach here is ideal for families as it is safe for children and there are various watersports available. Easy to reach on foot from St Ives, there is a footpath along the cliffs - at low tide the more adventurous may like to walk along the exposed sands to Lelant.

THE BADGER INN,

Fore Street, Lelant, near St Ives, Cornwall TR26 3JT
Tel: 01736 752181 Fax: 01736 759398

Dating back to the 1800s and found in the heart of Lelant, **The Badger Inn** is one of Cornwall's top places and it comes highly recommended for its food and hospitality. Managed by landlords, Robin and Mary Allen, this charming inn has award winning gardens to the rear, complete with sun trap patio seating and the interior is just as attractive - the conservatory restaurant is more like an indoor garden. As well as being just the place to come to for a fine pint of real ales, there are always several from which to choose, The Badger Inn has a superb menu that must be seen to be believed. Featuring plenty of fresh local produce and fish from nearby Newlyn and St Ives, the inn's chefs create a wonderful array of dishes and they are particularly noted for their heart-warming casseroles and pasta dishes. Meanwhile the splendid carvery, served throughout the week and not just on Sundays, also proves to be a draw here. Add to this the marvellous en suite accommodation in six beautiful guest rooms and The Badger Inn is an ideal country inn.

Bay View Private Hotel,

Headland Road, Carbis Bay, near St Ives,
Cornwall TR26 2NX
Tel: 01736 796469 Fax: 01736 796469

Just a short walk away from the beautiful beach at Carbis Bay,
the **Bay View Private Hotel** is an outstanding establishment
that provides guests with a real homely atmosphere whilst
also offering excellent hospitality. Originally a bungalow built
in the 1960s, well designed additions have created a
comfortable and relaxing environment that is both spacious and stylish. Owned and personally run
by Llew and Linda Beaven since 1988, this charming couple take great pride in ensuring that their
guests have an enjoyable holiday. There are nine well appointed en suite guest rooms which are, like
the rest of the hotel, exceptionally well decorated and furnished. A cosy bar provides the ideal place
to relax with a drink before being treated to Linda's home-cooked dinner. The meals, both breakfast
and dinner, are a feature of the hotel and the delicious dishes can be complemented with a bottle of
wine from the well chosen list. Already in the lovely position, a short walk to Carbis Bay railway
station followed by a coastal train ride to St Ives makes a great day out with no car parking worries.

The Bucket of Blood Inn,

Phillack, near Hayle, Cornwall TR27 5AE
Tel: 01736 752378

Found in the heart of Phillack, a once flourishing port, **The
Bucket of Blood Inn** has an intriguing history that is very
much linked with that of the village. There has been an inn
here for hundreds of years and, as well as being a haven for
travellers, sailors and fishermen, it has also been the haunt
of smugglers and pirates. One morning during those more
desperate days, the innkeeper was drawing water from the
outside well when he found not water but blood in his bucket drawn up from the well. The resulting
search uncovered a corpse - identity unknown. Today, things are much less sinister at the inn, though
it is said to be haunted and, having been in the Shackleton family since 1963, it is now personally run
by Ricky and Sue. A traditional pub with an olde worlde atmosphere it is easy for customers to imagine
the various outlaws who frequented this place. As well as offering a convivial and comfortable
environment in which to enjoy the excellent selection of drinks from the bar, Ricky and Sue also serve
a superb menu which features the very best in fresh local produce.

Nanterrow Farm,

Gwithian, near Hayle, Cornwall TR27 5BP
Tel: 01209 712282

The best way to find **Nanterrow Farm** is to follow owner
Linda Davies' helpful signs from Gwithian through the
country lanes to this splendid and secluded site. Found
in the heart of a 100 acre working farm, the charming
late Georgian farmhouse is a real hidden treasure that
sits surrounded by a small and traditional cottage
garden. The home of Glyn and Linda Davies since the
late 1970s, the couple have been offering wonderful
bed and breakfast accommodation for many years and
the situation certainly could not be more idyllic. Very popular with families who have stayed here
before, Nanterrow Farm offers its visitors a comfortable and pleasant stay in a house where everyone
will feel at home. There are three well furnished guest rooms and children can easily be catered for, and
at breakfast all the visitors sit together for their delicious home-cooked meal - more like a family than
guests. An evening meal can be served on request.

Carbis Bay

GWITHIAN
4 miles E of St Ives on the B3301

This ancient village of thatched cottages and houses, surrounded by sand dunes to the south of Godrevy Point, remains unspoilt. The high dunes, known as **The Towans**, back the long stretch of sandy beach that forms the eastern side of St Ives Bay and they have numerous footpaths running through them that provide perfect picnic areas. A sizeable prehistoric settlement is said to lie buried beneath the Towans, along with a 7th century oratory founded by the Irish missionary, St Gothian.

PERRANUTHNOE
7 miles S of St Ives off the A394

From the village a steep flight of steps lead down to **Perran Sands**, a rocky, sandy beach off which a sand bank sometimes forms that can make swimming hazardous. Overlooking Mount's Bay, to the southeast, the cliffs lead to the jagged **Cudden Point**, where many ships have floundered, and which is now owned by the National Trust.

MARAZION
6 miles S of St Ives off the A394

A port as long ago as the Bronze Age and for

THE VICTORIA INN,

Perranuthnoe, near Penzance, Cornwall TR20 9NP
Tel: 01736 710309 Fax: 01736 710309

Dating back, in parts, to the 12th century, **The Victoria Inn** lies in the heart of the picturesque village of Perranuthnoe and is an ideal place to stop whilst exploring the area around Penzance, Helston and St Michael's Bay. As full of character and olde worlde charm as the exterior would suggest, this cosy, ancient pub provides just the right atmosphere for relaxing and enjoy the splendid hospitality offered by licencee, Sarah Heims. As well as the excellent array of drinks served at the bar, The Victoria Inn has an enviable reputation for the high standard of food served here. Every dish is prepared to order, but is well worth waiting for and, from freshly filled crusty baguettes at lunchtime through to the tasty dishes on the specials board, there is sure to be something here to tempt even the most jaded palate. Having won awards for its food it is necessary to book both at weekends and in the evenings to avoid disappointment at the popular pub. Finally, Sarah also offers bed and breakfast accommodation in three delightful rooms, which blend the charm of this old building with the needs of modern day comfort.

THE CORNER HOUSE,

Fore Street, Marazion, Cornwall TR17 0AD
Tel: 01736 711348

As its name suggests, **The Corner House** can be found on a corner down the main street through this picturesque and historic town. With views over the sea, this premises, which dates back over 100 years, is just the place for both excellent food and good accommodation. Owned and personally run by Richard and Heather Tucker, situated on the ground floor of this attractive building is a cosy and intimate restaurant that has an enviable reputation in this area. The emphasis at this licensed restaurant is very much on home-cooking and fresh local produce and the menu, which is supplemented by a daily specials board, is a tempting list of delightful treats which feature plenty of fresh seafood and fish. Meanwhile, Richard and Heather also offer comfortable bed and breakfast accommodation in a choice of six well appointed en suite guest rooms found in the rest of the building. With a separate entrance from the restaurant and a lovely rear garden for guests to enjoy this is a charming place from which to explore the most southwesterly tip of mainland England.

OUT OF THE BLUE,

The Square, Marazion, Cornwall TR17 0AP
Tel: 01736 719019

Out of the Blue, situated in the heart of this popular Cornish village, is very hard to miss as the exterior of this old building is painted a bright and cheerful blue. Owned and personally run by Glyn Macey, a local painter who was born in nearby Newlyn, this gallery has, since opening in 1995, gained a reputation for the solo exhibitions that it shows on the first floor. Meanwhile, on the ground floor, there is a vast collection of paintings by local artists including Glyn's own work and also the work of local potters and other craftsmen. The simple decor of the gallery shows the work to great effect and whilst there are many original pieces on display there are items here that will suit all pockets and that will also provide a lasting memory of a visit to this charming part of Cornwall.

many centuries the most important settlement around Mount's Bay, Marazion is Cornwall's oldest charter town (the first charter granted here was by Henry III in 1257). Its long history, throughout which the port continued to prosper with the export trade in tin and copper, has left a legacy of fine old inns and residential houses which overlook the fine expanse of sandy beach. Now a windsurfing and sailing centre, to the northwest of the town is **Marazion Marsh**, an RSPB reserve with breeding colonies of grey herons and visiting waders and wildfowl species from the Mediterranean.

ST MICHAEL'S MOUNT
6½ miles S of St Ives off the A394

Situated a third of a mile offshore and connected to Marazion by a cobbled causeway that is exposed at high tide, St Michael's Mount is a remarkable granite outcrop that rises dramatically out of the sea. The steep sided islet has been inhabited since prehistoric times and its Cornish name, 'Carrick luz en cuz' (meaning 'the ancient rock in the wood'), suggests that, at one time, the coastline here was covered in trees. Indeed, the fossilised remains of a forest that once covered the land around St Michael's Mount can be seen at low tide. The rock is named after the Archangel St Michael who, according to legend, appeared to a party of fishermen in a vision in the 5th century.

A place of pilgrimage for centuries, it was Edward the Confessor who, in the 11th century, founded a priory on the mount as the daughter house to the famous Benedictine Mont St Michel in Normandy. The monastery was fortified after the Dissolution in 1539 and, in 1660, it became the home of the St Aubyn family who have lived here until the 1950s when it was donated to the National Trust.

St Michael's Mount

medieval remains, including the Chevy Chase Room which was the original monks' refectory, and there are other interesting details here such as the Strawberry Hill Gothic plaster work in the 18th century Blue Drawing Room, the artefacts in the Map and Museum Rooms and paintings and portraits by artists including the Cornishman John Opie.

PENZANCE

For centuries, this was a remote market town which made its living from fishing, mining and smuggling and, today, it is not only popular with holidaymakers looking to stay in the area but also for those taking the ferry from here to the Isles of Scilly. Along with nearby Newlyn and Mousehole, Penzance was sacked by the Spanish in 1595 and, at the end of the Civil War, it suffered a similar fate as the town had supported the Royalist cause. A major port in the 19th century for the exporting of tin, the fortunes of Penzance were transformed by the arrival of the railway in 1859. Not only could the direct despatch

Incorporating the old monastic buildings into their home, the family have created the marvellous embattled **St Michael's Mount Castle** which shows differing architectural styles from the 17th through to the 19th century. The house contains some impressive

THE MEXICO INN,

Gladstone Terrace, Long Rock,
near Penzance, Cornwall TR20 8JB
Tel: 01736 710625

A famous establishment that is signposted off the main road to Penzance, **The Mexico Inn** is named after a local mine and, although its age is unknown, it has obviously been serving the people of this area for many years. Owned and personally run by Vyvyan and Sally Jenkin, a couple with a great deal of experience in the catering trade, this inn is full of surprises as well as being warm and welcoming.

Full of character and olde worlde charm inside, where the cosy atmosphere is enhanced by the roaring real fires, a collection of excellent paintings by local artists are on display here that are also for sale. Well known for the high quality of the real ales served here, as a Cornish man Vyvyan always ensures that there are two Cornish brews available, but the range of drinks is extensive so that everyone can enjoy their favourite tipple. What, however, makes The Mexico Inn so different is the menu. An comprehensive list of traditional pub food along with a tasty and tempting range of international dishes, where fish features heavily, Sally and Vyvyan have incorporated dishes which use Slimming World's sin value scheme. An excellent idea that has certainly taken off here, everyone in the family can enjoy a meal here whether they are watching their weight or not.

THE OLD INN,

Lower Quarter, Ludgvan, near Penzance, Cornwall TR20 8EG
Tel: 01736 740419 e-mail: clifford@walker70.freeserve.co.uk

The Old Inn, in the heart of Ludgvan, is known to have been here since the mid 18th century though it is probable that the building is older still. A traditional English country inn, in every sense, this is the place to come to for excellent food, drink and hospitality. As full of character and charm as the exterior would suggest, this pub has exposed stone wall, a fire roaring away in the stone fireplace and a mass of gleaming brassware and other memorabilia hanging from the walls. An ideal place to stop for refreshment whilst exploring this part of Cornwall, the bar serves a good selection of all the usual drinks as well as three real ales. The tempting menu of home-cooked dishes ranges from freshly cut sandwiches through to what are now becoming traditional pub dishes such as lasagne, chilli and curry. The ever changing list of daily specials makes a choice harder whilst the house specialities, including the mammoth mixed grill, are always popular. Landlords, Cliff and Jackie Walker, as well as welcoming visitors and locals alike to their delightful inn also provide bed and breakfast in three comfortable guest rooms.

of early flowers, vegetables and locally caught fish to the rest of Britain be undertaken with ease but the railways also brought a great influx of holidaymakers and boosted the town's fledgling industry.

A bustling town and harbour today and home to Cornwall's only promenade, which stretches to Newlyn, Penzance has plenty to offer the visitor. Indeed, along the promenade lies the **Jubilee Swimming Pool**, a wonderful open air sea water pool that still has its original art deco styling. Most of the town's most interesting buildings can be found on Chapel Street which leads down from the domed **Market House**, that was built in 1836, to the quay. Outside the Market House is a statue to Penzance's most famous son, Sir Humphry Davy, the scientist who is best remembered for inventing the miners' safety lamp. One of the more exotic buildings along this narrow winding thoroughfare is the **Egyptian House**, built in the 1830s and restored by the Landmark Trust. Meanwhile, behind the Georgian façade of **The Union Hotel**, opposite, is an impressive Elizabethan interior where, from a minstrels' gallery in the assembly room, was made the first mainland announcement of the victory of Trafalgar and the death of Lord Nelson.

Further down is Penzance's **Maritime Museum**, home to a fascinating collection of artefacts that not only illustrates how ferocious the waters along this stretch of coast can be but also displays many items recovered from shipwrecks. Chapel Street was also the childhood home of Marie Branwell, the mother of the famous and ill-fated Brontë sisters. Down around the harbour lies the **Trinity House Lighthouse Centre**, where the interesting story of lighthouse keeping is told. Elsewhere in Penzance, local history and the work of the Newlyn School of artists can be seen at the **Penlee House Art Gallery and Museum** and the county's long association with the mining industry led not only to the foundation of the Royal Geological Society of

The Prom at Night, Penzance

The Egyptian House, Penzance

Cornwall in 1814 but also to the opening of the **Cornwall Geological Museum** which explores all aspects of geology and the industry.

Finally, anyone who saw the television adaptation of Mary Wesley's novel *The*

Camomile Lawn will recognise Penzance as the town was the place to which the three main characters, Calypso, Walter and Polly, came for their annual summer visit.

AROUND PENZANCE

NEWLYN
1 mile SW of Penzance on the B3315

The largest fish landing port in England and Wales, Newlyn has long been associated with the fishing. Its massive jetties were built in the 1880s to enclose some 40 acres of Mount's Bay and they also embraced the existing 15th century harbour. The whole fishing industry, like other industries, was spurred on by the arrival of the railways at Newlyn in 1859 - which allowed the swift transportation of

Newlyn Harbour

NEWLYN MEADERY,

The Coombe, Newlyn, near Penzance, Cornwall TR18 5QF
Tel: 01736 365375 Fax: 01736 365572

Found next door to Newlyn's Pilchard Museum, **Newlyn Meadery** is a popular family restaurant that has a very unique appeal. The striking black and white building dates back to the 1920s when it was constructed as a cinema and films were shown here right up until 1963. Purchased then by Cyril's brother, in 1974 the present owners, Cyril and Chris Leiworthy, bought the business and it has continued to go

from strength to strength. Though the exterior is very firmly rooted in the early 20th century, the interior decor of the Newlyn Meadery takes visitors back to a completely different age. Reminiscent of the Middle Ages, the mass of heavy timber work and the colourful stained glass windows created exactly the right atmosphere in which to enjoy the small but well selected menu served. Here the medieval theme continues and the house speciality is Chicken in the rough - a specially flavoured roasted half chicken served on a wooden platter that, it is suggested, is eaten with the fingers. Dining at the Newlyn Meadery is certainly an experience and one that the whole family are sure to enjoy.

Pilchard Works and Meadery

fresh fish and seafood to London and beyond. Today, it is the base for around 200 vessels, which vary greatly in size, and whose valuable

catches are now shipped around Britain and Europe in massive refrigerated lorries. The **Pilchard Works Heritage Museum** offers a unique insight into the fascinating history of the industry in Cornwall and the company can speak with authority as it is the sole producer and exporter of the county's traditional salted pilchards.

However, fishing is not the main reason that people visit Newlyn. Drawn here by the exceptionally clear natural light, Stanhope Forbes came here to paint outside rather than in a studio in the 1880s. He was soon joined by other artists keen to experience the joys of working here and the **Newlyn School** of art developed with the help of artists such as Lamorna Birch, Alfred Munnings, Norman

THE RED LION,

36 Fore Street, Newlyn, Cornwall TR18 5JR
Tel: 01736 362012

Occupying a marvellous position with views across Newlyn's harbour to St Michael's Mount in the distance, **The Red Lion** is certainly an inn that is an interesting place from which to watch the boating activity. Believed to date back to the 15th century, this attractive stone inn has been run by landlords Jacqui and Thomas Rowe since the late 1980s. A traditional inn with, naturally, a mass of nautical

memorabilia on display inside, The Red Lion also has a tucked away beer garden to the rear that is ideal

on warm summer's days. There is always an excellent range of beers, ales and lagers on tap as well as two real ales to be found at the bar. Delicious food too is served here, throughout the day and into the evening, and, with the harbour so close, fish and, crab in particular, are the house specialities - the home-made fresh crab soup is famous having appeared in local newspapers, radio and even national TV. A small and friendly inn with and warm and friendly atmosphere, the combination of good beer and food and charming hospitality found here have gone to make this a very popular inn.

THE SMUGGLERS RESTAURANT,

12-14 Fore Street, Newlyn, Cornwall TR18 5JN
Tel: 01736 331501 Fax: 01736 331501

Overlooking Newlyn's fishing harbour, **The Smugglers Restaurant** is housed in a charming 200 year old building that is very much entwined with the pilchard industry - once landed the fish were salted here and there was also a net loft. Although they are now blocked, there are tunnels between the building and the harbourside and from the large ground floor picture windows there are superb views out over the still busy harbour. Owned and personally run by Allan and Mary Owen, this small and intimate restaurant has built up an

enviable reputation locally for their excellent cuisine. Allan is the chef of the partnership and the style of the menu here reflects his experience and imagination. Fish features heavily amongst the dishes and the range is extensive whilst The Smugglers Restaurant also specialises in vegetarian dishes. This is a very popular restaurant for which a booking is essential during the season. Meanwhile, Allan and Mary also have a holiday cottage available for hire where both children and pets are welcome.

Garstin and Laura Knight. Still a favourite place for artists, the **Newlyn Art Gallery**, founded in 1895 by the Cornishman Passmore Edwards, shows the paintings of those living and working here today.

MOUSEHOLE
2½ miles SW of Penzance off the B3315

Described by Dylan Thomas, who honeymooned here in July 1937, as "the loveliest village in England", Mousehole

Mousehole Harbour

(pronounced *Mowzel*) is indeed the epitome of a Cornish fishing village. Certainly visited by Phoenician tin merchants in around 500 BC - it is thought that the village's name is derived from the Phoenician word for 'watering place' - Mousehole has a long and sometimes disturbing history. Some 2000 years after these first known visitors, in 1595, the Spanish arrived and ransacked the village leaving only the former manor house in Keigwin Street relatively unscathed. However, this attack was not that unexpected by the villagers as they saw it as the fulfilment of a prophecy that can be seen inscribed on **Merlin's Rock**, near the quay. The stone bears these words:

> *"There shall land on the Rock of Merlin*
> *Those who shall burn Paul,*
>   *Penzance and Newlyn."*

The village was rebuilt and went on to become an important pilchard fishing port until the stocks of fish dwindled in the early 20th century. Up on a hill, to the north of Mousehole, stands the village church and here can be found the grave of Polly Pentreath, a Mousehole fishwife who, when she died in 1777, was thought to be the last woman to speak Cornish as her native language.

Every 23 December, **Star-Gazy Pie** - a local speciality made with whole fish whose heads stick up through the pastry crust - is made in commemoration of Tom Bawcock, a local fisherman who saved Mousehole from starvation by setting sail in a storm and bringing home a large catch of seven varieties of fish. Less fortunate were the eight man crew of the Penlee lifeboat, *Solomon Browne*, who were lost in hurricane conditions while attempting to rescue the last four crew members from the coaster *Union Star*, in December 1981. Every member of the lifeboat crew was a Mousehole man.

LAMORNA
4 miles SW of Penzance off the B3315

This isolated hamlet is set in the craggy **Lamorna Cove** that was immortalised by the

Lamorna Cove

artist Lamorna Birch and author Derek Tangye, who were among several artists to be attracted to this area between 1880 and 1910. Once only licensed to sell beer, Lamorna's pub, The Wink, got its name from the old custom of winking to the landlord to obtain something stronger from under the counter.

To the west of the hamlet, amid excellent walking country, is the exception Bronze Age stone circle known as the **Merry Maidens**. The standing stones are said to be all that remains of 19 young women who were turned into granite for daring to dance on the Sabbath. **The Pipers**, two large menhirs nearby, are thought to be the musicians who suffered the same fate for providing the dancing music.

ST BURYAN
5 miles SW of Penzance on the B3283

This village is home to one of the finest churches in the county whose 14th century tower dominates the landscape and provides a daymark for shipping around Land's End. The first church here was built in the 10th century by King Athelstan and, apart from the Celtic crosses beside the porch, the most interesting feature here is a gravestone that reads:

"Here lie John and Richard Benn
Two lawyers and two honest men.
God works miracles now and then."

To the north of St Buryan is the **Boscawen-Un Stone Circle** which, though not the most impressive in the country, certain has much appeal; not only because of its isolated location but also because of the central standing stone - an attractive leaning pillar of sparkling quartz.

TREEN
6½ miles SW of Penzance on the B3315

Sheltered from the worst of the weather as it is situated in a shallow valley, Treen is an unspoilt hamlet that lies only a short walk away from the spectacularly sited Iron Age coastal fort, **Tretyn Dinas** - found on the headland that also bears this name. Despite having been constructed over 2000 years ago, the earthwork defences on the landward side can still be made out.

Also on the headland is the famous **Logan Rock**, a massive 60 ton granite boulder that was once so finely balanced that it could be rocked by hand. The rock was a popular tourist attraction until 1824, when Lieutenant Hugh Goldsmith (the nephew of the poet and playwright Oliver Goldsmith), egged on by some Royal Navy colleagues, pushed the stone on to the beach below. After many complaints by the locals, the naval officer was instructed to replace the rock - an extraordinary feat of engineering in itself - at his own expense but the fine balance the rock once had has never returned. This act of misadventure is recorded in the local inn.

THE PORTHCURNO HOTEL,
The Valley, Porthcurno, near St Levan, Cornwall TR19 6JX
Tel: 01736 810119 Fax: 01736 810711

Found just a short walk from the beach and standing within its own extensive terraced garden, **The Porthcurno Hotel** is a comfortable and friendly hotel that makes a perfect base from which to explore southwest Cornwall. Dating back to the 1934, this spacious property is owned and personally run by Terry and Julie Goss and their family who aim to provide guests with a quality personal service. The bright and airy dining room, with glorious views out over the gardens to the sea, is just the place to start the day with a hearty breakfast. Meanwhile, in the evening guests can relax in the licensed restaurant over a delicious dinner which is prepared by Terry and Julie from locally sourced ingredients. Throughout, the hotel is stylishly furnished and decorated and this extends to the guest bedrooms which have been designed to create just right environment for a good night's sleep. Nothing here is too much trouble for Terry and Julie and they are happy to prepare picnics and lend blankets to guests visiting the well known Minack Theatre, which is to be found a short walk away.

Minack Theatre, Porthcurno

underground wartime centre situated above the cove.

This interesting and picturesque village is also the home of the **Minack Theatre**, an open air amphitheatre cut into the high cliffs that was founded by Rowena Cade, the daughter of a textile tycoon who grew up in Cheltenham. The first production staged at this classical Greek style theatre was *The Tempest* in 1932 and a summer series has continued ever since.

PORTHCURNO
7½ miles SW of Penzance off the B3315

Overlooking one of the most dramatic and atmospheric coves in southwest Cornwall, Porthcurno's triangle of beach, made up of crushed sea shells, is sheltered by **Gwennap**

Porthcurno Beach

Head to the west and **Cribba Head** to the east. It was from here, in 1870, that the first telegraph cable was laid, linking Britain to the rest of the world, and this little bay soon became known as 'the centre of the universe'. The **Porthcurno Wartime Telegraph Museum** explains the technology that has been developed, from Victorian times to the present day, to enable global communications. The museum is housed in a secret

PORTHGWARRA
8 miles SW of Penzance off the B3315

This quaint old fishing hamlet lies just northeast of the high cliffs of Gwennap Head from which there is a spectacular coastal walk to Land's End although walkers should be aware that the terrain is sometimes rugged.

The small and cosy cove, with its sandy beach and backdrop of steep cliffs, was once known as **Sweetheart's Cove** as this is where, many years ago, Nancy said goodbye to her forbidden lover before he joined his ship. She

Porthgwarra Beach

watched for his safe return from then on and, one moonlight night, as she sat on a rock in the cove, an old woman observed her and seeing that she was in danger from the rising tide climbed down the cliffs to warn her. As the old woman approached, she saw that Nancy was not alone but was in the arms of a young sailor and she sat down to watch. Suddenly the couple floated out to sea and vanished. Nancy was never seen again and, the next morning, word arrived that her lover's ship had been lost with all hands.

LAND'S END
9 miles SW of Penzance on the A30

A curious mix of natural spectacle and manmade indulgence, Land's End, mainland Britain's most westerly point, is certainly one of the country's most famous landmarks. It is here that the granite on which most of Cornwall stands finally meets the Atlantic Ocean in a series of savage cliffs, reefs and sheer sided islets that provide some of the most awe inspiring scenery in the country. Known to the Romans as Belevian, or Seat of Storms, from this headland can be seen

Suspension Bridge, Land's End

Longships Lighthouse, which protects shipping from the Longships reef just offshore and **Wolf Rock Lighthouse**, some seven miles away.

Naturally, this place has given rise to numerous legends over the centuries. One

THE LAND'S END HOTEL,

Land's End, Cornwall TR19 7AA
Tel: 01736 871844 Fax: 01736 871812
e-mail: info@landsend-landmark.co.uk
website: www.landsend-landmark.co.uk

Situated at one of the most famous sites in England and proudly perched on the top of the 200 foot cliffs, **The Land's End Hotel** - open from March to October - is a warm and welcoming place. An attractive building that has had, over the years, to withstand the buffeting of the strong winds coming off the Atlantic, the views from the cliff tops are spectacular and the sunsets out over the sea are fabulous. However, whatever the weather, this comfortable hotel is sure to provide a quiet and peaceful haven to escape the harshest winds.

Overlooking the Atlantic, the Longships Restaurant, which is open to non residents, provides the opportunity to enjoy a unique dining experience. The comprehensive menu of classic dishes, including fresh fish from nearby Newlyn, and the extensive wine list ensure that guests will have a dinner to remember with a view that is quite out of this world. The accommodation here too is excellent and each of the 33 en suite guest rooms have been named after famous people or local landscape features. Designed to provide the perfect environment for a refreshing night's sleep, this is an ideal way to enjoy the spectacular scenery of Land's End in comfort.

claims that Land's End was once the entrance to Lyonesse, the fertile kingdom that stretched from here to the Isles of Scilly some 25 miles to the southwest. Said to have been engulfed by the sea some 900 years ago, one man, Trevilian, escaped from Lyonesse riding a white horse and the Trevilian family crest still depicts a horse rising from the waves.

Of the attractions here, other than the scenery, there is the **Land of Greeb** where visitors can explore a cottage furnished as it would have appeared in the late 18th century, watch the farm animals and see craftsmen and women at work. Stories of smugglers, shipwrecks and pirates are told at **The Last Labyrinth** whilst, at **Miles of Memories**, the stories of those who have travelled, some by very curious modes of transport, from Land's End to John O' Groats. The power of the sea and man's struggle with its is told in **The Relentless Sea** and, at **Air Sea Rescue Alert**, visitors can see a dangerous rescue mission out in the Atlantic that was filmed with the help of the air sea rescue services.

SENNEN
8 miles SW of Penzance on the A30

The most westerly village in the country, there are superb cliff walks along the coast to Land's End and, close to the massive Pedn-men-du headland, lie the remains of a clifftop **Castle**,

one of the country's earliest - this one dates from 300BC. The wide sandy beach at **Sennen Cove**, voted the cleanest in Britain in 1998, is ideal for both bathing and surfing whilst the former windlass house of the lifeboat station has been converted into a crafts gallery.

BRANE
4½ miles W of Penzance off the A30

Just to the west of this lovely hamlet is the fascinating Iron Age courtyard village of **Carn Euny**, founded around 200 BC by an early Cornish farming community. By far the most impressive building here is the **Fogou**, that was first discovered by miners in the 19th century. Taking its name from the Cornish for 'cave', this underground chamber was constructed in three separate stages and this 65 foot long room was entered by a low, 'creep' passage at one end. It purpose is still unclear although it may have been used for storage or for religious ceremonies.

SANCREED
3½ miles W of Penzance off the A30

In the churchyard of 15th century St Credan's Church can be found five Celtic Crosses, some of the many that are scattered around Cornwall. One in particular, at nine feet high, and of the wheel-head shape is the best

example of its kind in the county. The existence of **Sancreed Holy Well** nearby and the curious circular formation of the site suggests that the church is built on much older foundations.

In the surrounding area are two Bronze Age monuments, the **Blind Fiddler** and the **Two Sisters** and, like many Cornish menhirs, they are said to represent human beings turned to stone for committing irreligious acts on the Sabbath.

Sennen Cove

THE WELLINGTON HOTEL,

Market Square, St Just, near Penzance, Cornwall TR19 7HD
Tel: 01736 787319 Fax: 01736 787906

Found in the heart of St Just, a quiet area of Cornwall that is often overlooked for its famous neighbours such as Penzance and Land's End, **The Wellington Hotel** is an excellent place to stay whilst discovering the superb beaches, relics of Cornwall's mining industry and the glorious inland countryside. Built before the Battle of Waterloo in 1815, this attractive old hotel was named after the victorious Iron Duke following his stay here. Now fully modernised but fortunately without loosing any of its olde worlde charm, this friendly hotel has been managed by Rod and Jennifer Gray since 1988. AS well as having a well stocked bar, The Wellington also has a fine reputation for the high standard of food served here, whether it is a light snack or a full evening dinner. The prize winning ploughman's lunches here are a popular choice for lunch and with a varied range of dishes, including plenty of fresh, local fish and seafood, there is sure to be something to tempt even the most jaded palate. With 11 en suite and well appointed guest bedrooms, this is also a comfortable and relaxing place to stay where a warm welcome is guaranteed.

BOSAVERN HOUSE,

St Just, near Penzance, Cornwall TR19 7RD
Tel: 01736 788301 Fax: 01736 788301
e-mail: marcol@bosavern.u-net.com website: www.bosavern.u-net.com

Lying just to the south of St Just and set within extensive grounds, **Bosavern House** is a splendid old dwelling whose history spans several centuries. Built in 1625, probably on the site of an older building, it became the property of the Millet family later that century and stayed in their hands until the early 20th century. One member of the family, Grace Millet, married Robert Davy in 1776 and it was their son, Sir Humphry Davy, who famously invented the Davy Safety Lamp. Today, this interesting house is owned by Allan and Corinne Collinson who offer superb bed and breakfast accommodation all year

round. Most of the eight well appointed guest rooms are en suite and breakfast here is a real treat as Allan is a qualified chef. Guests also have a separate lounge which overlooks the pretty gardens and here they can enjoy a drink from the house's licensed bar. Throughout the season the couple serve cream teas, morning coffee and light lunches and they have a safe and secure camping and caravan site complete with showers, toilets, laundry facilities and electric hook-ups.

ST JUST

6½ miles NW of Penzance on the A3071

The westernmost town in mainland Britain, St Just was one of the copper and tin mining centres of Cornwall and the area surrounding this rather sombre town is littered with

Shoreline, St Just

industrial remains. However, the 15th century church contains some fascinating early relics, including two medieval wall paintings, and a 5th century burial stone on which is carved one of the earliest English Christian inscriptions. Near the town's clock tower, at the centre of St Just, is a shallow grassy amphitheatre that is known as **Plen-an-Gwary**, which means 'playing place', where medieval plays were performed up until the 17th century and which is now the setting for an annual carnival.

A narrow road leads from the town, westwards, to **Cape Cornwall**, the only cape in England and Wales and from where there are views of Land's End and of Longships Lighthouse. On the way to the tip of the cape the road passes a tall chimney, all that is left of Cape Cornwall mine, the country's most westerly, which was working up until the 1870s.

On the southern side of the headland lies **Priest's Cove**, a quiet boulder strewn beach, and further along the **South West Coast Path**, with follows the clifftops, there is an unusual Bronze Age burial chamber, **Ballowall Barrow**. Cape Cornwall marks the supposed boundary between the English and St George's Channels.

BOSWEDDEN HOUSE,

Cape Cornwall, St Just, near Penzance, Cornwall TR19 7NJ
Tel: 01736 788733 Fax: 01736 788733
e-mail: relax@boswedden.org.uk
website: www.SmoothHound.co.uk/hotels/boswedd.html

Built in 1828 as the home of a mine captain and his family, **Boswedden House** is a superb establishment that stands within two acres of mature gardens. The home of Thelma and Nigel, the couple offer excellent bed and breakfast accommodation in a choice of eight en suite guest rooms. Each room has been decorated and furnished to a very high standard, as is the rest of this wonderful Georgian house, and families with children are catered for well and evening meals are available. After a day out exploring this interesting area of Cornwall, guests can relax in the garden which also contain three fish ponds. However, the more energetic, as well as children, might like to take a swim in the indoor heated swimming pool. Whilst Boswedden House is certainly a very splendid place to stay that is sure to provide guest's with a peaceful and tranquil environment those still feeling the stresses and strains of modern day living will be glad to hear that Thelma and Nigel also offer their guests reflexology and massage treatments.

KENIDJACK
7 miles NW of Penzance off the B3306

Close to this old mining village lies **Carn
Kenidjack**, where one dark night two miners
encountered a black robed horseman.
Inviting them to a wrestling match, the
frightened miners accepted only to find that
the horseman was joined by a host of
fearsome demons which, as he was the Devil,
he commanded. During the fierce fight, one
of the demons was thrown against a rock and,
overcome with Christian charity, the two
miners whispered a prayer into the ear of the
dying creature. Immediately the ground
trembled and the whole demonic party
disappeared in a black cloud. The terrified
miners hid on the carn until daylight before
making their way home.

BOTALLACK
7 miles NW of Penzance on the B3306

Almost overlooking the coast lies the remains
of the old engine houses of **Botallack Mine**
where, amongst the derelict buildings, lies a
1908 'calciner' that was used to refine the tin

Botallack Tin Mine, St Just

The North Inn,

The Square, Pendeen, near Penzance, Cornwall TR19 7DN
Tel: 01736 788417 Fax: 01736 787504 e-mail: andrew.coak@btinternet.com

Found in the heart of this tranquil village is **The North Inn**, an early 18th century pub whose creeper
clad front overlooks Pendeen's village square. However, things have not always been so quiet and
peaceful here as Pendeen was once a busy tin mining village and this is how the inn got its name as
the miners referred to this area as the North Country.

Now that the mines have closed this remains a popular inn with locals and visitors alike and
landlord John Coak, along with his brother Andrew and sister-in-law Veronica, have been offering
excellent, traditional hospitality here since November 1998. As well as the superb range of real ales,

beers, lager and other drinks found
at the bar, The North Inn has a fine
reputation for its cuisine. A
tempting menu of sandwiches and
bar snacks are prepared for lunch
by Andrew and Veronica whilst, in
the evening, the menu takes a
more formal turn and the curries
here are a house speciality not to
be missed.

Finally, John also offers
accommodation in a comfortable
self-catering cottage and, behind
the inn, there is a field for tenters.
All the family, including the dog,
are welcome at this charming inn.

ore and to produce arsenic. The smell of arsenic can still be detected in the old flues.

PENDEEN
6½ miles NW of Penzance on the A3306

Tin has been mined in and around this village since prehistoric times and, from the 19th century, Pendeen also became a centre for copper extraction. Not surprisingly, it is this industry that dominates and to the northwest of the village there are two interesting old mines that are now open to the public. The last of 20 or so mines in the area to close, production ceased at Geevor Tin Mine in 1990 and, today, it has been extensively preserved as the **Geevor Tin Mine and Heritage Centre**. Guided tours, including some underground, the museum and a film highlight the lives and conditions of the miners who worked in the tunnels that once extended over four square miles and went right under the seabed.

Near by is the **Levant Beam Engine**, the oldest steam engine in the country that now stands in the engine house of the old Levant tin mine, which was incorporated into the Geevor mine in the 1960s. In 1919, Levant saw a tragic accident when the 'man engine' which carried miners to the surface failed and 31 men and boys were killed.

Further to the north, on the slate promontory of **Pendeen Watch** stands **Pendeen Lighthouse** that has been guiding ships for nearly a century. Since all lighthouses were fully automated, Pendeen

has been opened for guided tours around the light and the engine house.

MADRON
1½ miles NW of Penzance off the A30

The part 14th century Church of St Maddern was once the mother church to Penzance and inside can be seen a Trafalgar Banner, placed there during the celebrations for Nelson's victory. Close to the village centre, down an overgrown path, lies the source of **St Maddern's Well** that was thought to have curative powers especially to those with rickets who tied a rag to the small thorn tree

Lanyon Quoit

KING WILLIAM IV,

Church Road, Madron, near Penzance, Cornwall TR20 8SS
Tel: 01736 363022

An ancient old inn stand in the historic and picturesque village of Madron, the **King William IV** is a charming place which offers customers old fashioned hospitality. As olde worlde inside as the exterior would suggest, this delightful inn has heavy ceiling beams decorated with gleaming horse brasses, some interesting memorabilia hanging from walls and an splendid feature fireplace to add to the cosy feel of this already inviting inn. Landlady, Christine Ede, was born in this parish, and, along with her husband Peter, they have certainly put the King William IV on the map in the time that they have been here. Well known for the excellent selection of quality ales served from the bar, the inn is also a popular place for food. Served at lunchtimes and in the evenings the tasty menu of bar snacks includes home-made soups and pasties that are well worth trying. Sunday lunchtime is a special occasion here as roast meal is not only good value for money but a delicious treat. As well as catering for children, this is one inn where dogs too are welcome so that the whole family can enjoy the delights of this lovely village inn.

growing here. Further along the path are the remains of **St Maddern's Cell**, the place where the saint baptised villagers over 1000 years ago and which was destroyed by Cromwellian soldiers in 1646.

Just to the south of the village lies **Trengwainton Gardens**, the National Trust owned woodland gardens that are particularly well known for their spring flowering shrubs, walled garden and fine views of Mount's Bay.

The land to the north of Madron is rich in ancient monuments and, in particular, there is **Lanyon Quoit** and the granite **Men-an-Tol**, a holed stone that was originally the entrance to a tomb chamber. For centuries, this granite ring was thought to have curative powers and children were passed, naked, through its centre nine times to cure all manner of diseases.

ZENNOR
5 miles N of Penzance on the B3306

This delightful village, situated between moorland and coastal cliffs, is one of only a few settlements along this stretch of the north Cornish coastline. An ancient village, where evidence has been found of Bronze Age settlers, the 12th century Church of St Senara is famous for its bench end which depicts a local mermaid holding a comb and mirror and resembles the Greek goddess of love, Aphrodite. A famous local legend tells of a mysterious young maiden who was drawn to the church by the beautiful singing of a chorister, the squire's son Matthew Trewhella. An enchanting singer herself, one night she lured him down to nearby Pendour Cove where he swam out to join her and disappeared. On a warm summer's evening it is said that their voices can be heard rising from beneath the waves.

For an insight into the history of Zennor and the surrounding area, the **Wayside Folk Museum** has numerous exhibits that tell of this regions industrial past - tin mining - which is also referred to in the name of the local inn, The Tinners. It was at this pub that DH Lawrence spent many hours whilst living with his wife Frieda in the village during World War I. Originally intending to set up a farming cum literary commune, the couple

rented a cheap cottage at Zennor and whilst here, under police surveillance, he wrote *Women in Love*. However, eventually his pacifist tendencies and Frieda's German heritage (her cousin was the flying ace the Red Baron), caused them to be 'moved on' in October 1917.

Just to the southeast of Zennor, on the granite moorland, lies the Neolithic chamber tomb, **Zennor Quoit**. One of many such ancient monuments to be found in this area, the tomb has a huge capstone that was once supported on five broad uprights, with two standing stones marking the entrance to the inner chamber.

NEW MILL
2 miles N of Penzance off the A30

To the northeast of the village and on a windy hillside lies **Chysauster Ancient Village** that is under the ownership of English Heritage. Built around 2000 years ago, this Romano-Cornish village has one of the oldest identifiable streets in the country with two rows of four dwellings. Each is built around a

Chysauster Ancient Village

central courtyard and, during excavations, an assortment of pottery and domestic rubbish was found. Occupied from 100BC to around the 3rd century AD the villagers were obviously farmers - cattle sheds have been unearthed - but they supplemented their livings by working tin beside the nearby stream. Only discovered during archaeological excavations in the 1860s, the land surrounding the village also displays the irregular pattern of small Iron Age fields.

List of
Tourist Information Centres

BODMIN

Shire Hall, Mount Folly Square,
Bodmin, Cornwall PL31 2DQ

Tel/Fax: 01208 76616

BUDE

The Crescent, Bude,
Cornwall EX23 8LE

Tel. 01288 354240 Fax: 01288 355769

CAMELFORD

The North Cornwall Museum, The
Clease, Camelford, Cornwall PL32 9PL

Tel/Fax: 01840 212954

FALMOUTH

28 Killigrew Street, Falmouth,
Cornwall TR11 3PN

Tel: 01326 312300 Fax: 01326 313457

FOWEY

The Post Office, 4 Custom House Hill,
Fowey, Cornwall PL23 1AB

Tel/Fax: 01726 833616

HELSTON & THE LIZARD PENINSULA

79 Meneage Street, Helston,
Cornwall TR13 8RB

Tel: 01326 565431 Fax: 01326 572803

LAUNCESTON

Market House Arcade, Market Street,
Launceston, Cornwall PL15 8EP

Tel: 01566 772321 Fax: 01566 772322

LOOE

The Guildhall, Fore Street, East Looe,
Cornwall PL13 1AA

Tel: 01503 262076 Fax: 01503 265426

NEWQUAY

Municipal Offices, Marcus Hill,
Newquay, Cornwall TR7 1BD

Tel: 01637 854020 Fax: 01637 854030

PADSTOW

Red Brick Building, North Quay,
Padstow, Cornwall PL28 8AF

Tel: 01841 533449 Fax: 01841 532356

PENZANCE

Station Road, Penzance,
Cornwall TR18 2NF

Tel: 01736 362207 Fax: 01736 363600

ST IVES

The Guildhall, Street-an-Pol, St Ives,
Cornwall TR26 2DS

Tel: 01736 796297 Fax: 01736 798309

TRURO

Municipal Buildings, Boscawen Street,
Truro, Cornwall TR1 2NE

Tel: 01872 274555 Fax: 01872 263031

WADEBRIDGE

The Town Hall, Wadebridge,
Cornwall PL27 7AQ

Tel: 01208 813725 Fax: 01208 813781

Index of Towns, Villages and Places of Interest

Hidden Places Order Form

To order any of our publications just fill in the payment details below and complete the order form *overleaf*. For orders of less than 4 copies please add £1 per book for postage and packing. Orders over 4 copies are P & P free.

Please Complete Either:

I enclose a cheque for £ [   ] made payable to Travel Publishing Ltd

Or:

Card No: [   ]

Expiry Date: [   ]

Signature: [   ]

NAME: [   ]

ADDRESS: [   ]

POSTCODE: [   ]

TEL NO: [   ]

Please either send or telephone your order to:

Travel Publishing Ltd
7a Apollo House
Calleva Park
Aldermaston
Berks, RG7 8TN

Tel : 0118 981 7777
Fax: 0118 982 0077

	PRICE	QUANTITY	VALUE
Hidden Places Regional Titles			
Cambridgeshire & Lincolnshire	£7.99	....	....
Channel Islands	£6.99	....	....
Cheshire	£7.99	....	....
Chilterns	£7.99	....	....
Cornwall	£8.99	....	....
Derbyshire	£7.99	....	....
Devon	£8.99	....	....
Dorset, Hants & Isle of Wight	£7.99	....	....
East Anglia	£8.99	....	....
Essex	£7.99	....	....
Gloucestershire & Wiltshire	£7.99	....	....
Heart of England	£7.99	....	....
Hereford, Worcs & Shropshire	£7.99	....	....
Highlands & Islands	£7.99	....	....
Kent	£8.99	....	....
Lake District & Cumbria	£7.99	....	....
Lancashire	£7.99	....	....
Norfolk	£7.99	....	....
Northumberland & Durham	£6.99	....	....
North Wales	£7.99	....	....
Nottinghamshire	£6.99	....	....
Potteries	£6.99	....	....
Somerset	£7.99	....	....
South Wales	£7.99	....	....
Suffolk	£7.99	....	....
Surrey	£6.99	....	....
Sussex	£7.99	....	....
Thames Valley	£7.99	....	....
Warwickshire & West Midlands	£6.99	....	....
Yorkshire	£7.99	....	....
Hidden Places National Titles			
England	£9.99	....	....
Ireland	£9.99	....	....
Scotland	£9.99	....	....
Wales	£9.99	....	....
Hidden Inns Titles			
West Country	£5.99	....	....
South East	£5.99	....	....
South	£5.99	....	....
Wales	£5.99	....	....

*For orders of less than 4 copies please add £1 per book for
postage & packing. Orders over 4 copies P & P free.*

Hidden Places Reader Reaction

The *Hidden Inns* research team would like to receive reader's comments on any visitor attractions or places reviewed in the book and also recommendations for suitable entries to be included in the next edition. This will help ensure that the *Hidden Inns* series continues to provide its readers with useful information on the more interesting, unusual or unique features of each attraction or place ensuring that their stay in the local area is an enjoyable and stimulating experience.

To provide your comments or recommendations would you please complete the forms below and overleaf as indicated and send to:

The Research Department, Travel Publishing Ltd,
7a Apollo House, Calleva Park, Aldermaston, Reading, RG7 8TN.

Your Name:

Your Address:

Your Telephone Number:

Please tick as appropriate: Comments ☐   Recommendation ☐

Name of *"Hidden Place"*:

Address:

Telephone Number:

Name of Contact:

Hidden Places Reader Reaction

Comment or Reason for Recommendation:

....

....

....

....

....

....

....

....

....

....

....

Hidden Places Reader Reaction

The *Hidden Inns* research team would like to receive reader's comments on any visitor attractions or places reviewed in the book and also recommendations for suitable entries to be included in the next edition. This will help ensure that the *Hidden Inns* series continues to provide its readers with useful information on the more interesting, unusual or unique features of each attraction or place ensuring that their stay in the local area is an enjoyable and stimulating experience.

To provide your comments or recommendations would you please complete the forms below and overleaf as indicated and send to:

The Research Department, Travel Publishing Ltd,
7a Apollo House, Calleva Park, Aldermaston, Reading, RG7 8TN.

Your Name:

Your Address:

Your Telephone Number:

Please tick as appropriate: Comments ☐   Recommendation ☐

Name of *"Hidden Place"*:

Address:

Telephone Number:

Name of Contact:

Hidden Places Reader Reaction

Comment or Reason for Recommendation:

....

....

....

....

....

....

....

....

....

....

....